Nick McKenzie is one of Austr[alia's ... jour]nalists. He works for *The Age* and the *Sydney Morning Herald* and occasionally reports for ABC TV's *Four Corners* program. He has won Australia's highest journalism award, the Walkley, three times for his work exposing corruption and organised crime. His work has triggered several major inquiries, including Australia's biggest bribery investigation. In his free time he surfs and reads.

THE STING

NICK McKENZIE

AUSTRALIA'S PLOT TO CRACK A GLOBAL DRUG EMPIRE

VICTORY BOOKS
An imprint of Melbourne University Publishing Limited
187 Grattan Street, Carlton, Victoria 3053, Australia
mup-info@unimelb.edu.au
www.mup.com.au

First published 2012
Text © Nick McKenzie, 2012
Design and typography © Melbourne University Publishing Ltd 2012

This book is copyright. Apart from any use permitted under the *Copyright Act 1968* and subsequent amendments, no part may be reproduced, stored in a retrieval system or transmitted by any means or process whatsoever without the prior written permission of the publisher.

Every attempt has been made to locate the copyright holders for material quoted in this book. Any person or organisation that may have been overlooked or misattributed may contact the publisher.

Cover design by Nada Backovic
Typeset by Megan Ellis
Printed in Australia by Griffin Press, South Australia

National Library of Australia Cataloguing-in-Publication entry:

McKenzie, Nick.
The sting: Australia's plot to crack a global drug empire / Nick McKenzie.

ISBN: 9780522860924 (pbk)
ISBN: 9780522861532 (eBook)

Includes index.

Organized crime.
Organized crime investigation.
Criminal investigation.
International crimes.
364.106

Contents

Cast of characters   vi

Author's note   ix

Prologue   xi

Part 1: December 2006 – June 2007   1

Part 2: June 2007 – December 2007   61

Part 3: December 2007 – August 2009   87

Part 4: August 2009 – April 2010   181

Part 5: April 2010 – July 2011   209

Epilogue   252

Acknowledgements   256

Index   257

Cast of characters

ACC (Australian Crime Commission): Australian Government national criminal intelligence agency

AFP (Australian Federal Police): Australia's national law enforcement agency

AUSTRAC (Australian Transaction Reports and Analysis Centre): Australia's anti-money laundering regulator

Erkan Ayik: Hakan Ayik's brother

Hakan 'Hux' Ayik: Comanchero and Triad associate, international traveller and police target

Bilal: wharf worker, Wissam's second cousin by marriage

Harry Blackburn: former NSW police superintendent

Buds: former boxer and Comanchero enforcer

Bruce Bullock: ACC Melbourne operations manager

Comancheros: outlaw motorcycle club

Van Dang Tran: Vietnam Airlines pilot

Bob Debus: Minister for Home Affairs, responsible for the ACC (2007–2010)

Erkan Dogan: Hakan Ayik's nephew

Kelly Edmonds: runner for Hakan Ayik

Errol Gildea: president of the Hells Angels, Queensland

Mahmoud 'Mick' Hawi: president of the Comancheros

Steve Hutchins: Labor senator for NSW and chair of the Parliamentary Joint Committee on Law Enforcement

Gregory James: ACC acting general manager (Financial Crimes)

Lam family: Vietnamese crime family living in Sydney

Duncan Lam Sak Cheung: Sydney-based Asian underworld boss
John Lawler: ACC chief executive officer (2009–)
Andrew Lee: police undercover operative
Joseph 'Mizza' Micalizzi: Comanchero drug runner
Alastair 'Jock' Milroy: ACC chief executive officer (2003–2009)
Mark 'Ferret' Moroney: sergeant-at-arms for The Finks, an outlaw motorcycle club
NCA (National Crime Authority): predecessor to the ACC
Daux Ngakuru: Comanchero sergeant-at-arms
Mike Purchas: ACC Sydney operations manager
Smiley: Sydney heroin trafficker
Hun To: nephew of Hun Sen, Prime Minister of Cambodia
Triads: Chinese criminal organisation
Ly Vi Hung: Sydney-based Asian underworld boss
Patrick Vikingsson: ACC senior criminal intelligence analyst
Dylan Welch: *Sydney Morning Herald* reporter
Wissam ('Waz'): junior bikie, second cousin by marriage to Bilal
Jason Wood: Liberal party MP and member of the Parliamentary Joint Committee on Law Enforcement
Steve Wu: Chinese businessman and triad
Wei 'Will' Wong: Chinese national living in Sydney, close associate of Hakan Ayik
Yakuza: Japanese criminal organisation

Author's Note

The Sting is based on one of the biggest organised crime probes in recent Australian history. The drug, cash and weapon busts described, along with the related political and media activities, are all based on real events. Where possible, people's true identities have been used.

In the main, events follow the chronological order of the operations described in the book, save for some minor changes made only for ease of the reader. I have reconstructed the events depicted from in-depth research, although some parts of the story have been altered or fictionalised in order to respect Australian laws, including those that prohibit publishing law enforcement activities covered by the secrecy act.

The actions of the criminal figures are also inspired by real events and have been reconstructed by speaking to those who know them or are aware of their behaviour. However, some of their activities have also been altered or fictionalised.

The names and identities of five main characters have been altered to protect their welfare or for legal reasons: Wei 'Will' Wong, Gregory James, Bilal, Andrew Nguyen and Steve Wu. The identities and activities of all informers have been altered for the same reasons.

The book is written from the evolving perspectives of each of the main characters, capturing that person's view, rather than my view, of events as they unfold.

While the subjective points of view of some of the characters can be disputed, there are few involved in the fight against organised crime that would dispute the core themes this book explores.

It is also important to note that an organsied crime probe needs many people to succeed; the activities of only a few of the key investigators are dealt with in this book, although the operations described relied on the dedicated work of dozens of policing officials from the Australian Crime Commission, Australian Federal Police and other federal and state agencies.

Prologue
July, 2011

'I am always getting bloody jacked up,' he swore under his breath as the flashing red and blue strobed behind him.

Glancing quickly at himself in the rear-view mirror, he wished he'd shaved and got his teeth done as his wife was always asking. His eyes were bloodshot.

He eased out of the car. I look like a shitman, he thought. Maybe there's just a light out. I wish the boys would look after the car. Fuckin' jacks.

Chatter from the pub floated through the lane. A lady shrieked, followed by the roar of male voices and clapping.

Footy. At least I can down a fuckin' pint when they're done. He forced a smile, cleared his throat and turned to the approaching men. What the fuck? They're not …

Diving back into his car, he thrust his arm under the seat, his hand clawing a bottle, then a T-shirt, desperately hoping to land on metal. He felt the hands strike him, his head ground into the seat and something cold touching the back of his neck. His right hand, the one looking for his own piece, was now shaking.

'Calm down, Smiley,' one of the men said.

That voice, he thought, it's that fuckin' nut job Comanchero with the tattoo that said something about how he'd rather be carried by six than judged by twelve.

They walked him towards their car, the flashing police light still visible depite his head being held down by an ugly hand.

'You want to see the wife and kids again, you better not fuck around.'

Another roar erupted from the pub as he stared at the bluestone rocks moving beneath him, roughly hewn and ancient. I wonder if convicts laid those cobblestones? he thought, and then cursed for having such a stupid idea. I should have listened to the whispers. They'll want all of my share of the smack, all seventy kilos.

He was pushed roughly into the car and the passenger's side door slammed shut. The sounds from the pub became faint. His gut constricted and his legs twitched with nervous energy.

'I wanna call my wife. Tell her I'm gonna be out for a bit.'

He turned to the man next to him holding the piece. He hadn't said a word yet. He was grinning.

'Shhhhhhhh,' he said, a finger to his lips. 'You ain't calling nobody.'

Part 1
December 2006 – June 2007

December 2006 – June 2007

Mike Purchas

Mike Purchas felt the cool morning air dry the sweat running down his forehead as he pounded up the hill. Children were already out tossing balls. He ran past a father struggling to order his children into the back of a car and nodded a greeting.

He was glad he had managed to duck out early, beating the summer heat and finding a little peace before the inevitable chaos. His girlfriend's relatives would soon be arriving in a frenetic stream, bearing plates piled with spring rolls, prawns and Vietnamese salad, and tailed by screaming small children and their mute teenage siblings.

At least they learnt to shut up as they got older.

His thoughts drifted from how much he missed the snow of a London winter to his police partner, Bruce Bullock. He'd fought the urge to call him that morning but was now reconsidering. He wanted to workshop the tip-off that he and Bullock received prior to knocking off from the Crime Commission on Christmas Eve. But it was Christmas Day, and Bullock wouldn't appreciate the call. Nor would his wife.

Bugger it. I'll call him anyway, he thought. The drug stash could be bigger than anything we've seized before. And it will get us back in the game, give us leverage with the bosses in Canberra. He'll understand. It's not like Christmas is a one-off. For Christ's sake, Bruce, it comes every year.

Then again, Bullock's wife would probably stuff him in the turkey if he took a work call over his Christmas lunch. Even if Bullock told her what it was about—how, in a single swoop, they could destroy conventional wisdom about the size of Australia's drug trade.

As Purchas turned the corner, a child wobbled out in front of him on a new bike, forcing him to leap to the left. He could still move pretty well, despite his sixty years, he thought, turning around to glare at the child, who, absorbed with the task of staying upright, hadn't noticed him. He wiped the sweat off his forehead with his sleeve and lengthened his stride, feeling pain shoot through his knees.

They'd run some miles, he and 'Melonhead'. He had given Bullock the nickname when a motorcycle helmet from the United States had to be imported because none in Australia fit his partner's expansive skull.

Bullock didn't seem to mind the jibe. Everyone in the office had a name: 'Good News Glenn' was a manager who disappeared around bad news; 'Startrek' was the intelligence analyst who was often off in space; 'Turniptop' referred to a senior investigator whose head looked like it had been dug out of the ground. And he was 'Skeletor', thanks to his skinny frame, or 'Blakey', in reference to the pommy conductor from the old British comedy *On the Buses*.

He smiled as he ran, remembering the undercover job when he'd posed as a drug buyer. The crook had looked him up and down suspiciously, before blurting out, 'Mate, you don't need cocaine. You need a fuckin' feed.' One of the office smart-arses had it printed on a T-shirt.

I should probably leave Bullock alone, he thought. He's earned his time off. And I owe him one. He had wanted to say something meaningful to Bullock when they knocked off for Christmas leave the day before, but hadn't. It wasn't his or Bullock's style. Emotions weren't their forte. And anyway, Bullock would know what was on his mind.

It was Bullock who'd revived Purchas's career when other managers hadn't wanted to touch him. As usual, it was his mouth that had got him into trouble. He hadn't been able to contain himself when two female colleagues had asked for time off, mid-investigation. It had hit the courts and the press, and embarrassed his bosses. He grimaced as he recalled the newspaper reports: 'Mr Purchas berated her about her leave … Mr Purchas said that her children seemed to catch everything that went around …'

He had nothing against women. It was just that they often couldn't work the hours the job demanded because of kids and school pick-ups and whatever else happened in their lives. He'd also fallen out with male investigators who didn't share his work ethic. At the Independent Commission Against Corruption in Hong Kong and

December 2006 – June 2007

Sydney, or at the Australian Crime Commission's predecessor, the National Crime Authority, there was always a long line of the sick, the lame or the lazy. If by chance these staff were in the building, they would be arranging a multicultural breakfast or diversity training. Work was not high on their agenda. And he told them so. He'd never been able to shut up when he spotted laziness. Colleagues, bosses, it didn't matter.

That was one of the reasons he liked Bullock so much. He was a born detective who fearlessly spoke his mind, among the best he'd worked with in almost forty years. And they shared the same mad work ethic, despite Bullock having children. Each morning over the past twelve months, he'd called Bullock from his car at 6.00 a.m. to plan the day's operations in Melbourne and Sydney. They'd canvass everything: phone interceptions, secret cameras, star-chamber hearings, arrests, charges, rollovers. 6.00 a.m. every single day. He should have mentioned something to Bullock when they had knocked off …

Bullock had saved him from the office dead in 2005 by putting him in control of the Sydney end of Operation Gordian, the Crime Commission's biggest money laundering investigation since the agency's inception in 2003. Bullock had largely conceived the operation and was running the Melbourne end of the probe.

They were a perfect fit. They spurned office politics and the lazy or obsequious. As operations managers, they were tolerated by the senior executive only because they produced. And produced.

Gordian had exceeded all expectations, uncovering twenty-one drug syndicates moving $300 million to Asia through several small Vietnamese-run money-remitting companies in Sydney and Melbourne. All in just eighteen months.

The investigation had ripped up the manual on chasing the proceeds of crime. Instead of the usual retrospective tracing of a paper trail, they followed the tainted cash as they would a package of drugs. The result had been almost a hundred arrests, including dozens for money laundering, and the seizure of half a billion dollars' worth of drugs.

Bullock led a team of the commission's best investigators from Melbourne, and as the commission's Sydney-based operations manager, Purchas had coordinated a team of elite analysts. The pair had achieved an extraordinarily rare thing in Australian law enforcement: breaking down the inflexible, military-like hierarchy and getting staff in different states to work together over borders. No one called him boss. Just Mike. Or Skeletor.

Bullock called him Gordian's 'helicopter', because of the way his team in Sydney provided a broad overview of the project's operations while Bullock and his Melbourne investigators ran things on the ground. They bounced off each other continuously, always bluntly, sometimes explosively, but with the same aim in mind. They wanted results, wanted their work to have meaning. And they loved the game. That meant hating, despising, loathing the idea of a crook walking away from them. Which is why he and Bullock remained unsatisfied when Gordian wound up. They knew the real story

As the arrest phase had unfolded over the previous six months, the commission bosses, along with their political masters in Canberra, began briefing the media about one of Australia's most successful anti-drug and money laundering operations. But a week ago, during a routine traffic stop, uniformed Victorian police had discovered 340 litres of pure liquid ecstasy, enough to make $50 million worth of high-grade gear, in the back of a white HiAce van. The man at the wheel was a runner for a syndicate that Operation Gordian was meant to have wiped out.

Since then, intelligence had flowed in suggesting the drugs in the van were part of much bigger shipments stored along Australia's east coast. Searching for them was like looking for the proverbial needle. But their existence would prove what he and Bullock had suspected for months: of the two hundred or so suspects they had interviewed in the course of Gordian, almost none of these bottom feeders knew who they were really working for. They were all low- to middle-tier runners and money movers, and their arrests and the corresponding drug seizures had barely dented the drug supply. The bosses controlling the flow of heroin, ecstasy, ice and cocaine into Australia and internationally were still unknown, untouched and undisturbed.

He and Bullock wanted to find a way to extend Gordian so they could not only cast a wider net over suspicious money flows, but also find a way to track them once they had left Australia. The money marching offshore was not only money lost from Australia's economy; it was almost certainly financing fresh drug imports. It meant a new round of addicts pumping shit into themselves and ending up in hospital beds or crawling through the windows of other people's houses. And drug dealers shooting each other wherever they could get a clean shot: at football clinics, in pubs and on suburban streets. Melbourne's gangland war claimed more than twenty lives in just a few years and was one of the rare times the battle to control the drug market was fought in public.

Purchas slowed his pace to a walk as he turned the corner and neared the front of his girlfriend Huong's house, complete with neo-Georgian columns that had never really fit the bushy, gumtree-dotted suburb.

She glared at him as he walked through the door. 'The turkey, Mike!'

He felt himself grinning meekly. Bullock was right. For a supposedly feared senior police officer, he was remarkably adept at following orders at home. Huong wasn't shy about giving them. A successful lawyer, she was tough, uncompromising, and fiercely independent and protective of her own space. But it worked for them: she was spontaneous; he was fastidious. They were both quick-tongued. 'The little princess,' he would call her, but not before bracing for a withering riposte.

He was quietly looking forward to being swamped by her relatives, people who treasured family and loyalty. The thought conjured up, just briefly, a memory of his parents long gone, and his siblings overseas, whom he rarely spoke to. He wiped it from his mind, slipped into the bathroom, turned on a tap and dialled his phone, studying himself in the mirror as he waited for an answer. For many years his face had looked younger than he expected, but now it surprised him with age. His cheeks were still taught and slightly inverted, but the skin around his jutting jaw was lined. He dialled again.

'For fuck's sake, Mikey. It's Christmas Day.'

He ignored the rebuke. 'I've been thinking about the liquid ecstasy, Bruce. We can't sit around waiting for it to disappear. If it's out there, we have to find it.'

Bullock's wife was saying something in the background, although he couldn't make out the words. 'Mikey … it's my first day off in months.'

'This is our best chance at giving our plan a shot, Bruce.'

Another pause. 'Well?'

Bullock cleared his throat. 'I'll need a week with my boys. But I can be there New Year's Day. And Mike?'

'Yes?'

'Merry fucking Christmas.'

Hakan 'Hux' Ayik

Hakan Ayik felt the bass pulse through the air as he scanned the faces, seeking out his crew. *Doof, doof, doof.*

Buffed-up men in their twenties and thirties stood in circles, out-talking each other while downing shots of chartreuse and Jägermeister, gym-worked arms imitating bicep curls as they brought shot glasses to their lips.

He nodded at a couple of Lebanese guys whom he recognised from fight nights. They both wore tight T-shirts bearing the name of their gym. *Doof, doof, doof.* So many of the boys had been locked up, and were buff in a way that only came through full-time gym obsession or jail. The Islanders were the exception. They're all monsters, he thought.

He had felt at home at this club since the Comanchero motorcycle club had taken over the door. Half the blokes here were of Turkish descent, like him, or from Lebanon. They dressed like him; spoke his language. Here, he was among his own.

As his eyes kept moving, he felt his body ache dully, the product of two hours pumping weights that morning at the gym he part-owned. At times like this, when he was at the height of his training—five times a week—his muscles felt like they were in a constant state of semi-contraction, restricting his limb movement, making him walk as if he had an invisible surfboard under his arm.

Depending on his training, his body weight fluctuated. In peak form he weighed in at 90 kilos; his skin was tight, his body rippled, and with his pronounced jaw, even features and short hair, he looked handsome. Out of training, he would quickly fatten up, hitting ninety-five plus on the scales.

He breathed in and held a short flex, recapping the morning session. Three sets of power bench press, a heavy fly times three for the chest, lat pull downs for the neck and shoulders, and then ab crunches. No wonder I feel fuckin' ripped, he thought. And like partying.

He put his hand in his pocket and checked for the small, sealed bag. He loved these nights when he recognised half the patrons, the girls were dressed up in short skirts and everyone was drunk, high and out for a good time.

It hadn't changed since finishing James Cook High in … how many years was it? And it was still the same old shit: same friends, same bars, same girls, same kebab shop on the way home, same headache waking up. He grinned. He'd talked the same shit for years: cars, girls, footy, boxing, computer games and business. Business. Now, more than ever, he talked business.

'Hey, Hux.'

He glanced over the sea of bodies and saw the big Maori who had yelled his name moving slowly towards him. Daux was one of those at the Lincoln who didn't need to work out. He was born a monster.

On the T-shirt stretched across his vast chest was the word 'Comanchero' along with a large eagle, the club emblem. Unlike many members of bikie clubs who only wore their colours at bikie events or in the clubhouse, Daux wore his Comanchero gear almost everywhere. A heavy gold necklace spilled over the shirt. Thick and chunky, it was the sort of chain rapper Snoop Dog would wear in film clips, surrounded by bitches and cars. He wondered whose chest Daux had ripped it from.

He had known Daux since primary school, but even now he was wary. Violence came too easy for Daux. It was always about kneecapping someone or hanging them off a balcony. There wasn't a problem that couldn't be solved with a pipe and a blowtorch. Becoming the Comancheros' official enforcer, the sergeant-at-arms, had only made matters worse. Especially now club business was booming.

'How are you, brother?' He felt Daux's bear-like palm strike his back with a sharp whack. 'You comin' to my area tomoz? We need to talk.'

He knew what Daux wanted. 'My area' was Brighton-le-Sands, the suburb in which Daux fancied himself as the unofficial mayor. The talking would be about a plan cooked up by one of the Comos, a guy known to most as Mizza but whose real name was Joseph Micalizzi. Mizza had devised a clever way of getting gear interstate through a bloke willing to make deliveries in his light plane. It would be a huge cost and time saver that would lead to some easy multi million-dollar earns. The state of security at most of the nation's regional airports meant that planes were almost never searched.

'Are we safe to talk here?' Daux stared at the ceiling, looking for cameras.

'Bro, I can barely hear you, so no one else can hear shit.'

It was safe talking inside the club. Amid the music and chatter, a police bug would be useless. But he still leaned over to Daux and whispered into his ear. 'They've run a test flight and it went smoothly.'

'Good news, man,' said Daux. 'I'll have a chat with the pres.'

On paper, Daux answered to Mick Hawi, the president of the Comancheros and another James Cook alumnus, but in reality it was Daux and Hux who ran the show.

Ayik felt one of his mobiles buzz in his pocket but had to take out all three to find which one was ringing. It was Will. He walked into the club toilet to take the call.

'Hey, bro. You're meant to be at mine. I thought we were going to play the new Xbox. And you were going to drop around the you know what.'

He could hear the neediness and disappointment in Will's voice. 'Watch your mouth, dumb cunt.' How stupid could Will be? He'd told that prick a million times never to talk business on the phone. 'I can't make it tonight. One of the boys will be round to say hi in a few days.'

He hung up and stepped back into the club, wondering if Will had picked up his reference to the impending drop-off. He let the thought disappear into the warmth of the body heat and the thump of the bass. He spotted Daux clutching a scotch and eyeing off a girl whose skirt very nearly wasn't there. She was a very tasty piece. He'd get in there before his mate did. But first, business.

He walked over to Daux and leaned towards his ear. 'I got some good news, brother,' he whispered. 'I'm back off overseas pretty soon. I think we're all about to get fuckin' loaded.'

Senator Steve Hutchins

It had been a disaster. There was nothing more to it. Squinting to avoid the glare of the sun, Senator Steve Hutchins blocked out the sounds of splashing and laughter. The reassuring smell of sunscreen pervaded his nostrils. It was only a few weeks but he still wasn't over it. A bloody disaster.

Kim Beazley should have beaten Kevin Rudd for the leadership. Beazley was a decent man who wouldn't leave anyone behind, but he may have trusted too easily. He should never have had faith in Senator John Faulkner and the Victorian Left, but Beazley was a true believer—a real politician who believed in power *and* policy.

Rudd … Rudd believed only in his own advancement. Bugger it. Rudd had played the better game, aligning with the supposed Beazley loyalists who were instead white-anting their leader, all the while knowing that Beazley's decency put him at a disadvantage. It was a complete, bloody disaster.

Hutchins was distracted momentarily by his twin daughters splashing around, wearing their new Christmas bathers. If he could arrange to get his kids from both marriages together around Christmas time, surely they could have pulled it off for Beazley.

It wasn't just the loss that galled him, but what had followed. Straight afterwards, Beazley learnt that his brother had died. His family hadn't told him before the leadership ballot because they didn't want him to lose focus. Yet, when he lost, it meant the whole bloody world crumbled. Hutchins and the other Beazley supporters had crowded into his office, a throng of emotion and despair.

At any rate, he was stuffed. He had been one of Beazley's loudest backers, canvassing politicians in the Labor Party's right faction to vote for Beazley as the man to lead the party out of the wilderness of Opposition for the first time in a decade. The moment Beazley lost, he knew he was a marked man.

'Madeline, Georgia, not too deep!' he yelled. Had they heard or were they just ignoring him?

He'd been here before. He knew what it was like to have the party leave you for dead, he thought, smiling wryly. A few years back, while he lay in the oncology ward, he'd got word that buzzards from the state branch were circling, plotting his replacement. His body wasn't even cold.

He'd dispatched a letter from his surgeon to make his point: he was still alive and had prospects of recovery. They could fill his shoes when the priest was telling the mourners what a great bloke he was and not a second before.

Still, he was as good as buried now. Rudd wouldn't forget. If Rudd took the prime ministership, he would be in political Siberia.

December 2006 – June 2007

imports, gifts around holiday time and so on.' Vikingsson was now speaking rapidly. 'As I predicted, there was a huge discrepancy in the figures. All up, the remitters were sending back several hundred million more than could be accounted for in my estimates of legitimate transfers. Even when I bumped up the average earnings of those Vietnamese using the remitters, there was a huge difference. I then ran algorithms over those excess money flows to find which remitters were responsible for them. Sure enough, some of the remitters I flagged were run by the same corrupt money movers we uncovered in Gordian or had come up in other police inquiries. But the thing is …' Vikingsson was straining, getting louder with each sentence. 'I identified all of this by using the High Risks Funds Program. It helped me to find the needle in the haystack, the slime in the river.'

Vikingsson hesitated again, as if expecting applause.

'Keep going, Patrick.'

Glowing proudly, Vikingsson handed him the file. 'As soon as Gordian shut down those remitters sending the drug money offshore, several other Vietnamese money remitters in Sydney and Melbourne suddenly began sending far more funds offshore. Turns out they were picking up the business formerly held by the remitters we took out. The funds these new guys are moving are almost certain to be one great big filthy river of …'

Purchas studied the file, blocking out Vikingsson's voice. Absorbing the graphs and accompanying notes, he felt an odd hollowness permeate his body. The analyst was right. New corrupt remitters had simply taken over from those Gordian had shut down. Six weeks after Gordian had wrapped up, suspected narco-dollars were flowing out of Australia at an even greater volume than before.

'It's like trying to trap water by squeezing it in your hand. It simply moves. We've done nothing to stop the flow,' Purchas whispered. Closing the file, he turned to Vikingsson and, with renewed urgency in his voice, asked, 'Are you able to track where the funds are ending up offshore?'

Vikingsson shrugged. 'I mostly lose sight of it once it moves through different banks. But I am working on it.'

'Could the High Risk Funds Program run in almost real time?'

The analyst nodded.

'And you could feasibly do it with the entire Australian economy and come up with an estimate of the total black economy leaving Australia?'

The analyst paused. 'If we had enough solid data, we could probably give it a real crack. My early modelling suggests the official estimates of the size of Australia's criminal economy are laughable. It is likely to be much, much bigger …'

Purchas interrupted again. 'I want you to run another test case. Something outside of Asia, to prove that the High Risk Funds Program truly works.'

The analyst looked at him curiously. 'What are you going to do with it?'

'Nothing yet,' he said. 'First I have to find a needle of my own.'

Wei 'Will' Wong

By God, he needed a root. Will reached for the phone and dialled.

'Asian Dreams, how can I help you?'

'You got any Koreans on tonight?'

'We have three free now. Very good. Very nice. Very young.' The woman spoke with an unpleasant, shrill voice, dragging out her vowels. She sounded like the ladies in the dress shops his mother dragged him to as a child in Beijing.

He checked his wallet as he spoke. It was full of fifties. 'How old is very young?'

'She is twenteeee. Very nice massaaaage, very good fuuuun.'

He gave his address twice to make sure they didn't go to the wrong apartment—he didn't want that happening again—and waited. He considered cleaning up the mess in front of him, the Xbox consoles and empty take-away containers, but then dismissed the thought. What would she care? More to the point, what did he care? He had an hour to kill and business to take care of. He had to check the brothel had got the new linen, towels and shampoo, and receive the drop-off.

Hux was also due to call from somewhere in Asia. He looked at the two phones in front of him. He'd made a mistake getting two handsets so alike. Unforgivably, he'd used his personal phone to conduct business too many times. He shuddered thinking at how it displeased Hux. He hated annoying his friend. Hux had to know that he was a good soldier, and was up to what was asked of him and more. He thought back to the last time Hux had sat him down.

'I'm telling you, Will, unless you want to go inside or lose your visa, you can only talk on a clean line. You gotta believe that some cunt is always listening. And stop blowing so much on sluts.'

It wasn't so much what Hux had said, but how he had said it. He wasn't sure, but it was as if Hux was implying he wasn't sharp enough. That was unfair. None of Hux's other mates had his business degree, or even knew jack shit about revenue, overheads, tax and marketing.

He shrugged off his doubts. They got on better than most realised, he and the Turk. They were both entrepreneurs with a taste for finer things: computer games, cars, money and girls. Especially girls.

Now that he was flush, he was banging more fine chicks than he ever dreamed of back home. Chinese, Koreans, Japs, Thai; he loved them all. What's more, he knew how to please them. It was about staying power. If he'd paid for an hour, he'd go for the full sixty minutes. With a bit of luck, he'd blow right on the buzzer. How many guys could say that?

He started as the intercom buzzed. It must be the cash.

He hit the button and, on the way to the door, diverted to relieve himself. As he pissed, he felt pain shoot through his groin. That was the down side with pros. Still, he wasn't about to start using condoms; they interfered with the rush, the whole business of getting down.

Sliding back the door chain, he braced for a monster. He got one. The man at his doorway would not be passing through it, not if he could help it. 'You got it?' He tried to sound casual.

The man, who had tattoos snaking around his neck and down his arm, eyed him with disdain before passing over a backpack and, without saying a word, marched away.

Well, fuck you very much, too. Hux's bikie mates were like … he searched for a word, smiling as it came to him. They were s*huǐ niú*, big useless creatures who treated him as they would a bird feeding off their hides. That was the difference with Hux. Hux understood the Asian scene, understood *gei mianzi*, respecting those who needed to be respected. In turn, they respected him.

Hux *got it*. Bikies usually looked fearsome, and sometimes were. Triads rarely looked fearsome, but always were. He thought back to the skinny, wild-eyed triad soldiers in his old neighbourhood, covered in scars from being chopped and hacked. Brawn didn't equal courage.

One of his phones began buzzing. It had to be Hux.

'Wei. Wei.'

Shit. It was his mother. She was the only person who called him by his real name. He'd confused the phones again. She was speaking Mandarin in her usual breakneck style, launching into a fresh question before finishing the last. Health? Food? Girlfriend? Study? Visa? Business?

He mumbled an excuse and hung up as the intercom buzzed again.

The squeaky voice piping through the speaker caused him to smile. She sounded young. 'Come on up. Level thirty-three.'

He greeted a short, pretty, dark-haired girl wearing a tiny red miniskirt; she was hot and somehow familiar. Did he know her from a club or food joint? Or had he had her before?

'You want shower or massage?' she asked as he peeled off three fifties from the bundle and handed them to her. She was eying the lump of notes still in his hand, so he stalled on putting it back in his pocket. They loved a man with means. He shook his head and pointed her towards the bed, undoing his own shirt. He wanted to fuck, not join a hygiene class. What was she worried about, anyhow? She was a pro. There was nothing clean about that.

He checked his watch, calculating how long until his girlfriend was due to arrive. There was no risk of another crossover—he'd sworn to avoid a repeat of the last time—but the sooner he was finished the better. He needed time to recharge his batteries.

He finished with the hooker two minutes short of the half hour. He was a machine, he thought to himself. After ejecting her, he decided he needed some air and headed for the escalator and the streets of Chinatown, towards his baby. It sat on a lane corner, in the heart of the precinct, surrounded by the restaurant hustle and a smell that reminded him of his mother's kitchen. He and Hux had decided on the name a few weeks ago: Club de Melody. He spoke the words out loud and felt a rush of pride.

His phone vibrated, and he hoped again for Hux.

'Where the hell are you?'

Wrong phone again. It was his girlfriend. If only she liked the bed as much as she liked to argue. He turned tail, steeling himself for the encounter. Pros made for infinitely simpler companions. Club de Melody would have to wait.

He braced himself and slid the key in the apartment door. 'Hello? You there?'

There was no reply. The apartment was still. He checked the bathroom, but it was empty. Same for the bedroom. His phone vibrated again and this time he made sure it was the business phone. 'Hello?'

'Hey, bro.' It was Hux, finally.

'Hey. How you going?'

'Yeah, all good. Been here a week or two. Did they drop by?'

The question prompted him to look towards the corner of his room where he'd dumped the bag. There was nothing there. He spun around, scanning the room for it. Still nothing. He froze momentarily, before rushing through the apartment, searching for the dough.

'Fuck. Fuck. Fuck.' He heard questions coming down the phone line, but they sounded mumbled. With his free hand he flung the pillows and doona cover off the bed. Nothing.

'Fuck, fuck, fuck.' He felt his stomach seize up as he walked into the bathroom. Nothing. As his misdemeanours flashed through his mind—the spare key, the unattended apartment, the bag of money—he was drawn back to the increasing irritation in Hux's voice.

He drew breath and forced the words out of his mouth. 'It's gone. That fuckin' bitch has taken the whole bag.'

Gregory James

'I want you to get the agency to break some new ground in the money-laundering area. To really *do* something.' Sitting alone in the commission's cafe, Gregory James replayed the words of one of the agency's Canberra bosses in his head.

It was easier said than done. He'd been given no plan, no suggestions, no nothing. All he had was his title, Acting General Manager, Financial Crimes, which gave him responsibility for an underperforming portfolio. He was busy enough already cleaning up the Taskforce Wickenby mess.

Wickenby, a major tax fraud probe targeting some of Australia's biggest sporting and entertainment celebrities, including actor Paul Hogan, was being spruiked in the press by the commission and the tax office as one of the nation's biggest crime probes. James winced at the tag. Celebrities avoiding tax through offshore banking might be illegal, but it wasn't in the realm of the crime syndicates who were the agency's reason for being. Crocodile Dundee was hardly a crime boss, and the investigation into Hogan was heading for a major shitfight as well. He had already briefed his bosses that he was sceptical about the case against the film star and that it would become endlessly bogged down in expensive legal challenges.

December 2006 – June 2007

Hunting Crocodile Dundee wasn't why the agency had been created as an organised crime buster in 2003, he thought to himself. It certainly wasn't the reason why he had returned to law enforcement. Wickenby was turning into one of those politicised inquiries whose momentum was partly down to someone's empire building. He learnt long ago that while supposedly being an independent law enforcement agency, the ACC operated at the discretion of the state and federal police chiefs on its board, and at the mercy of the federal government, which funded the agency and often directed it to investigate certain and sometimes politically motivated areas.

If you wanted to avoid the politics, you had to learn to play the political game. An inquiry would go nowhere if it didn't hold out at least something for the commission's political and policing masters: busts, news headlines, political kudos. At least his boss was giving him an opportunity at something new. But what? All he had was a blank page.

A gravelly voice, straight from old London, interrupted his thinking. 'You escaped from the nursing home?'

It was Michael Purchas, the commission's Sydney operations manager.

'I followed you out the window, Mike.'

'Mind if I join you?'

He nodded, watching Purchas head to the coffee counter. There was something reassuring about Purchas's London turn of phrase. It took him back to his own time in the UK. If you were clever, you had a dose of the smarts; if you were annoyed, you had a dose of the shits. A corrupt copper was in on the joke; a stupid cop, with no ambition, was a wooden top who would need retraining after a long lunch.

He watched Purchas as he waited for his coffee, phone stuck to his ear and face lined with a cool intensity. He'd first come across Purchas's work while auditing an informer and deep cover unit. Purchas's name had come up in over a dozen informer-based operations. It appeared that most of the agency's Asian sources belonged to him.

James knew why several of the commission's senior executives were wary of Purchas. The man was like an ungrateful volcano, a bubbling force of energy and aggression. He could be sour and appeared endlessly restless, frustrated.

Much of what Purchas did was considered high risk. Yet he guarded the safety of his informers and colleagues as zealously as he disregarded the ability of many of his bosses to do the same. With Purchas, you did it his way or you got out of the way. Purchas explained operational concepts with what he called his 'one-liners', the simple analogies he designed to get through to even the thickest of his bosses. When things turned nasty, his favourite one-liner contained only two words: get fucked.

It was no wonder some of the commission's bosses had relished parking him in the corner after a discrimination complaint. Yet most in the game, even those who couldn't stand him, acknowledged him as one of Australia's most successful organised crime fighters, especially when it came to Asian organised crime.

His expertise and experience were unquestioned. In the 1970s, Purchas had made his name as a detective investigating roving gangs of gypsies robbing houses in wealthy English towns; 'travelling criminals' Purchas called them. He moved into homicide and drug investigations, and then corruption and organised crime probes in Hong Kong and Sydney.

Along the way, Purchas had gained a better grasp of criminal law around drug and money laundering investigations than many lawyers and barristers. He took them on, as well. He famously challenged a Supreme Court judge's knowledge of the law from the witness box, extracting a rare, red-faced apology from his honour.

As most of his contemporaries were growing comfortable in office-bound senior management positions, Purchas was still out on the street. Even in his fifties, he'd worked as an undercover officer.

James guessed that the reason Purchas had warmed to him was due to his background in intelligence gathering. James had worked as an undercover operative for European intelligence services, infiltrating arms-dealing and terrorist networks. Purchas hadn't said so, but he knew it had given him a rare credibility in the eyes of the old investigator. It meant that Purchas was, if only slowly, starting to trust him and show a side most rarely seen: his quiet, but boundless, kindness and loyalty.

Purchas returned with his coffee, sat down and grinned. 'You look like shit, Jamesy. What's going on?'

He noticed a knowing expression dance across Purchas's face as James explained his blank page conundrum. He guessed Purchas knew of it already. It was probably the underlying reason for this morning's banter.

'I heard our genius leaders in Canberra want to make up for some lost ground. You know, I may be able to fill your blank sheet with a few ideas. Bruce is coming up in a day or two to chase up some post-Gordian leads. Could be nothing. But it could be something.'

James responded with silence. If you wanted answers from Purchas, it was often better not to question him. But, after a few awkward seconds, Purchas excused himself. He watched the gangly figure stride off, phone again to his ear, and then noticed Purchas had left his coffee sitting untouched. Something was up. He wondered how long he'd have to wait before Purchas brought him into the loop.

Bilal

As Bilal watched Waz work, he felt his sense of disgust building. There was nothing about Waz that was remotely attractive. The man was small, maybe five feet six, with stumpy, short legs that held up a barrelling torso and an impossibly wide and ugly head. For reasons known only to Him, God had forgotten to give Waz a neck. The mere sight of him was annoying.

Waz, short for Wissam, was at that moment tipping a bottle of chemicals into a large plastic barrel with a tap on the bottom, the sort usually filled with cordial at a junior football clinic. He had bought the barrel two hours before at Kmart as part of a trip that had taken him to two hardware stores and a chemist to buy toluene, Epsom salts, glucose and hydrochloric acid.

'How am I going, Bilal?'

He shook his head, saying nothing. Waz was his second cousin by marriage. He was also a twenty-two-year-old bikie nominee who, six months ago, had been assigned the task of hiring a factory, registering a health food and soap importing business, and guarding the barrels of chemical precursors that his associates had apparently sourced from some sort of shipment from China.

Waz had been breezily talking up the prospect of doing a cook for the last three months, as if it amounted to nothing more than popping on a roast. He had endlessly pestered him to help out, and offered him twenty grand—or, as Waz liked to repeat ad nauseum, 'twenty mutha-fuckin' large'. When he had refused, Waz called in his wife, Bilal's second cousin, to lobby him.

Bilal thought back to the call as he watched his cousin prise open one of the containers. At first, he had told her what he had told Waz. 'No, no and no. I have done one year of university chemistry. I work as freight forwarder at Port Botany, not in a lab … It ain't gunna happen.'

Waz's wife had responded by bursting into tears and, through her sobs, told him that Waz would be bashed or worse if he didn't do the cook. It was part of his non-negotiable duties as a bikie club nominee.

He had later tried to convince Waz that maybe, just maybe, being a nom wasn't worth it, given it meant taking on all of the risk in a highly risky, highly illegal enterprise. The factory was in Waz's name and it was his grubby arms that would be elbow deep in shit if any cops burst in.

Waz had responded to his tirade with a grin. 'So, you in or not, cuz?'

He'd agreed, saying he didn't want to have Waz's blood on his hands. In truth, he needed the money. His job on the wharves brought in only a grand a week. He had a mortgage, a son and another baby on the way. So here he was, helping possibly the dumbest man he knew mix up $20 million worth of speed.

'You gotta let it sit, Waz. The toluene has to bind with the meth.'

He hadn't said so, but he found himself secretly enjoying the chemical side of the cook. He'd always loved chemistry, both at high school and, before he'd dropped out, at university. He had been good at it, as well. There was something wonderful about knowing how things were made; how the bubbles formed in soda; how the alcohol in beer was produced; how the toluene molecules would attach to those in the methamphetamine precursors, separating them out from the heavier oil-based molecules and bringing the meth to the surface, leaving the oil at the bottom to be drained out.

'Try it now,' he said.

Waz opened the tap and a thick syrupy oil poured out into a plastic tub. 'At least this is better than punching out tablets, eh cuz?'

Bilal responded with a glare. At first, to get his foot in the club door, Waz had been assigned the job of sitting for days on end in a safe house pushing pseudoephedrine tablets out of thousands of cold and flu packets sourced from every chemist between Sydney and Byron Bay.

'You know Waz, it might be fucking great being in a bikie club ...' he said, pausing to make his point, 'if you're the president. Otherwise, it seems to pretty much suck.'

'You're dead right,' Waz said dreamily. 'Imagine being president. All that pussy and power. It would be siiiick!'

Bilal glared again. 'Let's just get this shit over and done with. I gotta get home,' he said. Glancing at the precursor-filled containers lined up against the factory wall, he added, 'And if you think I am doing this again, you are off your fucking face.'

Each container was sealed and covered in Chinese characters. He had tried to do the maths on how much meth could be made from the liquid if it was pure pre-cook precursor, but gave up when he passed $100 million.

'Just the one cook, bro. Then your work is done. What's next?'

He began explaining the next step when he noticed Waz reaching for a cigarette. He leapt over, grabbing his arm. 'For fuck's sake, Waz. You want to blow us up, cocksucker? Sniff the air. You smell it? It's solvent vapour. You really, truly are a dumb cunt.'

Waz's face began burning red and he immediately felt guilty. 'You can have a smoke later. First you gotta add the drain cleaner. It will neutralise the acid and help form crystals. Then we'll test the pH.'

His nostrils twitched as Waz poured the caustic soda into the meth solution and he covered his nose with his T-shirt as he watched the liquid harden into translucent crystals. 'We need the pH at 7. Any more and your shit is going to be just that.' Bilal thought back to early high school, when he had first learnt about the body's pH level. If the meth wasn't pH 7, it would burn the mucous membranes in the nasal passage or rupture a user's veins.

'Now, pass it through the filter.' An oily, gluggy mass formed on the paper as Waz tipped the mixture onto the gauze. All they needed now was hydrochloric acid to get the pH right.

An hour later, he was pouring a 10-kilo bag of glucose mixed with Epsom salts onto a mound of white powder. The mix was roughly one to one, although he knew that by the time it reached the street, it would probably be around ten to one.

'Who can we get to have a taste?' he asked Waz.

'Follow me.'

Waz grabbed a dime bag and filled it with a pinch of the cut product. As he followed Waz out of the factory, Bilal found himself scanning the street looking for any movement. It was dark and quiet. Ten minutes later, he was standing next to Waz outside a rundown weatherboard house decorated with two rusting cars on the front lawn.

'Nice place,' he said under his breath as Waz knocked on the door.

A muscular guy appeared wearing a singlet that said, 'Singha Beer'. He had scabs around his mouth and yellow teeth. Bilal had seen speed heads like him before. They hit the gear like they hit the gym.

'Hey, bro. We need your expert advice for some new shit. You want a free taste?'

The man eyed Waz and then Bilal warily.

'He's cool, bro. He's my cuz. Bilal meet Mo.'

He had to stop himself correcting Waz—it's second cousin by marriage, dickhead. He followed Waz and Mo into the house, his curiosity rising over whether their batch was any good.

He and Waz had already mapped out a game plan if the guinea pig keeled over. They would wipe the doorknob for prints, take their meth sample and remove any drug paraphernalia which had come into contact with it. He didn't know for sure, but he suspected every batch had its own chemical fingerprint.

Waz had responded in typical manner: 'You're fucking CSI, cuz. Siiiick!'

Bilal watched Mo as he filled a metal spoon with crystals and a few drops of saline. Hip-hop was pumping from the bedroom, and body-building mags were strewn around the longue room. The carpet looked like it hadn't been cleaned in years. Using a lighter, Mo heated the saline and crystals until it became a bubbling liquid, which he sucked into a syringe.

Most who would end up buying this speed in nightclubs and bars would snort it in the belief that it was somehow cleaner. Not Mo, he thought. With one deft stroke, their product tester picked up a tie and, keeping an end in his mouth, wrapped it tightly around his arm. Within seconds, the blue lines on his arm rose from the skin and he plunged the needle into a vein.

'Ahhhhh.'

As Mo's head rolled back and he closed his eyes, Bilal wondered anxiously for a half a second if their test bunny was dead. But then he exclaimed, 'Ahhhh. Ahhhhhhh. That's some fucking good shit, boys. What a rush.' Mo leapt to his feet, pumping a fist into an open palm—*Slap. Slap. Slap.* 'I got to pump some iron, boys.' He looked like he was itching to hit someone. Bilal hoped it wasn't Waz.

When Mo disappeared into his bedroom, he whispered to Waz, 'Let's get out of here mate.' Waz nodded at the wisdom of leaving this junkie to his high.

An hour later, after Waz dropped him off at his house, Bilal crept through the front door like a teenage thief, past the small bedroom that, in quiet prayer for another son, he had painted blue the week before.

'Is that you, Billy?' his wife yelled from the bedroom. 'Where have you been?'

'Nowhere,' he said. And then, as if to avoid the lie, 'Just catching up with Waz.'

Purchas

The streets were empty, save for the odd group of stumbling New Year's Eve revellers who hadn't yet made it home. Purchas drove in silence, his eyes switching between the road and Bullock, who was studying a map laid out on the dashboard.

Whenever he saw Bullock in the flesh after an absence, he always thought back to their first conversation, when he'd picked up an office phone to cop an earful from a husky voice about how the ACC's Sydney office had bungled a surveillance job. Before Bullock could finish, Purchas had barked, 'Get fucked', and hung up.

A few days later, Bullock had appeared in the Sydney office for the first time—all 6 feet 2 and 110 kilograms of him. 'I'm Bruce. It's good to meet you. It was a pleasure speaking to you on the phone the other day,' he had said with a twinkle in his eyes.

Bullock interrupted his daydreaming. 'It's got to be it, Mikey. I'll try the real estate out-of-hours number again.'

When he was on the chase, Bullock was like him. He never gave up. Never. Who else would see in the New Year by trading their family holiday for a wild goose chase?

This time, Bullock connected. 'Yes, I'm sorry … yes, I know what day it is … but …' Purchas heard his colleague drop the friendliness in his voice. He knew that tone well. 'Listen, mate. I'll say it only once. We're working on a law enforcement inquiry of great priority. It's very important you assist us. We need to urgently identify a premise you're renting out, a premise that may be tied to serious criminality. I'm asking for your help. Do you reckon you might be good enough to give it?'

Bullock hung up the phone. 'I think he was still in bed. He'll meet us there in twenty.'

It was now two weeks since the bust on the van filled with liquid ecstasy. In that time, the Crime Commission had received a single piece of intelligence. The chemicals in the van had most likely been sourced from a stash in an industrial complex in Sydney's north-west. There were two possibilities.

The first, circled on the map in front of Bullock, was a small industrial enclave with a dozen factories that they had already discounted on the basis that they had been rented for a minimum of twelve months and had open shopfronts. The modus operandi of the Gordian syndicates was to set up, import, distribute and shut down within a matter of weeks. Liquid ecstasy was a highly volatile and odorous substance, so it would need to be stored in a closed garage or warehouse premises.

That left a much bigger industrial complex with hundreds of shops, offices and factories spread across several kilometres. 'One hell of a bleedin' haystack,' was how he'd begun describing it. Approaching it now, he was struck again by its immensity. It was as big as it was cheaply designed and constructed. It looked liked someone had built a small city out of an IKEA catalogue.

He and Bullock entered the estate management office, where the agent was waiting with a sour expression. He looked either badly ill or desperately hung over.

'Happy New Year, fellas. What's going on?' he grumbled.

'We are trying to identify some of your tenants.'

The estate manager stared blankly. 'Welcome to my world. You'll need the rental agreements. What is the, uh, the ... legality of all this?' Before either he or Bullock could answer, the estate agent slid a thick, heavy binder towards them. 'Bugger it. Go for your life. It's ordered by shop number. The sooner you get what you need, the sooner I'm back to bed.'

They both stayed mute, neither acknowledging the minor victory. Getting a warrant on a public holiday would have been a nightmare. As he thumbed through the lease agreements, with Bullock staring over his shoulder, he noticed the estate agent watching them curiously.

'How do we know which are open shopfronts and which are garage door set-ups?' Bullock asked him.

'Garage doors are the cheaper rental packages. What exactly are you guys looking for?'

Purchas ignored the question. The garage front or warehouse needed to be a short-term rental, almost certainly less than three months. After fifteen minutes, he reached the halfway mark of the folder, and the agent sighed and excused himself for a cigarette. When he returned, he was three-quarters of the way through.

'Maybe I can help you guys speed up your search?' the agent asked hopefully.

Neither he nor Bullock raised his head. Flicking through the pages, Purchas paused at each Asian name or recently signed rental agreement. He discounted potential candidates in whispered conversation. Been there too long. Open front. Too small. Nearing the end of the binder, he noticed a rental agreement on paper that was whiter, with pen marks less faded than the other documents. It had been signed five weeks before. Purchas traced the signature with his eyes once and then twice. He turned to look at Bullock. He could tell Bullock had seen the same thing, although his face gave away nothing. The signature bore a name that was very similar to that of one of the syndicate runners who had been arrested driving the liquid ecstasy-filled van.

'Can we use your photocopier please? We have a few premises we may need to take a closer look at.'

When they were out of earshot of the agent, Bullock asked, 'What do you think?'

'It's got to be it.'

Bullock nodded, his face now bearing a familiar, intense look. He was thinking ahead. Whenever an operation was ready to unfold, Bullock was completely absorbed. Nothing else mattered.

'We need to do a quick drive by now and then call in the dogs and techs for a sneak and peek. If it seems like the place, we need to pull into the background and call the feds.'

'Or give it to Deb's crew,' Purchas interjected. Superintendent Deb Wallace was with the NSW police Asian Crime Squad. If the feds weren't interested in taking a chance on the raid, she had enough manpower and hunger to take the risk.

'*If* it is there, and *if* it is as big as we think, whoever seizes it will be thrilled. But if there's nothing there, we'll be a laughing stock,' said Bullock

'You know, Bruce. We might just be back in the game.'

'We have to nail this first, Mikey. Then we focus on our next move.'

Dylan Welch

Dylan Welch trudged through the morning dark, willing the pounding in his head to recede with each step. He hated having a hangover at work, and as he entered the lift, he silently swore an oath that he wouldn't drink again—not without a good reason. Or at least, not tonight.

It was difficult trying to keep up with the old cop and court reporters. They drank like they worked—hard. 'Fucking Gibbsy,' he whispered to himself as the lift opened in the middle of the twenty-fifth floor. After a heavy session a few months before, Stephen Gibbs, a seasoned crime reporter, was accused of pushing a small revolver into the stomach of another journo as he sat at the bar.

Welch had been roped into giving testimony in the court case triggered by the incident and had found the witness box was no place for a trainee reporter. Luckily, he'd seen nothing incriminating, a fact that strengthened Gibbs's argument that there was no gun in the first place. The charges were dismissed and Gibbs had walked, a free—albeit unemployed—man. Despite his reporting ability, Gibbsy was too hot for the *Sydney Morning Herald*. Snubnosed revolver or not.

Welch scanned the office as he walked towards his desk among the online reporters. The office was almost empty. He didn't mind the early starts, the quietness of the newsroom. Anyway, most of the office resented the online team and regarded them as omens of the digital future. He would probably have thought the same if he hadn't got the job there. He'd wanted to be in newspapers but couldn't land a gig. Online had its own thrills; he pumped out six or so stories a day on all manner of news events, uploading fresh copy on the hour and then counting the webpage eyeballs like a scoreboard attendent. That was the future the old newspaper hands were holding at bay. One day, they'd all be measured by online hits but even Welch wasn't sure it was a good thing.

He quickly scanned down the email list, opening messages of potential worth. Along with monitoring the morning radio programs, his next few hours would involve churning through the media releases on the night's woes: the fires, car crashes, murders and stick-ups. What a job.

His eyes landed on an email from the NSW police media service. There had been some sort of drug bust overnight, with press conferences scheduled for Canberra and Sydney. Senior police and politicians would be fronting. That had to be something big.

The police media liaison line was engaged so he redialled and was put on hold. Other outlets must also be chasing the story. He felt his mind twitching with anticipation as he waited. He'd been doing an increasing number of crime stories and enjoyed the rawness of the police beat, the absence of the sophisticated spin that cloaked business or politics. It was as newspaperish as a beat could be: sources still whispered over beers and coffees, and crooks and cops—at least the old-school ones—still had their own strange codes.

There were two cities in Sydney: the one above the surface and the one that lay under the belly. The more he delved, the deeper his interest. Before the *Sydney Morning Herald*, when he'd worked in pubs, travelled and stayed busy doing nothing, he'd got to know a few heavies. As a reporter, that world was growing.

His thoughts were broken by the police media liaison officer.

'It's, ah, Dylan ...' His head was still hurting. 'Dylan Welch from the *Sydney Morning Herald*. Just wondering if you guys are putting anyone up to be interviewed on the bust?'

'We're working on it. Have you got the updated release?'

He thought about bluffing and then decided against it. 'Nup. What's the story?'

'They reckon it's the biggest liquid ecstasy bust in Australian history. The Asian squad pulled it off last night in Castle Hill. I'll be back with someone shortly.'

Before he had time to jot down any questions, a female voice was on the end of the line, introducing herself as Deb Wallace, superintendent of the NSW police Asian Crime Squad. She spoke rapidly, and he guessed she was reading from prepared lines.

He scrawled as he listened, putting quote marks around the key words. One week before Christmas, a random traffic stop in Victoria had uncovered a stash of liquid ecstasy. The discovery had started police on a trail that eventually led them to a storage shed in an industrial complex in Castle Hill in Sydney. The cops had opened the door to be hit by 'a very, very strong smell'. They sent in the chemical and fire guys, and they declared it 'a hot zone'. Police searching the storage shed found seventy boxes, each holding about six bottles, containing a total of 1900 litres of liquid ecstasy, known in science speak as methylenedioxyphenyl-2-propanone, or MDP2P for short.

His hand was now competing with his head in the ache stakes as he clutched his pen, trying to keep up with Wallace.

'It is such a large amount, with the potential for 2 tonnes of MDP2P to hit the streets, that it would cause, I would assume, a huge disruption to the marketplace and have a national impact.'

As the officer continued, appearing to barely draw breath, he attempted the maths. Two tonnes of liquid ecstasy could make tens of millions of tablets. For thirty bucks a pop, the haul would be worth at least … too many bloody zeros … at least half a billion dollars. It was enough to buy a small country. He had to get a few questions in.

'Have there been any arrests?'

He heard the superintendent pause. When she answered, he thought he detected a flicker of hesitancy, although he couldn't be sure. She was certainly speaking more slowly and being very careful with her words.

'We've got a lot of work to do to ascertain the source. We'll be working with our counterparts overseas and with the Australian Federal Police, who have been called in to assist us. So we'll be now working backwards to try to locate the source.'

Hanging up, he began to shape the story in his mind. The sheer size of the bust meant it should lead the website. The state government and federal justice minister were likely to spruik the bust as a big win in the drug war, so he could give the story a fresh top throughout the day.

The website attracted most readers before 9 a.m. and he wanted his copy to be there. He felt the usual rush of nerves that came with a breaking story as he punched out the first few lines.

> A lucky break for uniformed police in Victoria has led to one of Australia's biggest drug seizures in Sydney, police say.
>
> The NSW State Crime Command's South-East Asian Crime Squad, Victorian Police and Australian Federal Police last night raided an industrial complex in Castle Hill, where they found the chemical, which had the potential to make up to 2 tonnes of ecstasy (MDP2P).

It was one of the biggest drug seizures in Australian history, NSW Police said. No new arrests have followed last night's seizure.'

He stopped typing for a moment and yelled at the online copy editor, who had just sat down. 'I'll have something coming in about a big drug bust shortly.'

'Okay.' The news editor sounded unimpressed.

He paused for a moment, thinking back to some advice he'd got from Gibbsy, or one of the other old hands. 'You have to sell your stories to the news desk, Dylan, 'cos no other fucker will.'

Welch yelled again, 'It's one of the biggest busts in Australia.'

'Has anyone big been locked up?'

He knew what underlined the question. There were half a dozen major crooks in Sydney whose infamy had turned them into quasi-celebrities. The media loved them, and if they featured in a story, it would almost guarantee it a healthy run.

'There're no arrests yet. They made the bust off a lucky break. I'm guessing the cops don't have much of an idea at all about who is truly behind it.'

Purchas

Glancing at the empty driver's seat, Purchas thought of Bug. The three-hour return trip to visit Harry Blackburn up on the Central Coast always brought up memories of his Doberman. Blackburn, a former NSW police superintendent, had been there when he'd first bought the dog in 1989. It had been a flea-infested pup, jumping around like a lunatic, but it had responded when spoken to. 'Come here you buggedy git,' he'd said. And the name Bug had stuck.

He'd always joked to Blackburn that Bug would outlive the gruff ex-copper, who had a pacemaker and seemed to have a second home on death's door. But Bug was gone and Harry was still kicking—old and gruff with a bone-dry manner, but still full of life. 'The good ones always go first,' he'd joked to Blackburn when Bug had died after thirteen years spent staying an inch from his backside.

Glancing out the window, he tried to make out the shapes of trees as they flashed by, twisted black ghosts reaching into the sky, illuminated by the passing headlights. It was a boring drive in the daytime, but at night he felt like he was passing through a black hole. At least it gave him time to think.

Whenever he visited Blackburn—he was now nearing eighty-five—they'd slipped into their old banter. 'You're too horrible to die, Harry,' he unfailingly reminded the old cop whenever he moaned about his latest ailment. Blackburn never made a big deal of his visits, but he knew the ex-cop was grateful for the company. And so was he. They shared a quiet bond, having survived the worst of the bad old days, when half the detectives from certain squads were 'in on the joke'.

In an infamous case, some of those NSW detectives had charged Blackburn with several rapes. He was later cleared by a royal commission and paid out over a million dollars in compensation. Purchas's mind wandered to corrupt cops. It was corrupt detectives who later targeted him at the NSW Independent Commission Against Corruption, spinning a line that he was a suspect in an armed robbery. It was bullshit, a fix-up, and he hadn't backed away. Most of the crooks in uniform were booted out or charged, and he'd been promoted to ICAC's chief inspector.

Purchas's battle with one of the worst of the bunch, Roger Rogerson, had lasted until a few years ago, when the notorious ex-detective had spread the word that he deserved a flogging—or worse. The National Crime Authority, where he then worked, had made him carry a gun just in case Rogerson wasn't kidding. Seeing Blackburn reminded him that a bullet could soon be the least of his health problems. At least it would be quick.

Stop being so bleedin' morbid, he told himself. He glanced again at the passenger seat. A few years after Bug had arrived, his wife, now ex, had finally relented and allowed the Doberman to travel in the front passenger seat, while she sat in the back. It was only because

Bug refused to sit in the back, but it would have driven the equity officers mad had they seen it. He laughed aloud and wound down his window, scanning the black sweep of the Hawkesbury River, the bobbing lights of boats and the twinkle of small towns in the distance.

He thought briefly of Huong; it had been a few days since they'd spent any proper time together. And then of his old job—lights on water always made him think of Hong Kong. Sydney Harbour at night had the same effect. The two cities were not unalike: citadels of water and light that, for outsiders, were filled with strangers. Beneath their facade of respectability, each hid underworlds heaving with wealth and power that reached everywhere, from the banks to the parliaments. They both stank. But Hong Kong stank literally; he'd never got used to that smell, despite prospering in it.

The Chinese were masters of wheeling and dealing, and systemic corruption pervaded almost every government institution. Within weeks of arriving at Hong Kong's corruption commission in 1982, he began to avoid the other expat detectives drinking and lazing their way towards British pensions. He'd never drunk, nor did he root around. It left him running with the hungriest Chinese corruption investigators and with the pick of the jobs. They had their fun, too: if an arsehole boss or local official sprang a visit on the ICAC and demanded the usual perks—whores and drink—they'd point him to the brothel where their guest would run a strong chance of getting the clap. Then they'd get back to work: corrupt multinational companies, high-finance scams and, inevitably, the triads.

Hong Kong was crawling with them: 14K, the Wo Shing Wo and Sun Yee On were all busy expanding across Asia, building empires from gambling, prostitution and loan sharking to drug trafficking and money laundering. Hong Kong and Macau were perfect bases for the latter. The pegging of the Hong Kong dollar to the US dollar made it a stable place to send, store and invest money, while Macau—Asia's Las Vegas minus the regulation—was an easy place to wash it. Triads bought into some of the casinos, controlling high-roller rooms that then doubled as money-laundering bases.

As Purchas drove, he felt himself swamped by memories. He hated nostalgia. It made him feel old. Back in Hong Kong, he'd never once thought that he, ICAC Superintendent Mike Purchas, would strain to hear conversations or have growths on his eyes that blurred his vision. He was invincible. It was he who had faced off a young triad soldier who had leapt around like a speed-addled Bruce Lee, clutching a Samurai sword and with a face so scarred it looked like he shaved with a cheese grater. It was he who had kicked the triad soldier down twenty flights of steps so that the neighbours knew that the ICAC was nothing like the corrupt Hong Kong cops, and wouldn't be bought off or stood over by anyone.

He glanced at the dashboard. He was forty-five minutes from home. As he got older, the triads got smarter. A decade after he left Asia bound for Sydney, when Hong Kong returned to the mainland in 1997, they went truly global: Vietnam, Taiwan, mainland China, and into the Chinatowns of Los Angeles, Toronto, London, Sydney and Melbourne.

The mostly Vietnamese-Australian launderers and drug and money runners they identified in Operation Gordian were almost certainly servicing Asian organised crime syndicates. The triads, who years before had begun using the Vietnamese as their runners, were almost certainly pulling the strings for the liquid ecstasy he and Bullock had discovered. The bust had gone down as planned. It was all over the media, with no mention of the Australian Crime Commission, and the politicians had lapped it up, describing the $540 million haul as one of the biggest and most important in Australian history.

Of course, it was bullshit. They had no means of measuring the true impact of the bust, and it was likely to be minimal. Operation Gordian and Vikingsson's latest work had fortified his belief that an endless supply was feeding an insatiable demand, regardless of police interdictions.

Forty minutes until he was home. He wound down his window further, and breathed in deeply. It was time to stop dreaming. He needed to think. There had to be a more effective way to confront offshore drug bosses supplying the local market. Gordian had rammed home to him and Bullock, investigators who lived to make a difference, that they weren't. But it had also given them a fresh insight into the money-laundering game.

Policing agencies usually sought to infiltrate crime syndicates by posing as drug buyers. Even when it worked, they mostly ended up taking out the runners and those stupid enough to be hands on. The smartest operators worked from overseas, out of sight and reach. The only thing that connected them to a deal was the repatriation of funds. If Bullock and he wanted to get into the game, they needed to get into the money stream. Fuck! That was it. How come he hadn't thought of it before? They had watched remitters operate and knew their game. Corrupt money movers operated on trust and on their reputation for efficiency, reliability and competitive rates. It was the gentleman's side of the drug trade, and rip-offs were rare. Why couldn't the commission set up an undercover drug money remitting business? They knew how it worked. They knew some of the players. With his and Bullock's stable of Asian informers, they could send out the word that a new player wanted business. It would be a honey pot, attracting criminals. If it worked, they could infiltrate the international money-laundering game and follow the drug dollars all they way back to the importers.

It was high risk, but it would get them a piece on a board game that they had only ever observed from a distance. Bullock's operational nous would ensure the laundry met management and legal requirements. They would need a controlled operations certificate, legal opinions, and reliable undercover operatives to be the face of the venture. Vikingsson could build his High Risk Funds system to accommodate the concept. They just needed to sell it. They needed a guardian, someone able to sway the bosses in Canberra when they bolted from the plan. He could hear them now, 'You want the commission to move drug money offshore? You must be crazy.'

Jamesy. He'd be the man. As a former undercover operative turned senior commission lawyer, James had run high-risk stings before and knew the value of long-term covert work. He had the operational experience to win the respect of the investigators and analysts, but he also had a seat at the executive table and the ear of the bosses. He was smooth, well educated and articulate, but he also possessed a fiercely competitive, hungry edge. James liked winning, and he had a blank page to fill. He'd start hassling him tomorrow. And he wouldn't let up. He'd just have to keep it simple so the wooden tops in Canberra could get it. It would be a money-laundering sting like no other.

'Getting in the money gets us in the game.'

That was it. He found himself grinning, his car hurtling through the black, as full of energy as he'd ever been.

Ayik

Whack. As the sound of glove smacking skin carried into the crowd, Ayik found himself moving his upper body just slightly to the left, as if avoiding a punch. He feinted again, this time forward, as if he was laying one.

Whack. And again. *Whack. Whack.*

He was on the edge of his seat. It wouldn't be long now. The boxer, *his* boxer, was all sweat and muscles, pummelling his bigger opponent. He knew what the guy was capable of. The boys had seen him in the gym, training and pumping iron. His rep had travelled quickly. He was the perfect combination of speed and brawn. And he was winning. Ayik could see the larger fighter was already gone by the look in his eyes.

Whack. The other fighter looked scared. *Whack.* Just a few more blows. His boxer's frame was cut, real cut. He should try to get like that, Ayik told himself. Then again, he didn't need speed in his game.

Ding. Saved by the bell. Ayik relaxed, feeling the tension leave his body. He scanned the room. Fight nights were one of the few occasions when different crews could coexist without killing each other. It was a microcosm of the world he was trying to build on the outside.

Patches and feuds caused endless dramas. If they really wanted to earn, they had to work together. And who didn't want to earn?

The crazy thing was that the different clubs didn't know what they could achieve by working together. That was why he'd got in the ears of Daux and Hawi. And it was why they had listened.

Ding. It was back on. His shoulders tensed and he slid forward again.

Whack. It was about exploiting the potential of a ready-made distribution network: first Sydney, then Melbourne and Perth. Thanks to him, the Comos were already dealing across bikie lines, from the Lone Wolves on the NSW coast to the Rebels in Western Australia. It was the beginning of something beautiful.

Whack. It didn't mean they shouldn't be tooled up. At least that is what Daux had kept saying. The more they earned, the more they expanded, the more they'd run into …

Whack. Whack. Whack.

Ayik rose to his feet as the large man's nose erupted. The boxer tottered and the crowd roared as he slumped on the canvas. Ayik turned around and soaked it in, the jungle of men in suits, singlets and gold chains, all roaring, baying to see more.

James

James sat in his office and watched the two men in front of him. Purchas sat to the left and Bullock to the right. At that moment, Purchas was intensely describing what he had intensely described at least half a dozen times before, first over coffee and then everywhere: in the lift, his office, the car, on the phone. Purchas's dour persona appeared to have temporarily vacated, and been replaced by … well, by a wall of sheer intensity.

Fuelling Purchas's intensity was his plan to extend Operation Gordian into 2007 and beyond. James knew why Purchas had picked him. He had seen his opportunity and swooped. Financial Crimes would be the perfect home for the plan. And Purchas needed someone senior and presentable, with a voice on the Crime Commission's executive table that was listened to.

He knew Purchas considered him differently from the other managers. Purchas hated bosses who had done nothing—who'd run no real jobs, made no big arrests, never gone first through a door. What's more, Purchas knew James was one boss who could handle risk: his old life as an undercover agent had seen him operating alone in hostile zones. James understood risk. And he was a survivor.

James focused back on Purchas as he outlined his plan. Purchase and Bullock wanted to start a new operation to pick up where Gordian had left off, an inquiry that would again shift the primary focus of investigators away from drugs and towards the money that the criminal syndicates in Australia were moving offshore.

The scheme had potential to work well on several levels. Using a system pioneered by Vikingsson, the commission would attempt to cast a net over all money moving out of Australia via banks and Western Union remitters and, using filters and law enforcement intelligence, to identify suspicious, high-risk transfers.

'It's like fishing in a lake, Gregory.'

He tried to hide his annoyance as Purchas began another one-liner. If it wasn't a lake, it was a haystack. But he nodded anyway. It was useless to interrupt Purchas when he was in the moment.

'If a fisherman doesn't know where the fish are in the lake, he won't know where to cast his line. But if we can tell him where in the lake the fish are most likely to be, where the hot spots are, then he'll fish there. It's the same with drug money.' Purchas paused for effect. 'If we can find the hot spots, we will find those sending the drug money … And we'll get to those getting the cash sent to them overseas. All the way to the top.'

As he watched Purchas, James's mind was running, ploughing through the problems the plan presented. It was a skill he had mastered as a deep-cover agent, a job that required him to carefully craft his own words and listen, interpret and store every utterance of his target; every name, place or plan dropped. He had never worn wires or tapes but had relied solely on cunning, instinct and attention to detail. He could hold a conversation about almost anything, while simultaneously conversing with himself. Was his target suspicious? What was his exit plan if things turned to shit?

And now he was already wondering how he could sell the plan to the agency bosses. Vikingsson's High Risk Funds Program was already producing intelligence suggesting that the size of Australia's drug economy was far bigger than previously thought. The Australian Institute of Criminology was estimating it at around $390 million a year, but the recent $540 million liquid ecstasy seizure had already shot that to bits. Vikingsson's work was putting the nation's drug trade in the billions. It would be up to him, rather than Purchas or Bullock, to get it backed in Canberra.

He nodded again at Purchas, while his mind's eye moved to the man sitting to his right, sizing him up. Bullock had let Purchas do most of the talking, butting in only occasionally where he thought it would help. He was a hulking but good-looking man, with slightly greying hair, a large jaw and friendly eyes. He had no doubt Bullock could throw a punch if he needed to. He'd probably thrown more than a few in his former job as a state police detective. Bullock by name, bullock by nature, he thought.

But his brawn belied his ability as an investigator. Only those who hadn't worked with Bullock wondered how he'd risen to operations mananger. Watch Bullock run a job and you'd see a cop with a rare talent for strategy, who could instinctively exploit the weaknesses of the gangsters the commission chased.

He realised the room was silent. Purchas and Bullock were staring at him. Neither man had spoken directly about the subject they had raised at earlier meetings with him. He guessed they were avoiding it because it was their plan's most controversial element: launching an undercover money-laundering operation.

James finally spoke. 'I get it. But Canberra is not going to like the idea of letting suspected drug money fly offshore. What if we lose it?

And how do we explain to the minister that the money we are watching is going to fund the next drug shipment into Melbourne or Sydney?'

He sensed Purchas bristling at his questions, but it was Bullock who spoke. 'We've been through this already, Jamesy. This money is going to move offshore whether we like it or not. If we keep running the normal drug busts, we might pick up a few bunnies. But we're not going to stop the bulk of drugs coming in, or the money flying out. We either get in the game, or we get out. The covert laundry gets us on the board. As soon as the money starts moving, we begin playing.'

James inhaled loudly and stared at both men. The background of people mattered to him. Sensing a person's weaknesses, strengths and vices was a skill that he'd once needed to keep himself alive. It hadn't dulled. These men would be difficult to manage. Both were stubborn, relentless souls who thrived on the chase as much as they disliked politics, bureaucracy and, on occasion, their bosses. They were not against bending rules if it meant securing an outcome. For all their investigative smarts, Bullock and Purchas shared the same failings. They understood policing politics, but they didn't care to engage in it; they survived on their results alone. Despite this, or perhaps because of it, they were the best sort of cop.

They cared little for office friendships, but if they picked you as one of them, they were endlessly loyal. Their operational success in a cash-strapped niche organisation, along with their reputations as men who wore their hearts on their sleeves, regardless of the cost, imbued them with a unique freedom. They could speak their minds, take risks and think big. Today was a case in point. Here they were, addressing him, their boss, like an equal and proposing a plan that could well kill his career.

'You know what you are asking me to sell to Canberra, don't you?' he said. 'And you know they are going to shit themselves.'

The two men before him said nothing. It was near on a miracle that the ACC bosses had allowed James to even float the idea of heading a taskforce that would be operationally directed by Purchas and Bullock. If he was headstrong, then Purchas and Bullock were in another league. But, inwardly, he felt as excited about the scheme as they did. Its strategic significance and potential to take the commission further than ever before were exhilarating. But he wasn't about to share his enthusiasm with them just yet. There were too many hurdles, and getting over them would involve managing the operational risk and massaging the nervous souls in Canberra.

'At some point a senator, a journalist, someone, anyone is going to ask the agency about this. And they are going to say, "So, you mean to say you didn't just watch drug money move out of Australia. You actually helped to move it yourselves?"' said James, shaking his head, while smiling inwardly. The plan's strength was also its biggest weakness. While it could lead the ACC to the organised crime bosses offshore, it also potentially made the commission a party to their enrichment. 'If this is going to get up, we have to get Jock 100 percent on board.'

Alastair 'Jock' Milroy was the chief executive of the Crime Commission, a popular state police superintendent known for his decency who'd been plucked out of a sea-change retirement to run Australia's most powerful and secretive policing agency. 'Ultimately, he's going to have to run it past the AFP. Everything is going to need to be gift wrapped and covered by a controlled operation certificate that protects everyone's backside.'

Purchas and Bullock were now both nodding. James guessed that the pair now knew they had his support. 'I guess I'd better book a flight to Canberra,' he said, and turning to Purchas added, 'And you better believe that we are going to need more than your bloody one-liners. We are done for now.'

He was working though the possibilities before Purchas and Bullock were out of his office. He understood the need to commit to long-term operations, ditching convention and taking planned risks. He'd spent years navigating his way around arms dealers, drug importers, pornographers and corporate thieves, and he knew he could see through the complications of running a laundry and informers. After he'd found himself as an undercover agent moving up the hierarchy of an arms-running outfit in Europe, his policing bosses had sought to have him moved, saying he would either end up dead or in too deep. But he'd dug in for years, ultimately helping the authorities pre-empt the moves of global criminal networks. Purchas and Bullock were offering the same thing. They needed him to dig in again.

In the event the bosses decided to let the plan fly, he would be the first to the sacrificial altar if something went wrong. Bullock and Purchas's heads would follow. He frowned. Overseeing the plan would overwhelm the trio with paperwork. They'd be swamped with operational plans, risk-assessment strategies, matrix-evaluation reports, business case submissions, inter-agency memorandums of understanding, budget estimates, updates and endless committee briefings. Yet here was a chance at something real, a chance to get back in the game.

He knew who he had to convince. Apart from Jock Milroy, he would need the support of Milroy's right-hand man, ACC national operations manager Michael Outram, as well as the agency's intelligence manager, Kevin Kitson.

The commission hated taking risks, but the plan had its selling points. Operation Gordian was an effective test run. Despite its reported success, it had not led to the arrest of any big crime bosses. Yet the intelligence it had gathered had helped identify new syndicates and drug imports. His pitch would promise much more of that. And more big busts would be lapped up by those running the cash-strapped agency.

'The rewards must outweigh the risks,' James whispered to himself. No, not strong enough, he thought. 'The rewards will outweigh the risks.' He chuckled to himself, thinking back to his boss's instruction to get the agency to do something that mattered. Starting your own money-laundering business was certainly doing something.

To make it fly, he would need to build a coalition of the willing. AUSTRAC, Australia's financial intelligence and counter-terrorist funding agency, was an obvious partner. Some of the major banks would also have to play ball. Every dollar the agency sent overseas would need to be tracked. The state police forces had to be on board, as well as the federal police and customs.

Purchas and Bullock could farm off future drug busts to other agencies, letting them enjoy the headlines and political kudos. If he knew anything about the policing game, the plan would still be a hard sell. The idea of funding a long-term investigation concept without any firm organised crime targets or short-term outcomes would be an anathema to the nation's police chiefs and many others in Canberra.

He felt uneasy on another level. If the commission was serious about following money offshore, it would likely mean embedding informers into a long-term international operation, turning the Crime Commission into a mini Central Intelligence Agency. It was controversial when he'd done the same thing decades before in Europe. Australian law enforcement was vastly more conservative.

He picked up the phone and dialled home.

'Hello.'

As soon as he heard his wife's voice, he felt a pang of guilt. 'I'll be home late tonight. I have to organise a meeting and a flight.'

She asked him where he was going, but didn't bother asking why. She'd long ago stopped asking him about his work.

'I have to organise some meetings in Canberra. It's important.'

There was a long, awkward silence. 'Just come home as soon as you can,' she said tersely and hung up with out saying goodbye.

He held the phone to his ear for a few seconds, listening to the engaged tone and wondering if he really wanted to be back in the game.

Bilal

As his stomach lurched with the rocking of the yacht, Bilal focused on the shimmering blue around him. He tried to concentrate on the patterns made as the sunlight danced on the water and, when that failed, attempted to block out everything but the wind and warmth on his face. It was a perfect Sydney day, one he should have spent rolling around on the grass with his boy and a football.

His wife would be cursing him right now. She had said nothing to him as he walked out the door, brushing off his attempt at a kiss and glaring at him with what looked very much like unadulterated hatred.

'I should have listened to my sister, Bilal. You are one hell of a father. You promised me,' she had spat at him before slamming the door.

His stomach heaved again. He had to get off this boat.

He watched his cousin head towards him, a scotch in hand. He'd been holding that scotch for the last ten minutes, pretending to sip it while matching the laughter and cursing of the other bikies. Waz was wearing a T-shirt bearing the word 'NOM', bikie shorthand for nominee, the lowest of the rungs in the club. There was something very primary school about it, Bilal thought. Waz's unquestioning acceptance of the whole ritual was embarrassing.

'Rules of the club, cuz. Even the president was a nom once,' Waz had told him earlier. He had found that hard to believe.

Waz walked over and stared at him quizzically. 'You look green Bilal. You don't like boats?' Without waiting for an answer, he said, 'Come and meet the boys.'

He glared back. He knew this was going to happen. He knew it. He hadn't come here to meet anyone. 'Let's get our money and get outta here, Waz. That's the deal. I gotta go and see my own boy or I won't have a wife by the end of the day. Can't keep a pregnant woman waiting.'

'Relax, cuz. They just want to meet the famous cook.'

'They fucking what?' he part whispered, part yelled.

The urge to vomit intensified. 'I told you not to say jack shit about the cook. You told m-m-m-me you wouldn't tell anybody. That was the d-d-d-deal.' Bilal heard himself stuttering, a remnant of a childhood dysfunction he'd conquered with speech therapy and that only reared its head when he was stressed. He hadn't stuttered for the best part of a year.

He shouldn't have come. He should be in the park right now, covered in grass, kissing his wife, kicking the ball with his son, nowhere near a pack of maniacal, drug-dealing bikies who would sooner drown his second cousin than look at him. And all on board a boat. He swallowed, breathed in, swallowed again and grimaced at the taste of stomach acid in his mouth. He hated boats.

'Let's get our cash and get off this fuckin' thing,' he whispered.

'We got to wait for the dosh to come. It will be here in an hour. In the meantime, let me introduce you to some of the boys.'

'I'll give you one more hour. Then I'm going home. I should have never come, Waz. No more favours.'

Waz had begged him to come last night with the promise that it would be a five-minute ordeal. He'd only agreed because he didn't trust Waz with his share of the money they had earned from the cook. It wasn't so much that Waz might outright steal from him, but there was a risk he would get sidetracked and end up reinvesting their cash in some stupid venture. Waz had already suggested they take a load of drugs as payment instead of cash. 'We can cut it and make an extra 20 percent. Make a real fuckin' earn. It makes perfect sense.'

'And how are we going to sell it, Waz? Are you going to hit Kings Cross and start selling it yourself?'

Five minutes. That's all it was meant to take to get their money, *his* money, and get the hell off the boat. That is what Waz had promised.

'One hour and I'm gone,' he said, as Waz, arm draped over his shoulder, steered him across the deck to introduce him to a group of fresh-faced young guys.

'Boys, this is my cuz, Bilal.'

They all looked remarkably similar. Olive skin, singlets, caps tilted slightly upwards, gym-toned arms, thick necks and tattoos. At the end of the handshaking, he realised he'd forgotten every name he'd been told. While his first instinct was to loathe it, there was also something fascinating about this display of brotherhood.

'Wazza has been telling us about you,' said the bikie to his right, grinning. 'You pretty good with chemicals. You a scientist or something?'

The sickness swelled up inside him again. He turned to look at his cousin, but he was already swallowed up in another conversation. 'I work on the wharves at Port Botany. I'm a freight forwarder.'

'A what?'

'I get people's shipments, containers, through the wharves.'

'No shit,' said the bikie eyeing him up and down. 'You got an MSIC?'

How the hell did some shitbag bikie know what an MSIC was? The federal government's maritime security identity cards, required for anyone who worked in a secure waterfront area, had only been issued a few years before.

'How do you know about MSICs?'

'We got a few friends on the wharves. Let's just say that.' The bikie winked at him. 'Hey Wazza, you didn't say your brother was a wharfie!'

Freight forwarder, he thought. I am a fucking freight forwarder, a fact relayed to you not ten seconds ago. And I'm not Waz's fucking brother. Not even a first cousin.

'A cook and a wharfie! He's the whole package!' the bikie continued with delight.

Feeling his face reddening, Bilal forced a smile, thinking of a way to change the subject. 'What do you boys ride? You all got Harleys?'

His question was met with a fresh round of guffawing. At least he hadn't stuttered. He turned to Waz to find his face burning red.

'Wazza's having a few problems getting his licence,' another bikie explained. Bilal's wife had told him something about Waz's struggle to get his probationary motorcycle licence, but he hadn't paid any attention. Now he found himself shaking his head: a bikie nom without a leather jacket or a motorcycle licence. Fucking Waz. His cousin was an unmitigated disaster.

'Did you get to the fight?'

He issued a quiet prayer as the conversation moved on to a recent boxing match. 'I shit you not, his blow went smack bang up this dude's schnoz,' said the skinniest bikie, vividly re-enacting a recent kickboxing bout.

Bilal watched the two other groups of bikies standing on the deck of the yacht. One was made up of older men in their forties and fifties, their fading tattoos like black-blue bruises marking wrinkled, sagging skin, their moustaches and goatees flecked with grey. Unlike the younger guys, who mostly had darker features, the older bikies looked like skips. A few looked like they had just walked out of the Milperra massacre, grabbed a cab and headed for the harbour.

The third group of guys were dressed classier than the rest, with short-trimmed haircuts and solid builds. They looked like they were in their thirties. To a man, they were wearing glistening watches, gold chains or chunky rings. There was something sinister about this group. He couldn't put his finger on it. He watched them out of the corner of his eye. Three of them looked Arabic or Turkish, two others maybe Tongans or Maoris. The men wore different patches. Most were Comancheros, but he also picked a Rebel and a Lone Wolf.

'Who's that?' he asked his cousin when they were alone again.

'That's the pres and the sergeant and some of their crew. They are mostly James Cook boys. That bloke on the right is worth millions.'

'Why don't you ask them for what we are owed?'

'You fucking crazy?'

He felt his phone buzzing in his pocket. It was his wife's number.

'I tell you what, Waz. You get my cash and bring it over tonight. I'm out of here.'

Without saying goodbye, he leapt over the side of the yacht. For what could have only been a fraction of second, he panicked, thinking he'd misjudged the sway of the boat. But it was closer than it looked and he cleared the gap with a few feet to spare, hitting the planks and powering his legs onwards. He heard Waz calling his name, but he didn't look back.

Purchas

Purchas grimaced as he entered the prison visitor centre. It reminded him of a public hospital waiting room, with its cheap plastic chairs and grim faces.

A woman who looked about twenty sat near the counter, waiting for her call-up. She had a plain, pretty face and peroxide blonde hair, and was wearing a short skirt. He noticed a large engagement ring on one of her yellow-stained fingers. Sitting next to her was a gaunt woman with acne-pocked cheeks and thick eyeliner. Her hair was badly dyed, and while she looked like she was in her fifties, she could have been the girl's mother or grandmother. He picked her as a junkie, probably visiting a husband or brother.

He and another commission officer walked past the queue, ignoring a visitor who muttered, 'Fucking cops'. Someone else hissed something, but he couldn't make out the words. Nobody looked at them directly. All eyes were elsewhere. Prison visitors were almost all the same, ordinary people burdened by the ill deed of another, shuffling through the security check like Catholics heading for confession.

'What's your fella in for?' they would ask.

'An armed rob. Yours?'

'You don't wanna know.'

'Hey Mike, look sharp.' The man standing next to him gently nudged him as a prison guard scanned their Australian Crime Commission badges.

'G'day, fellas. Who you here to see?'

The familiarity with which prison guards treated police was another feature of visiting jails that he was tiring of. Prison guards he had never met before treated him as one of them; screws versus crooks, plain and simple. In this game, the screws claimed the cops. Anyone else was treated with hostility: the mother of an inmate was a potential drug smuggler; the girlfriend a weapon mule hiding a shiv behind the wire of her bra.

He hated the scene. It was counterproductive. As a copper, it often paid to be onside with the crooks. Treating someone like shit rarely loosened their tongue. He hated it, especially today. He'd been waiting all day for James's phone call. The future of their plan was resting on it.

'Fingers please, Mr Purchas.'

He stretched his hands on the finger print scanner. Spread out, they looked like the tails from overcooked chops, his fingers twisted and gnarled. He and his commission offsider were waved through the X-ray machine, brushed once over with a metal wand and escorted through bare corridors to a small interview room.

Before entering, he looked in through the peephole, immediately recognising the man sitting in the chair from a blown-up surveillance still taken by closed-circuit cameras at Sydney airport the year before, on the morning of 4 June 2006.

The photo had always struck him as oddly disconcerting. It showed Van Dang Tran striding through the airport wearing a Vietnam Airlines uniform and pilot's hat, his black bag on wheels in tow. Tran's chin was tilted upwards, his broad face smiling. A thick fringe spilled out from under his pilot's hat. It was blurred, slightly out of focus, but still managed to capture plenty: a man comfortable with himself, proud and purposeful, without the faintest idea that he was hurtling towards trouble. When he had first read his police file, he'd known why Tran looked pleased. The Hanoi-born forty-year-old had been trained to fly fighter jets by the Russians and, after landing a job with his country's national airline, had become the pilot for Vietnam's politicians and party leaders. When a foreign dignitary had arrived, he'd been the pick of the pilots. But this hadn't been enough for Tran. He was also greedy. And there was nothing quite like the feeling of clutching half a million dollars. Or, as the official police count had shown, $549,265.

As he entered the interview room, he wondered briefly what Tran must have felt when he'd noticed the group of customs officers and detectives heading straight towards him at the airport, hunters who'd known their prey was caught long before he'd even known they existed. Had the pilot realised then that the life that he had known for so long was suddenly over?

'Hi Tran. You remember me, don't you?'

Tran stared straight ahead. His skin was blotchy, his eyes dark. He'd lost weight. Purchas had seen prison do the same to others. There was nothing like a jail cell to drain a man.

'Let's try this again. I am Michael Purchas from the Australian Crime Commission and this is my corroborator. We met when you gave your first statement.'

Tran acknowledged nothing. He had already confessed to moving more than $6 million to Vietnam in his pilot's bag on behalf of a money remitting business operating in the Vietnamese districts of Sydney and Melbourne. Operation Gordian had already identified the remitter's primary customers as drug-trafficking syndicates and the money Tran was moving as narco-dollars, but Tran refused to give up any other Vietnam Airlines' staff involved in the money smuggling.

He bit his lip and watched Tran sitting so still. There was something about the pilot's quiet, resolute persona he understood. If he gave up other airline staff, he could further reduce his sentence. That he would get a long stint inside was a surety. With a small camera hidden in the Long Thanh Money Transfer Company shop, the Crime Commission investigators had filmed Tran filling up his suitcase on a dozen occasions before his arrest. It was illegal to move more than ten thousand dollars out of Australia without declaring it to customs.

But Tran had held his tongue.

'What about Li, Tran. We know you know about Li.'

Li was another senior pilot the Crime Commission had arrested. The case against him was strong, too, although there was nothing like having another witness on the stand corroborating your case.

'You have to think about yourself, Tran. You have a family back home.' He paused. Nothing.

'Well, what is it Tran? Can you tell us about Li?'

Tran shrugged, paused and then cleared his throat. 'Sorry, I don't understand. My English no good.' The smallest of smiles crept along the crevice in his mouth, before disappearing.

'What do you mean, you don't understand?'

'Sorry. No English.' Tran shrugged again.

He felt a ripple of annoyance and fought the urge to tell Tran that they already had the other pilot dead to rights and they didn't really need his support, but if he wanted to rot in jail longer than he had to it was his own prerogative. In other words, he was fucked.

But it wasn't really Tran who was the source of his frustration. Despite a promise, he hadn't heard from James all morning, and he wanted to get back to check his phone, which was sitting in a prison locker.

Tran was living proof as to why they needed backing to reach further than Gordian. He was one of a hundred or so suspects they had interviewed in the course of Gordian. Most knew almost nothing about who they really worked for. Those they had arrested were all low- to mid-tier runners. If he chose to, Tran could give them his fellow Vietnam Airlines money couriers, but that was about it. He had no idea where the money he carried was truly going, or who had sent to Australia the drugs that had generated the cash he'd smuggled.

He breathed in and smiled at Tran. He had made the trip, so he might as well do it properly. He had interviewed hundreds of crooks. His strategy was simple. If you heavied someone in an interview, which plenty of cops still did, you would be left with nowhere to go if they still stayed quiet. Better to find a way in. It could be an offer to support a bail application, a move to a more comfortable cell, or a promise to keep photos of a suspect's mistress away from his wife.

He locked his eyes on Tran's. Huong had taught him plenty about the culture. A proud Vietnamese man would not be openly shaken by threats. They would only strengthen his resolve. He needed to find a way to level with him. He cleared his throat. 'I find your sudden difficulty with the English language a bit strange, Tran. You see, my girlfriend is Vietnamese, and I have flown on almost as many Vietnam Airlines planes as you.'

Tran was now looking at him. Curious.

'One of the things I know about Vietnam Airlines pilots, Tran, is that they have to know very good English to understand what traffic controllers are telling them. On the basis of our conversation today, you have made me very relieved about one thing. Do you know what that thing is, Tran?'

He leaned towards the prisoner, held his gaze and continued speaking in an even, friendly tone. 'If that is your level of English, I am fucking relieved I have never set foot, let alone flown, on any plane you were piloting.'

He winked at Tran and a smile crept on the Vietnamese man's face.

'Come on Tran. Can you help us?'

..

An hour and a half later, he walked back into the commission. No call from James. No help from Tran. At least the pilot had levelled with him. He would stick with his guilty plea but he wouldn't give up his friend and fellow pilot. Not today. Not ever. There was something he respected about crooks who actually abided by their code, stayed staunch when it mattered.

Purchas was in the commission elevator when his phone finally rang, displaying James's number. He didn't bother saying hello, just 'What did they say?'

'They look like they are going to back it. Outram and Milroy were cautious, Kitson less so. The others will come on board subject to several requirements. They want some impregnable legal advice on the laundry. And you and Bullock will need to start assembling a team.'

When the conversation finished, he hung up the phone and wondered if James had told him all that had really gone on in Canberra. James was a man who didn't relish telling people things they didn't want or need to hear. Bugger it. Any bad news could be processed later. As he walked through the office, he dialled Bullock's number and got through to an answering machine.

'Bruce, it's Mike. I need you to pull together Melbourne's best operators. Forget the flatliners. We only need workers on this. I was figuring Blanch, Cohen and that bloke who is a whiz with the phones, Chris Price. And start looking for an undercover. We need someone who knows what they are doing, a face no one knows.' He was so excited he had briefly forgotten he was speaking to an answering machine. 'Looks like they are going to let us run, Bruce.'

Bullock would assemble another dozen or so staff, most who would work twelve-hour days without complaint. He already knew who he wanted working the job at his end in Sydney, although he guessed not all would be lining up to work with him. He had made something of an art form of rubbing people up the wrong way, so he needed those who would also be prepared to follow his lead. Work for him, really work for him, and you became family. Just don't think about knocking off early to see your own.

He spied Vikingsson at his computer. 'Permission to enter your quadrant, Patrick?'

'What is it, Mike.' Vikingsson didn't bother to look up.

'You know your work on the high-risk funds?'

Vikingsson spun his chair around to look at him. 'Go on.'

'There may be a chance to put it into practice. It looks like we are starting a taskforce. I can't say anymore yet. But I need you to get ready.'

As he turned to go, Vikingsson grabbed him gently by the arm. 'If that's the case, I should tell you this now. Some intel from the Dutch police has come in about our big liquid ecstasy seizure. Turns out some triads in Europe were picked up on phones talking about some of their brothers losing their portion of a shipment in Sydney. Whoever was behind the shipment, they have tentacles all over the world. I think we should …'

He interrupted him.

'There's no time for a bleedin' thesis, Patrick. I gotta run.' It was almost 2.00 p.m., which meant he still had half a chance of finding Bob Sutherland in his chambers before the court lunch break ended.

A few weeks before, he had asked the Sydney barrister to come up with an opinion about the legality of the agency setting up its own covert money-laundering business and sending drug dollars offshore. The advice could break them before they had even started.

He sweated as he walked down Elizabeth Street, past Hyde Park and towards Martin Place. If Sutherland gave them supportive advice he would need a full-time agency lawyer on the team. His preference was Andrew Adams, a gently spoken, devout Christian with a fiercely competitive streak and a knack for finding legal precedents to support risky undercover operations.

Sutherland was eating lunch when he entered his chambers.

'We are going need that opinion now, Bob.'

The barrister responded in a throaty, annoyed tone as he finished his mouthful. 'I'm well, Michael. And how are you?'

'I'll be better if you tell me what I want to hear.'

'Can I finish my sushi?'

'You charging the agency for eating, Bob?'

The barrister growled again. 'It is going to take me a bit longer to put it in writing, Mike. But I think you might be able to get away with it. The trick for the commission will be to ensure that the laundry does not cause any criminality that would not have occurred without its intervention. If you can show the money would have moved offshore regardless of your intervention, then you may well be able to go ahead.

'But there is a hitch. You need to show that the money moved will lead you to drug seizures. The money must be ancillary to the drug trafficking that it will help you uncover. In other words, you can join a money-laundering venture if it is stopping a greater act of criminality, such as drug trafficking. Without drug busts, there's no laundry.'

He was out the door before the barrister had taken his next bite, choosing a different route back to the ACC office. It was an old habit that made it harder for anyone watching him to follow. Powering through the city, he reached inside his jacket pocket and felt for his second mobile. It was his clean phone, bought with a prepaid sim card and used only for contacting his sources, whose numbers were recorded in code against various letters. He punched the security code and went to the letter H. As Purchas pressed the phone to his ear, he heard the sound of an overseas dial tone.

'Yes?' The Chinese accent was thick and familiar.

'It's me. We need to have a talk.'

'I fly in next month. Meet me at the usual place.'

When he returned to his desk, it was 4.00 p.m. Vikingson had left a large yellow Post-it note on his desk. Two Chinese characters were sketched on it, and underneath Vikingsson had written: 'Da-Yu, or Yu the Great, ruler of ancient China, was famed for stopping the huge floods that swamped parts of China. It is said that after learning about how the water moved, he devised a way to control it.'

He scrunched up the Post-it note and clicked on a link on his computer screen to the commission's operational briefing memo. When the prompt requested he select which staff members he wanted the memo accessed by, he entered eight names: James, Bullock, Vikingsson, Blanch, Cohen, Price and Adams. If they ever got up and running, many more names would need to be added to the list. But, for now, it was a start.

The next screen prompt asked him to select an operation name. He paused and then skipped past it, to the main content field. Quickly he typed:

> Operation Gordian and subsequent data modelling suggests that interconnected drug trafficking syndicates with suspected links to the triad organisers, along with other syndicates, are repatriating from Australia billons in drug dollars each year. These early estimates are still being questioned by other agencies and the Australian Institute of Criminology, but in reality are likely to be conservative. The recent seizure of liquid ecstasy had a street wholesale price of at least $540 million.

This agency is capable of running an operation in the mould of Gordian and aimed at better understanding the make-up of these Asian organised crime syndicates here and offshore, as well as the size of the nation's drug economy.

The operation will seek to infiltrate and understand the international drug money repatriation and laundering network which Australia feeds into. By understanding and infiltrating the flow of drug funds to offshore importers and organisers, a truer picture of international organised crime networks profiting from the Australian drug market may be gained. Sustained analysis using the High Risk Funds Program may eventually generate a more accurate account of the true size of Australia's criminal economy.

He clicked on the 'operation name' link. A prompt appeared, asking him if he wanted the computer to generate a random name. He hesitated and clicked 'no'. He retrieved the Post-it note from the bin, flattened it on his desk and whispered the two syllables Vikingsson had sketched out. The name had a certain ring to it. It would stick. He typed it into the blank box, hit save and spoke it aloud for the first time: 'Operation Dayu'.

Part 2
June 2007 – December 2007

June 2007 – December 2007

Ayik

The city reminded Ayik of the sci-fi film *Blade Runner*, with its arterial highways snaking through a sea of lights. He read the huge, illuminated signs suspended over the freeway: 'Welcome to Hong Kong. The jewel of Asia.'

'You here for business' said the driver studying him in the rear-vision mirror with a sleazy grin, 'or pleasure?' He obviously took great pleasure in dropping his passengers off at brothels.

'A bit of both, bro,' said Ayik, smiling thinly before looking back towards the skyscrapers.

The taxi driver persisted, despite Ayik's reticence. 'Mandarin Oriental, very nice hotel. You in big business?'

'Um, sort of,' he said reluctantly. 'Big business, bro. Big business.'

The cab driver looked unimpressed. 'You like Hong Kong?'

He nodded, thinking how he'd always felt comfortable here, ever since Sydney's Chinatown had become his second home. Daux might control Brighton le Sands, but he owned the block around World Square, with its Korean barbecue restaurants, massage joints and clubs.

Hong Kong had the same vibe, except everything was bigger. The local women were gorgeous and keen to meet foreigners—rich foreigners. Which was pretty fuckin' fortunate, he grinned to himself. Some of the boys back home thought Asian girls were reserved, demure types, but they could really go off in bed, and they loved a guy with a bit of bulk. And they loved his Coke can; it might be short, but it was the width that counted.

Squeezing his hand into a fist and feeling his bicep tense, he pondered his good fortune. These trips always reminded him of where he came from. He had made some decent earns after leaving school, shifting a few kilos of speed and selling cars. But even he'd been surprised by how quickly it had all expanded: from a suburban player to high-rolling entrepreneur. The more of the game you played, the better the network you built, and the easier it was to source bigger loads of product. Hong Kong. Turkey. Thailand. The simple economics of it was mind-boggling. Thirty kilos of high-grade methamphetamine could be sourced in Asia for a few million, and wholesaled in Melbourne or Sydney, uncut, for around double that amount. If the Comos cut it before wholesaling, they could quadruple their profits. And that was being conservative.

He thought back to an article he had read in a newspaper a few weeks before about a couple of guys who had grown up together, first in high school, where they'd had their initial business idea, then at university and, finally, running a billion-dollar multinational. He couldn't remember what they were selling: high finance, or computers, or some other shit. The point was his story was the same. His local crew's reach now spread from Rockdale and Brighton le Sands in Sydney's south to parts of King Cross and the eastern beaches. The boys had poured coin into tattoo parlours, security companies, clubs, building firms and gyms. And then there were his overseas connections. He stared out the window as the harbour and city came into view. He didn't feel right in the centre of it—he was the fuckin' centre.

Wooosh. A black Audi R8 with chrome mags and tinted windows flew by. It was all power and muscle, every part of it dedicated to flying forward. That's why he loved cars. He went to point it out to the taxi driver but thought the better of it. His nephew Erkan was looking after his R8 in Sydney. His face had erupted in a smile when he'd tossed him the keys.

'You serious, Hux? You're the man. You're a champ!'

The memory warmed him. Money was nothing without family. The Comancheros had their brotherhood. He had his family.

'Here we are, boss.'

He noticed the cab driver staring at the entrance, seemingly awed by the hotel's facade, and paid the fare along with a $50 tip, walking away before the driver registered his good fortune. He liked travelling light: just a small suitcase and a brown leather satchel for his laptop. In his bumbag were his two passports, two phones and two sim cards still wrapped in plastic.

'We have you in the deluxe suite. Would you like an upgrade, sir? There is a harbour-view grande suite free.'

He studied the receptionist's face as he thanked her. She was gorgeous, about twenty-one, with delicate Chinese features and rich brown eyes. 'You havin' a busy night?'

He enjoyed talking to girls, even if there was no chance—except there always was a chance. Anyway, it was about perfecting an art form, a game. May the best man win. Or the richest one.

He unzipped his bumbag and handed over his Turkish passport, watching the receptionist open up the photo page. He loved that shot. It had taken him a few attempts to get it right, his face taut and strong, his eyes dead down the barrel.

She smiled nervously at him and glanced back at the photo. 'Welcome to the Oriental, sir. Let me know if I can be of any assistance.'

He raised an eyebrow. 'Will do.' That's how you played the game.

A few minutes later, he was staring out onto a harbour framed by a glowing landscape of skyscrapers. Unbuttoning his shirt, he stood in front of the mirror, studying his own body. His pecs and arms looked ripped, the protruding flesh and muscle compact and defined, but he wondered whether his lats stuck out too much. He brought his arms together, as if posing for a body-building comp, and watched his chest compress. 'Sometimes you're a real faggot', he told himself. He squeezed into a fresh white shirt a size too small, leaving the top three buttons undone.

As he walked towards the door, a text message buzzed onto his phone. It was Will. It had to be about the interstate run. With a reliable source of gear, they would soon rule a big chunk of the Australian market. Selling the shit was easy; with bars and clubs full of cashed-up yuppies and bogans, they would make a killing. Even eskimos would be buying their ice. A young buck working a mine could earn more than his parents combined; half a grand on booze and gear in a night was nothing. Same for a cashed-up uni student. That was the thing with the drug market, he thought. Mad demand kept prices up, even as more gear came in. Buyers were everywhere, the children of cops and politicians included. All he was doing was meeting the laws of demand and supply. If it wasn't gear, he'd be shifting phones or cars or energy drinks. Whatever gave the highest return. You can't fuck with the market.

He would get back to Will later. He had enjoyed making him squirm ever since the 300 grand had walked. It took fifteen minutes to get to Lan Kwai Fong. The street was heaving with locals and expats spilling out of bars, clutching imported beers or sipping cocktails. The air was hot and humid, and his shirt was beginning to stick to his back.

It always felt like a holiday here, even on business. People knew how to party. The expats would flog themselves behind a computer in a highrise and at 8.00 p.m. hit street level and flog themselves in a bar. For a moment, he struggled to remember what night it was. Friday night. That made sense. The street felt electric. He walked into a convenience store and bought a prepaid sim card and a fresh mobile before spotting a boutique jewellery store.

Inside, his eyes were caught by a watch with a silver and gold band and a face studded with diamonds. A sign underneath declared it the Rolls Royce of Rolexes. The shop assistant eyed him warily, as if there was no way he could afford it. He pulled back his sleeve and displayed his own watch. 'You stock this?' It was a hundred G worth of timekeeping.

'No sir, but we have several in the same range. They are in our special cabinet. Would you like to take a look?'

'Nah, I gotta run.' They'd think again next time he walked in.

When he arrived at the club, he pushed through the crowd searching for Steve Wu. He was in a corner, wearing a purple shirt with a wide-open collar and gold chain. He looked like he had lost weight.

'Brother!' Wu smiled ear to ear and hugged him. 'Long time no see. You been runnin' Sydney?'

'Same as ever, bro.'

'Hey, what you drivin'?'

'Still got the Audi, and it still fuckin' flies, bro. You?'

'A sick little Mazda. It's over in the new territories with the wife.'

Trailing Wu as he weaved through the crowd towards the seating booths, he thought of the rumours that the former busboy turned dealer had lagged on a business partner to lessen a stretch inside Long Bay. He needed to keep him close. But with his Asian connections in Hong Kong and on the mainland, he was worth the risk. Wu had got him an in with the right players, or as he called them, the *dai los*, the big brothers, and schooled him on how they played the game. The most important thing was to make good on your word, to always follow through. Everything in the first year or so was a test; you do it right, and your opportunities multiplied.

He slid behind Wu into a leather booth. 'So, what's on the go?'

'There's a fresh contract. It is coming from one of the local *dai los*.'

There were several *dai los* above Wu, and several more above them. Wu mostly referred to them with code or nicknames: brother one, brother two, brother three and so on; or skinny brother, fat brother, tall brother. The higher they ranked, the more Wu deferred to them.

'Can you still fix the ports?' Wu asked.

Ayik nodded.

'We fulfil the contract six weeks after we pick up and return 40 percent. We do it right ...' Wu trailed off, grinning like an idiot.

'Go on,' he said, fishing it out of him.

'This is bigger than you think. The old *dai los* have people everywhere. It's global, brother. Like Coke or McDonald's!'

He ran the figures in his head as Wu talked himself up as a global gangster. Forty percent was a large slice to hand over, given it was his crew in Sydney taking all the risk while the Chinese pumped out high-grade precursors by the tonne for next to nothing. It would sting his boys to pay off those on the port as well.

Wu was staring at him, waiting for him to talk. His friend had done well for a Sydney dishpig moving a bit of gear on the side. As he studied Wu's greedy, expectant eyes, Ayik realised his Chinese friend wasn't waiting for an answer. It wasn't Wu who had the distribution and muscle in Australia. It was him. Wu was waiting for an order.

Purchas

Walking up the stairs of the Melbourne apartment block, Purchas scanned for anything out of place. Closed-circuit cameras, too many people or too few could spook a target. Those bringing cash to the laundry had to feel comfortable. There was a certain art to undercover work. He'd always loved the gamesmanship, the skill of casting a cover story to reel in a crook and of knowing when to walk away in order to stay in the game.

'What do you think, Bruce?' he asked.

Bullock had come along for the reconnaissance, along with a couple of agency techs who needed to ensure the space could accommodate cameras, listening devices and a panic room filled with armed officers if it turned bad.

'It feels good, Mike. With a few additions, it should meet our needs.'

He let the scenario play out again in his mind. The apartment appeared sound; new laminate surfaces, clean rooms, a place barely lived in by occupants who never entertained. It was a few floors up, which would give the security team time to lock down the ground floor exits if anything went wrong. The balcony offered a good view to the street. If any of their customers arrived with unexpected friends, they would know about it. The room would need some fresh furniture, a new television and a safe installed. But it felt good.

The undercover would be alone in the apartment to relax whoever was coming in. Crooks always expected cops to work in pairs, and in the past, when he was undercover, he'd always run solo.

For ten years, whenever it was called for, he was a pharmaceutical sales executive who played competitive squash, drove an average sports car but aspired to own something faster, and was willing to sell chemicals to unlicensed buyers for a healthy premium. A cooperative chemical company had assigned him an internal work extension, which diverted to his mobile phone. He was given a plastic company badge, etched with 'Mike'.

The character he played never pushed for a sale, instead presenting as a highly cautious opportunist. He recalled one of his favourite stings, when he'd been deployed to ensnare a paranoid crime figure. Shortly before the meeting, one of the target's intermediaries had called 'Mike' to test his bona fides. They checked out. When the meeting took place, it lasted less than thirty seconds. 'I told you that no one calls me at work to discuss business,' he'd spat at the crime figure. 'Not you. Not your friends. I don't take risks and I never deal with amateurs. You can get fucked.' The apology had come an hour later, along with the revival of the deal that ultimately landed the crook in jail.

It was crucial to know when to walk away, to never seem desperate. If they thought a potential drug money customer was getting nervous or asking too many questions, their undercover would refuse his business.

Their laundry had to follow the lead of the best Gordian-targeted drug syndicates. They were disciplined, with strict operating procedures, and consisted of small-shore parties who would fly into Australia for short periods and carry out their allocated roles without knowing anything about who they were working with or for.

Drugs shipped in would be picked up by one shore party and taken to a safe house where they would be cut, packaged and moved to a pick up house, where a second shore party would begin distribution to a network of mid-tier retailers. The gear would be cut and onsold. Ten kilos of high-grade ice could pass through ten hands, each who would cut it down, until it hit the streets or the clubs at around 5 percent purity.

Working on the assumption that most cops began an investigation after arresting a street level dealer who would agree to roll over and inform on those next up in the chain, the syndicates ensured that those most exposed were quarantined from the senior players. They also factored in the loss to law enforcement of a safe house or a few drug runners. If a bust went down, they would remove all shore parties and start again. To insure against any longer term police probes, shore parties would be replaced every few months, regardless of whether there had been any police attention. It was cold, clinical and extraordinarily efficient: the perfect model for the ACC's laundry.

Anyone who wanted money moved would be told to come alone. If they wanted their money counted, they could do so on the spot. Otherwise, they relied on the count of the house. If the count fell short, there could be no complaints, or their business would be refused. The more their clients felt like their business wasn't wanted, the better.

'Mikey. Wake up, mate. How are you going to get some bees to the honey pot?'

Purchas finally had a face-to-face with the old source he'd reactivated at the start of Dayu. The source was familiar with many of the mid-tier players in the Vietnamese and Chinese money-moving game, those who cleaned dirty cash through their restaurant tills, brothels and gaming parlours in the Chinatowns and little Saigons of Melbourne and Sydney.

Before becoming a source, the man was himself a player. His perspective had altered when his son was imprisoned over an assault and there were whispers that he would be killed in jail. Purchas had sought out the father and assured him that his son could be moved to a safe facility and could even get a lighter sentence. All the father had to do was help out the commission with intelligence; he would never have to testify, or appear in court, unless he was caught committing crimes himself. His name would never go down in any document that could be subpoenaed.

The father refused, until a fresh death threat floated through prison and his son panicked. Within hours, hands were shaken, papers were signed, and Purchas and his new source embarked on an understanding that had never been spoken about since. They both knew it could only truly cease when one of them died.

When they'd met recently, Purchas asked the source to put out a quiet word. 'I need you to let others know of a new money moving business. They charge a competitive rate, anywhere from 3–5 percent, depending on where the money is going and how much needs to be moved.'

The source didn't ask who was behind the new venture, although Purchas figured he would assume it was run by some fresh targets the ACC were hoping to catch in the act. The source had simply shrugged his shoulders and said that it wouldn't attract customers. 'There are trusted remitters who will undercut this new business. Unless it undercuts them or kills them off, no one will come to it. It's business, pure and simple, Mike. That's all it ever is.'

He smiled as he recalled the advice. It was sage. Undercutting the market would reek of desperation. The honey pot needed to attract a higher-end, more cautious client. That left option two. He smiled again. They had to find a way to kill off their money-moving competitors. Still grinning, he punched Vikingsson's number into his phone.

James

James skimmed the undercover's personnel file, storing the details in his mind as he flicked the pages. Andrew Lee had been with the Western Australia police for twelve years and had worked undercover for three. He was Australian-born with a Malaysian father and Chinese mother, and had done most of his work infiltrating low- to mid-level drug rings. His photos depicted him in various unwashed states: long hair, dreads, bearded or badly unshaven. He appeared lean and sinewy, like a junkie or a cross-country runner, but not your typical cop.

'UC 420 is able to adapt to situations with ease and has proven himself a capable UC. He is adept at working with Australian and

Asian targets and has a good understanding of Asian behaviour.' He couldn't rely on the notes, though. He closed the file. He needed to assess the man for himself. He left the file in front of him, so Lee's UC number would be showing when he entered. He wanted Lee to know he was being studied. There was a knock on his door and he told Lee to come in.

'I have heard plenty about you, Andrew.'

Lee shook his hand gently and smiled. 'And me you.'

He was obviously primed for the interview. He didn't look like the photos. He was cleanly shaven and dressed in a neatly pressed designer shirt with a gold chain peeping from under his collar, and he had expensive shoes on. He wore the kind of signet ring favoured by Asian businessmen. And he held himself well, with an easy, unimposing air. It was as if he'd already stepped into the role.

What they were holding out to Lee wasn't a tough assignment. He was only going to be used as a conduit in a commercial transaction. He was effectively a bagman; he would take the money and make sure it got to the next delivery point. But could he handle the unexpected?

'What do you say when they ask you where you are from?'

Lee replied without hesitation, 'My mother was born in Kuala Lumpur and she still lives over there; my dad died when I was young and I ...'

James interrupted. 'I don't and they don't need to hear your life story. That's a bullshit answer. Try again.'

Lee nodded. 'Gotcha. Mike has stressed that I should keep it as simple as possible. I'm just a gofer, sitting in a room and getting paid for collecting.'

James leaned over the table, narrowed his eyes and gave Lee a look of disgust. 'I don't like the fucking look of you one bit. You know what, mate. You look a lot like a fucking fed trying a lot not to look like a fucking fed.' He realised he was sounding angrier than he wanted to. But he needed to know if Lee was up to it.

James's mind flicked back to a meeting years earlier set up by a major criminal he'd been living with while undercover. He'd walked into a confrontation with a heavy, who'd placed a handgun on the spare seat at the table. There had been no backup to call, no panic button to press, no cavalry waiting. He'd walked out in one piece, but only after surviving a two-hour cross-examination, a fearful psychological hammering that had never left him. As Lee responded to his probing, the feelings from that old meeting reared up as if it had happened only yesterday.

Lee was quick to respond. 'I'm no jack, mate. I'm from the same place as you … If you don't like me, fuck off and don't waste my time.' Lee had responded naturally, barely raising his voice. He hadn't blushed, fidgeted or become tongue-tied. It was better.

James addressed the young undercover again. 'People speak highly of you, Andrew. But if you're not up for this, don't do it. If you can't work this out, don't do it. I'm not going to work this out for you or write a script for you to follow. In this game, accidents happen. If you feel at all uncomfortable about this operation, I need you to speak up.'

Lee still hadn't flinched. The undercover profession attracted cops who were risk-takers, people who thought themselves somehow immune to misfortune because, at their core, they cared little for consequence. Many of the best UCs didn't have to perfect the art of not looking scared. They simply didn't get scared or, when they did, they thrived on the feeling.

'That was me, two decades ago,' thought James. As Lee left his office, he resisted the urge to offer more advice. It had taken him years to come to terms with his own time as an undercover, the fact that he'd become a man who relished living among multi-layered lies. He had enjoyed perfecting his art, directing every word and action towards influencing someone's view of him, and always thinking that at some point, somewhere, someone would say, 'You're a cop, aren't you?'

It had cost him his first marriage, but at the time, he thought it was worth it. He still did. What a thing to think. He brushed away the past and pulled out the legal advice from Sutherland. It was good news, advising that the Crime Commission could run the covert laundry as part of a sanctioned controlled operation as long as they met several caveats. The criminality aided by the venture had to be in proportion to the overall criminality being investigated, and the laundry had to be used to gather evidence that would lead to arrests and drug seizures.

AUSTRAC had already agreed to play ball, and he'd contacted a major Australian bank with international reach and met with a senior executive, who had agreed to participate in the scheme. The bank would move the money and allow them to track it through the international banking system.

Legalities aside, he knew that over the last few weeks he'd invested the greater part of his professional standing selling the concept. The liquid ecstasy bust and Vikingsson's early economic modelling had helped make the case that, despite its much trumpeted success, Operation Gordian had failed to dent the amount of money being moved offshore to pay for fresh imports. If the laundry was given enough time to establish itself, they could infiltrate the international money-laundering game and get closer than ever before to the recipients of the offshore payments. It would be the mother of all long-term stings. But it didn't reduce the risks.

His last briefing to federal police chief Mick Keelty was far from seamless. He hadn't told Purchas or Bullock, but it left him dismayed. Other agencies, including the tax office and AUSTRAC, initially seemed impressed by the concept, but many couldn't move past what had concerned the feds: the perception.

'No matter how carefully you manage it, if it becomes public the media will accuse you of funding organised crime. And if the story sticks around, the politicians will shoot you down before you've had time to scratch your arse,' a law enforcement official had warned him. 'That said, it is the best operational concept I've heard in a long time.

Everyone knows it is almost as easy to buy an ecstasy tablet in Australia as a beer, but no one is prepared to say so publicly. Does the ACC really have the will to make a difference?'

If they were to run the laundry effectively, they couldn't wire the money directly to the recipients, the entities controlled by offshore criminals. Otherwise, overseas law enforcement agencies, unaware of the covert operation, might begin targeting it. They needed to create a clean break in the flow of money, so that anyone who came across the final money transfer to the end recipient could not easily trace it back to the commission. To create this break, they needed to utilise the offshore money movers they had already identified through Gordian.

The system they had agreed on involved sending the laundry's money through a bank, which would allow them to trace it to an account in an Asian country. There, a remitter known to be involved in laundering would move it to the destination specified by the commission's client. At this point they would lose physical control of the funds. It was an unpleasant fact, but it could not be avoided. And no one in law enforcement—no one—easily swallowed the idea of sending narco-dollars into a big black international hole. Neither did he.

Welch

Welch scanned the cafe, trying to imagine what the man he was due to meet would look like. The bikie was unlikely to be wearing his colours or, as a new recruit, any leather at all. There was no Harley-Davidson out in the street.

Welch thought back to the call he'd received that morning, shortly after he'd arrived at work. 'Why are you asking around about my friends?' an angry voice had demanded down the phone. Ever since moving from online to police rounds, and delving more deeply into the bikie scene—first by studying magazines such as *Ozbiker* and

Live to Ride, and reading old clippings about the 1986 Milperra massacre, which had left several Comancheros and Bandidos dead, and then by fronting bikies in court—he'd begun getting calls from shitty underworld types. One of his regular callers was an older bikie, annoyed by the challenge to the old world posed by so-called 'Nike bikies.' Each rant was the same: 'These cunts don't even ride a Harley. Why do you call them bikies?'

When he received the gruff call that morning, Welch had held his own on the phone, challenging the nameless caller to a meeting. He was surprised when the man had agreed, although on the way to the cafe had reasoned that he shouldn't have been. Bikies were mostly highly impulsive men who thrived on machismo and conflict.

Sitting in the cab, Sydney's suburbs flashing by, it had briefly occurred to Welch that this might be a set-up. His focus of late had been on the Ibrahim crime family, a Sydney underworld institution consisting of a number of brothers who had gained strong footholds in the Nomads outlaw bikie club in Kings Cross. Welch had heard mutterings that his enquiries were annoying some heavier types.

When he got to the cafe, Welch locked eyes with a man by himself at a table in the corner, his back to the wall. The man looked about thirty-five years old, with a shaved head and a garrish Christian Audigier designer T-shirt, which had recently become de rigueur for many gangsters. A pair of black designer sunglasses sat on the table, not unlike the sort his girlfriend wore, thought Welch: gaudy, expensive, with the brand running down the sides. The bikie had thick gold chains wrapped around his neck and wrist. He stayed seated as Welch arrived at the table.

'Dylan Welch from the *Sydney Morning Herald*. Good to meet you.'

His hand was swallowed by the bikie's fist. The man had jailhouse tattoos across his knuckles; homemade jobs that now looked like faded ink blotches.

The bikie didn't offer a name. 'It was me who called you,' he said, with a rough, husky voice, his accent part ocker, part something else.

In his designer T-shirt and white sneakers, with not even so much as a belt to provide a hint of leather, the man opposite looked every inch the Nike bikie.

'Can I get you a coffee?' Welch asked. Buying someone a coffee was a surprisingly good tongue relaxant. It was as if the act of sipping a free cappuccino was imbued with an obligation on the drinker to talk. But the bikie, already downing a Perrier mineral water, ignored the question.

'You been asking about my brother and that tattoo parlour. He ain't got nothin' to do with shit', the man spat.

Welch wracked his brain. He had no idea what the bikie was talking about. Bikie clubs were increasingly setting up their own tattoo parlours, as well as bombing those belonging to their rivals, but that was the extent of his knowledge.

'You keep asking about his involvement, soon enough people are going to think that he *is* involved.'

Welch opened his notebook. 'Do you mind?' he said, raising his pen. He still had no idea what the bikie was talking about.

'Why you asking anyhow? You think you're a jack?'

Welch adjusted his glasses, a slight nervous tic he couldn't shake, and looked his companion in the eyes. There was usually a sound formula for meeting people: maintain eye contact, chat instead of question, defer to your companion's better wisdom, listen more than you speak and don't bullshit.

He breathed in. 'Listen mate. I don't know who your brother is or what parlour you are talking about. All I've been doing is asking around about which bikie clubs are getting bigger.' He paused. The bikie was staring at him, with what looked like curiosity. With a little more time, the bikie might start chatting.

He thought back to a police intelligence report he'd been leaked a week before by a senior detective. It was the first file he had ever received that was marked 'secret'. The feeling of getting it made for an addictive rush.

He remembered wanting to absorb every word on the page the instant the file was in his hands, but resisting the urge, he'd slipped it into his notebook with the air of a man to whom absorbing secrets was like breathing. The file had described the links between different bikie leaders and their business and family connections. He'd picked up similar snippets of information before, but reading it in an official document, a genuine police file, somehow authenticated the information, even though it was just intelligence. The document blamed the recent shooting of the Nomads clubhouse on members of the Comancheros.

'I've heard the blue between the Comos and the Nomads is still raging. Some people say drugs, some say nightclub turf. Any ideas?'

The bikie eyed him suspiciously. 'Listen, buddy. We ride motorbikes. That is why we're called bikers.' He articulated the word 'bikers' slowly, as if he was speaking to a child.

Closing his notebook, he tried again. 'Well it sounds like the Nomads are intent on hitting back at the Comos.'

The bikie moved to stand up, but hesitated. 'Some cunts out there might get jealous 'cos the Comos are growin' and have the smarts. Listen mate, I gotta run. You stay away from my brother … or next time we'll be meeting at your house when you and your missus are asleep.'

As the bikie roared with laughter and pushed in his chair, Welch tried again. 'Who has the smarts?'

'Mate, I'll tell you once, and only once. Daux, Big Hux and their boys are running the show. You ever been to Rockdale or Brighton le Sands? Well, they own them.' With that, the bikie turned and walked out of the cafe, over the road and into a glistening black four-wheel drive. He'd heard of Daux before, but not the other name. He waited until the car had sped off before he opened his notebook and jotted the second name down: 'Big Hux'.

Purchas

Undoing his seatbelt and reaching for his laptop, Purchas felt a surge of confidence. Everything was in order. Few things compared to the feeling of being in control as an operation was about to go live, he thought. It was the pay-off for hours spent strategising, arguing and dreaming up scenarios involving armed crews bursting through the laundry door, guns blazing.

Bullock sat beside him, oozing intensity and concentration. He was holding a police radio and two mobiles, into one of which he was issuing the last instructions to the undercover. Bullock, who had been an undercover as well, was in charge of securing the UCs security throughout the operation. If it went pear-shaped, it was Bullock who would activate the security team.

His own role involved floating across the operation, looking for anything that could go wrong. Not that it would. He touched the semi-automatic pistol strapped in a holster on his chest. It was the closest thing he had to a talisman. If it all went south, it would not be down to a lack of thoroughness. But it wasn't going to happen. Not today.

Sucking in, he held his breath as the video feed on the laptop lit up, beaming vision of Lee sitting in the apartment dining room. It was empty save for a money-counting machine and three suitcases. Lee appeared to be bouncing what looked like a tennis ball against the wall. He turned up the volume of his earpiece. *Bum-bump. Bum-bump. Bum-bump.* He hoped it wasn't a sign of nervousness. It was too late for that.

It was an hour until kick-off, but the operations room back at the commission had been live all morning, lit up like a television studio, beaming sound and vision from the secret cameras and microphones hidden throughout the apartment. If anything went wrong, he could be at the apartment within minutes. First in the door, though, would be the two armed commission investigators monitoring the situation from an adjoining bedroom on another laptop.

He heard Bullock calling through to the security team. 'Car one to alpha. Waiting target arrival. If you're good to go, we now need to stay off air.'

Purchas took off his jacket and turned up the air-conditioning. It wasn't hot, but he was sweating. If anything worried him, it was the unknown, the irrational. The unknown could beat the best system. You could never guess a lunatic's next move.

They had done their best with what they had, rehearsing go-wrong scenarios. The first involved someone attempting to pull a heist on the laundry, believing it would be flush with dirty cash. The other risk was that the money brought in might have been ripped off from another syndicate, who might try to retrieve it. The two scenarios could be managed by sticking to the rules of the laundry. Customers must come alone or the door would stay shut.

For a moment, Purchas wished they could have had just a few more minutes with Lee, to eyeball him one last time and go through the rules. Once the laundry was active, the only unpredictable, unknown element would be whoever was bringing in the cash. He had seen crooks flip for the smallest of reasons, especially if they were pepped up on ice or coke. The truth was, if a gun was pulled by someone determined to squeeze the trigger, he and Bullock would be cleaning Lee's brains off the wall. At least the shooter's brains would be there too.

But it wouldn't go like that. Not today. Not while he was in control.

The laundry operation had got the final tick of approval from Canberra just a few weeks before. By then, he, Bullock and James had spent hours plotting and planning, coming up with a game plan that was acceptable to both the bosses and the crooks, and which could be reviewed, tracked, challenged and defended if anything went bad. It had to meet the commission's rules of operation and stay within the bounds of their controlled operations certificate, as well as withstand what was known as the Senate test, a reference to the grilling dished out by the politicians who sat on the Crime Commission's oversight committee in Canberra and who, depending on the politics of the day, could just as easily support the agency as savage it.

He knew there was another reason why he, a sixty-one-year-old operations manager, and Bullock, his equal in rank, were out in the field coordinating. They were senior enough to hang out to dry if anything went wrong. And if it did, a flagpole would be firmly up their arses and they'd be flapping in the wind before the sun went down.

Not that it was going to. Not on his watch.

The night before, Bullock and a tech team had set up a series of small traps, including wedging a small match between the door and its frame, to make sure the apartment wasn't interfered with. The apartment block was also watched all night.

The only movement now was the tennis ball. *Bum-bump. Bum-bump.* 'For Christ's sake, sit still,' he whispered.

The plan for attracting customers had gone smoothly after several sources had put out the word that there was a new business in town. Vikingsson, meanwhile, had killed off the competition. By using his High Risks Funds Program, along with other financial and law enforcement intelligence, he was identifying and directing the commission to the money movers who had taken over from the remitters shut down by Gordian. Once identified, the new corrupt players were immediately put through the law enforcement wringer: suspects were questioned, warrants issued and files seized. As they turned up the police heat, the dodgiest remitters melted away, allowing their own laundry to fill the gap.

Bum-bump. Bum-bump. Lee hadn't moved from his seat. If he was nervous, he didn't look it, thought Purchas. *Bum-bump. Bum-bump.*

Finally, his earpiece crackled to life. 'Okay guys, we have a possible eyeball walking to the building.' It was the surveillance team watching the front of the apartment block. 'Asian man carrying two big suitcases ... A very fat Asian man ... He's going at a snail's pace ... He is hitting our man's doorbell.'

The tennis ball stopped bouncing the instant the buzzer sounded. Purchas watched Lee walk to the security box and peer at the screen. The listening devices picked up the conversation in the apartment.

'You alone?'

'Yeah, yeah. But I am going to need some help bringing it up,' the man said with a strong Chinese accent.

'You know the rules. If you can't make it up the stairs by yourself, you can piss off.'

Purchas felt himself nodding, as if in agreement. He heard Bullock whisper 'Good lad' under his breath.

'Okay, okay. Let me in,' the Chinese man said.

Purchas glanced at his watch. Two minutes had passed since he'd been buzzed in. Then three. At four, he glanced at Bullock and noticed a line of sweat sliding slowly down his partner's face.

Bullock radioed the two investigators in the bedroom. 'This is taking too long. Something is not right. Stay sharp.'

At six minutes, a huge beast of a man appeared in the live feed from the camera outside the apartment door. He was waddling towards the door, dragging the suitcases behind him. Something didn't look right. The man had a huge patch of blood on his shirt. Purchas felt his entire body tense, but before he could speak, Bullock whispered to him, 'It's just sweat, Mikey. I'm guessing our tubby friend normally takes the lift.'

Purchas turned his attention back to Lee, who opened the door and led his sweat-drenched guest to a table.

'Stick to the script,' he heard Bullock whisper to Lee, even though the undercover could no longer hear him.

The conversation from inside the apartment crackled through Purchas's earpiece. 'Okay, boss. We can do the count here and now, or you can leave it to us and we will do it later,' said Lee.

The fat man said nothing. Purchas guessed he was catching his breath.

Lee pushed on. 'Your people know the rates. You can leave the suitcases here, but you won't get them back.'

'No, no. You empty them.'

As Purchas watched the money tumble onto the table, he felt a shot of adrenaline course through his system. The bundles stacked higher and higher, a small mountain of ill-gotten gains; it had to be at least a million dollars.

'You been doing this for long?' the fat man asked.

Lee didn't hesitate, 'Listen mate. I get paid to sit here and collect. I don't know shit about shit. If you're done asking questions, you know where the door lives.'

The fat man said nothing on his way out.

Purchas checked his watch. They had to move fast; the money had to begin its journey offshore that day. He revised the operational plan in his head. A surveillance team would peel off on the fat man while a second car would take the money to the bank.

The radio crackled again. 'Eyeball on the money car. Following to bank.'

Purchas dialled Nick Cohen, one of only two investigators who was a signatory on the laundry's bank account. As an anti-corruption measure, James had divided up the task of moving the money offshore and assigned different steps to different staff. Only Purchas and Bullock could direct that the money be moved. But only Cohen and another staff member could sign off on the covert laundry's accounts. If anyone at the ACC was considering topping up their own bank account with the laundry's money, they would need others to help. Purchas considered it an unpleasant but necessary step.

'Nick, the money will be there shortly. Stand by.'

He and Bullock had already assessed the risk of a rip-off as at its highest when the money was overseas, although this was negated by the nature of the laundering industry. Those moving the narco-dollars made a healthy living by taking an agreed cut of every dollar they shifted. A rip-off on their watch would sour their reputation and risk retribution from the underworld.

He checked his watch again. Vikingsson, along with several other analysts, was already working on identifying those behind the account to which the laundry's first client had directed their funds.

After he closed the lid on the laptop and unplugged his earpiece, he realised that three hours had passed since they had gone live. It felt like much less.

He heard Bullock on the phone to Lee, quietly debriefing him.

He gripped the steering wheel, and pulled out. They were finally in the game, he thought. They now had their chance to take it further than ever before, to change the way law enforcement fought organised crime.

How deep could they go?

Hutchins

The dew on the grass soaked through Hutchins's boots and socks as he trudged through the brush on his usual early morning walk from the small township of Glenbrook into the Blue Mountains wilderness. The air was cold and his breath appeared as puffs of steam before him. With the morning light creeping over the granite embankments to his left, he walked and whispered the rosary.

'Our Father who art in heaven, hallowed be thy name.'

He felt sweat drip down his brow as he neared Mitchell's Pass. The viaduct, built by convicts in 1832, was taking shape in the gathering light, the rough-hewn rocks that formed its base framed by untamed eucalypts, old friends from his morning route. *We are weathered, but we are still here.*

'Hail Mary, full of grace, the Lord is with thee.'

This was the only part of the day when his mobile stayed silent. There was very little sanctity in the life of an Australian politician, he thought. Here, in the wilderness, without a person in sight, he could find time for peace and prayer. The taste of acid from yesterday's wine was still in his mouth. That was the downside of his Catholic roots. He loved a drink.

'Glory to the Father, and to the Son, and to the Holy Spirit.'

He'd risen at 5.00 a.m. after a troubled sleep. The new regime of Prime Minister Kevin Rudd had served him something that seemed more like a shit sandwich than a shepherd's pie. It was to be expected. Rudd's vindictiveness hadn't been tempered by his ascent to the top job. Hutchins quickened his gait as the path dipped around an embankment covered in rich, green moss. Saint Kevin didn't see the value of humility in triumph.

To those who had backed Beazley all those months before, Rudd would hand out the crumbs of Labor's victory, the ministerial and committee posts that were either poisoned chalices, roads to nowhere or both. Hence last night's phone call from the party factional leader. 'Steve, we want you to chair the Australian Crime Commission committee,' he was told.

Hutchins wondered if he'd betrayed his disappointment on the phone. The ACC oversight committee was almost as low a rung as a senator could descend, chairman or not. He'd given the labour movement thirty-five years of his life, leading the Transport Workers Union and serving as the Labor Party's vice-president. And for what? To lead a committee that, when he'd served on it a few years ago, could barely muster enough members to hold a vote. It was Siberia, alright. Rudd had played him out of the park.

'At least you got something,' his wife had told him. 'See it as an opportunity.'

He valued her opinion; she was a political staffer turned successful businesswoman, but she'd be a politician one day and would probably scale higher than he. And she was probably right. Whatever Rudd thought of him, he still commanded enough numbers in the party, and had enough favours owed, to be given something.

Reaching the flat that marked the lookout, he bent over, hands on his knees. The sunlight was now wrapping around the mountain tops, illuminating great slabs of granite. He breathed in deeply and then out. If it was there, the imprint left by the cancer wasn't noticeable.

'Our Father who art in heaven, hallowed by thy name.'

Maybe the committee wouldn't be so bad. Starting his ascent, he picked his way over loose rocks, thinking through the little he knew about organised crime. Thirty years ago, it had been almost as big as terrorism post September 11, a political and media priority that generated royal commissions, new laws and agencies. Combing his mind, he searched for the name of the hitman suspected of killing NSW anti-drugs campaigner Donald Mackay in 1977.

Bazely. James Bazely.

When Hutchins worked as a union rep in the country area where Mackay had lived, people were still angry about the murder, with most blaming a local dope-growing Italian mafia cell. The headlines about Mackay's murder were soon followed by ones about crooks and bent police, including the notorious Roger Rogerson. Some politicians and judges were also said to be running with crime bosses.

But his knowledge of modern organised crime was limited. Save for the obsession with Melbourne's gangland killings and a few celebrity crooks, the media's coverage of the issue was sporadic: occasional stories about the popularity of ecstasy and ice, drug busts and bikie gangs. It didn't compare to the crime and corruption scandals of the 1970s–1980s or even the uproar when teenager Anna Wood died after taking an ecstasy tablet in 1995. It was as if organised crime had fallen off the political and media map, with the void later being filled by terrorism.

Maybe an opportunity could lie with the committee. If the system needed some stoking, he knew how to use a political poker. There was nothing stopping him from having a crack. Anyway, under Rudd, he would be a backbencher for the foreseeable future, and he was now free of any great personal ambitions. But he still had a fair bit of influence inside the party. He'd taken on dead-end parliamentary commissions in the past that had turned into catalysts for change. The inquiry into abuse in the military had rocked the entire defence force. He would have to play this new role carefully. Committees that lacked cross-party consensus usually went nowhere. But if anyone in the party thought he was about to languish, they were mistaken.

Brushing the sweat from his forehead, he realised his rosary had lapsed as the morning had finally broken through, drenching the brush with light. He felt better now, filled with promise.

'Our Father who art in heaven.'

Part 3
December 2007 – August 2009

December 2007 – August 2009

James

James watched his son topple over a footy. He shrieked with laughter and rolled in the grass.

'C'mon. Pick it up and toss it to me.'

The light was fading and they needed to head home soon.

James's son grabbed the ball and, directing all of his attention to the task of tossing it, flung it a few metres. He ran over to it, grabbed it, and tossed it again. His son was a determined creature. Not unlike himself. James felt strong and proud.

'C'mon little man. It's home time.'

Chatting to his son about working on his ball skills, James tried to push the day's events from his mind. Purchas and Bullock had impeccable timing, he thought darkly. He'd spent half the morning writing up a defence of the commission in response to a complaint from some federal police officers that the ACC had pinched an AFP job when they had taken out the huge haul of liquid ecstasy. The complaint was baseless, and the man appointed to examine it, AFP deputy commissioner John Lawler, was likely to find it so, yet it had created a hostile environment that they could do without.

The covert laundry was now successfully moving money without incident, and the commission was running hot on two suspected drug-trafficking syndicates. In one of their last briefings, Purchas and Bullock had revealed that an especially strong lead—from a Chinese–Canadian runner using the laundry to send suspected drug funds to Asia—had led them to a suspected drug syndicate whose fronts included several Vietnamese-run nail, beauty and foot spa businesses.

Vikingsson was also tantalisingly close to confirming the identities of the owners of some of the offshore bank accounts receiving the laundry's repatriated drug cash.

Trotting along with his son, James confronted what was bothering him: the risk that they might become the victims of their own success. The laundry's reputation for efficiency was already spreading around the Australian underworld, especially among Asian organised crime syndicates. Word had also apparently reached senior players offshore, and it had led to their laundry being offered a huge contract to move funds sitting in Macau to destinations across Asia.

Purchas and Bullock were urging him to assess the feasibility of extending the laundry to Asia and forming a partnership with the Hong Kong authorities. The pair had argued that the move would potentially get them far closer to the offshore phantoms responsible for the imports into Australia. They already had the contacts in Macau to set up in a gaming room, as well as the ability to track funds through the island's financial system thanks to a contact with high-level access to the island's casino computer and banking network.

There was merit in the idea, yet it was still troubling him. The covert laundry's initial money movements had got their foot in the door of the global money-laundering industry, but knowing how to fully infiltrate and exploit it would take at least a year, and probably much longer. It would mean a serious long-term commitment from not just the agency, but the Australian government as well.

The recent federal election had installed a new government and prime minister, which would most likely mean a new boss to replace Jock Milroy at the crime commission. A new regime was always an unknown and could spell trouble. Operation Dayu's concept of operations would need to find fresh backing and it would be up to him to sell it, not just for a year, but for two or three or more.

While it was worrying the hell out of some of the other senior managers, the idea of a covert laundry had never really bothered him. It was the long-term equation that ate at him. His anxiety led him back to the first piece of advice he had been given as a budding undercover operative: 'Anyone can get caught up in shit. But getting out of it is usually harder.'

Could they really stay alive for several years? And if they found the overseas phantoms, did they actually have the reach to deal with them? Most crucial was the question of whether Canberra would commit to an extended operation or opt to favour the old way of doing things: short investigations, quick hits, and regular front page coverage that made everyone look good. He'd seen it before.

James's son begun pulling on his father's hand.

'How are you doing down there?' he asked, but before the boy could answer, he added, 'What do you think about Dad going away for a while?'

Purchas

Standing over Vikingsson's shoulder, he listened to his colleague becoming increasingly excited.

'It actually works better than I expected, Mike.'

Ever since the laundry had began operating, he had noticed the analyst was sleeping less, sometimes spending twenty-four hours in the office, working on what Vikingsson had named the High Risk Funds Program geospatial database. One pack of smokes a day had become two, and he had lost weight. He wondered how Vikingsson's wife and kids were coping, but quickly shook off the thought. Christ. He was the last person to give family advice.

'Pay attention to this, Mike.'

Vikingsson deftly struck a few keys and the screen lit up with a three-dimensional model of the world. 'It's clunky, but it works.'

It occurred to him that Vikingsson looked like a child at show and tell.

With half an ear on the analyst, he began recapping the core developments in his head: their covert laundry had, over a series of weeks, conducted transfers to several different corporate entities in Asia, sending several million dollars in suspected drug money offshore; they had also been working backwards from the runners arriving at their laundry, including the fat man, identifying several suspected syndicates who were filling the void left by Operation Gordian.

One of the syndicates, a Chinese–Canadian outfit linked to Vietnamese nail and beauty salons, appeared to be sending suspicious money transfers to Hong Kong and Canada through several different money remitters. One of the transfers had been sent to a freight-forwarding company to cover customs and quarantine fees for the movement of goods through the port of Melbourne. It looked suspicious.

He focused back on Vikingsson and the computer model. Crude as it was, it allowed the viewer to clearly visualise what was happening with the funds after they left Australia. The computer screen depicted a Google map of the globe, with red lines between Australia and Asia representing the money the ACC's covert laundry had sent offshore during Operation Dayu. The green lines depicted the money transfers sent by the remitters used by the twenty-one Gordian syndicates between 2005 and 2007.

Vikingsson spun around and, with an air of theatre, said, 'You ready for the pièce de résistance?'

'Get on with it Startrek.' The analyst was, yet again, testing his patience.

Vikingsson swivelled back towards his screen and tapped the keyboard. 'I have entered in our laundry transfers, along with those from all known Gordian syndicates and any other High Risk Fund transfers going to South-East Asia that I've been able to identify. It looks ugly but it makes the point. Watch closely.'

Vikingsson appeared more magician than analyst, Purchas thought, as he watched dozens of lines representing wire transfers crisscross the globe, from Melbourne and Sydney to different parts of Asia. But the analyst was right. A huge portion of the drug funds had been sent to the same corporate entities or bank accounts. The modelling appeared to prove that the twenty-one Gordian drug syndicates, along with the replacement syndicates identified by Dayu, were sending drug money to some sort of interlinked overseas organisation headquartered in Asia.

He felt his mouth go dry as Vikingsson continued.

'Much of the money ends up in a small number of major casino, hotel or online gambling businesses in Asia. Cambodia is featuring heavily, as are Macau and Thailand. There is also a truckload pouring into multi million-dollar property companies in Hong Kong and a massive construction company in Vietnam—early indications suggest that it is closely aligned to the Vietnamese government.'

It made sense. Members of certain South-East Asian governments and militaries controlled many of their countries' major private enterprises, were notoriously corrupt, and had a long history of involvement in drug and arms trafficking. But Australian drug money?

He thought back to one of the covert laundry money transfers that had stalled in Vietnam. It was alarming at the time because the laundry relied on speedy transfers. Instead, the money had lingered in a Vietnamese account before being shifted several days later. The explanation that had filtered back to them through their sources suggested that two high-ranking officials within the Communist Party who were usually used by corrupt remitters to shift bulk funds out of Vietnam had, for some reason, failed to do so.

Vikingsson's work was pointing towards some sort of powerful international crime network which was importing drugs into, and repatriating funds from, Australia, and which had contacts in senior government and business circles throughout Asia.

Vikingsson watched Purchas examine the computer screen and said, 'You know, Mike, if we can extend the laundry to Macau and Hong Kong, it will get us even closer to the slime.'

Purchas nodded, his mind racing. 'Who are they?' he muttered aloud. He wasn't looking for an answer—not right now, at any rate—but Vikingsson obliged him anyway.

'It's too hard to say at this stage. We're still crunching data and intel. Hopefully some of your sources can further enlighten us. But put it this way: if there is an Asian mafia, some sort of global entity controlling the drug trade, it is highly likely we are now working on it.'

As Purchas turned to leave, Vikingsson stopped him. 'There is one other thing that has jumped out at me. Up until now, it has been Chinese and Vietnamese dominating the picture. But one of the suspicious money movements flagged on the system doesn't come from an Asian entity. The funds appear to be associated with a company in Sydney. It might be nothing, but it appears to be linked to an Australian national who features in some NSW police criminal intelligence holdings.'

He squeezed Vikingsson on the shoulder. 'Good work, Patrick. Can you create me a briefing note on it?' Noticing what looked like deep exhaustion in the analyst's eyes, he added, 'And do us all a bleedin' favour. Go get yourself some sleep while you still can. I have an inkling that things are about to heat up.'

Bilal

'Make sure you don't run over my nipple.' Bilal winced as he spoke, straining his eyes downwards to watch the needle travel across his upper chest like a fire ant.

'Don't worry, brother. The last time I did that I got fuckin' sued.' The tattooist laughed. 'Just fucking with you. This tat is a piece of piss. I've done millions of 'em. How long you known Waz, anyway?'

Far too long, he thought. But he answered politely, 'He's family. Married in.'

'You can't pick your family, eh?' The tattooist chuckled. 'Fuckin' with you again. Waz is a good lad. Not much of a rider, though. Still no licence. What a retard.'

'Tell me about it,' said Bilal.

The tattooist removed the gun from his skin and examined it before pressing it again on his chest, to retrace the outline.

'What does he owe you, anyhow?'

The tattooist was referring to the fact that Waz had organised for him to get a tat gratis. It was Waz's way of saying thanks after endlessly stuffing him around with the money from the cook.

'We just had a friendly bet. I'm not sure if I won or lost.'

Someone walked into the shop, and the tattooist excused himself. Bilal waited, scanning the far wall and the detailed sketches of flaming skulls and Harleys, and naked, busty women wrapped around knives and guns. 'Death before dishonour' and 'Comanchero always, always Comancheros' seemed to be the favourite slogans; must be a bikie-affiliated parlour, he thought.

Shifting his attention to the wall itself, he noticed it was smudged with soot, as if it had been recently burned. His eye followed the black traces up the wall to the roof, which also had signs of smoke damage. When the tattooist returned to the job, Bilal gently asked about the black walls. 'A heater catch on fire?'

The tattooist's face turned sullen and he spoke quietly. 'Someone tried to burn the shop down a few months backs. Had bricks through the window the other day. It's starting to heat up out there. I've been tattooing patches on blokes like never before. The clubs are recruiting and everyone is jumpy as fuck. Okay, buddy, you're done. Take a look at my magic.'

He sat up straight and examined his chest in the mirror. It was perfect: a three bar Maronite cross etched in dark blue. The same cross that hung above his mother's kitchen table and around his wife's neck.

It would serve as a reminder that bad deeds could lead to good. And to keep his head down and stay the hell away from Waz.

James

It reeked of rampant excess. James studied the gold leaf wrapped around the Roman columns as he and Bullock strode through the entrance. Next to a column, a sign said: 'The volume of sand used in the reclamation of land for this casino resort is enough to build one of Egypt's largest pyramids!'

The hotel's shopping strip ran parallel to a mock canal lined with Sherlock Holmes lampposts. If it was designed as a nod to the island's European roots, it had missed the mark. Apart from the whores, this place was everything old Europe was not: crude, garish and obscene.

The only thing it truly had in common was the sea of tourists passing through. If he and Bullock were under surveillance, they wouldn't have the faintest.

'Wake up, 007. She wants your card,' said Bullock.

His wallet felt lighter than usual. They'd left their official ID in a safety deposit box across the street from their Hong Kong hotel before heading to the ferry terminal.

'How many nights will you be staying, sir?'

'Just the one, thank you.'

His eyes were drawn to the wall behind the concierge, where another sign proclaimed: 'As many as 11,000 construction workers and 900 trucks a day were needed to build this resort … your playground!'

There was no better international melting pot of illegitimate and legitimate capital and labour than Macau: from the funds spun through the roulette tables to the construction and sex workers plucked out of the backblocks of Manila, Beijing and Eastern Europe to service the island.

The poverty he'd noticed on the streets disappeared inside the ugly edifices in the sky that housed the casinos and hotels. The cleaners and hotel staff were the only reminders of the real world. And the prostitutes. The place was teeming with them: Asian and Russian dolls with plastic breasts, miniskirts, fake designer handbags and sad eyes.

'I'll make one bet while I am here,' he said to Bullock, nodding towards the sign. 'None of those 11,000 workers would have ever stayed a single night in this joint.' And they weren't missing anything, he thought. The higher class the casinos pretended to be, the more garish they got: the chandeliers too big, the waitresses too friendly, and the punters trying too hard not to look like they were losing.

Canals! At least the smaller joints hadn't forgot what they were: money pits. Still, he was glad he was here, let loose into the real world instead of drafting another report or attending another meaningless meeting. He grew up on the streets, and despite the disdain he felt for much around him, he was comfortable mixing in a place like Macau, comfortable to be back undercover.

'Let's dump our bags and meet outside. First contact is coming up.' Contact. He hadn't used that word for years. He felt a small pulse of excitement, but brushed it off. 'And Bruce …'

'Yes, Jamesy?'

'Change your shirt. We are going to the high-roller rooms and you look like a cleaner.'

'Understood. Over and out, Mr Bond,' said Bullock, winking before he strode off, bag slung over his large shoulders.

He watched him go, thinking what a good partner Bullock would make in the field. While James was 5 foot 9, wiry and fit, with a well-rounded English accent, Bullock was 5 inches taller, at least 30 kilograms heavier and, even on his better days, charming but gruff. Bullock could easily pass as a heavy. That would be their cover tonight: the well-heeled businessman and his muscle.

His hotel room was, as with all five-star casino resorts, far too big for any guest who wasn't intending to host an orgy or an in-house cards racket. As he buttoned up his freshly ironed white shirt, he stared at himself in the mirror. His face was still trim, his hair greying but thick. He did up the last button, had a final look over himself and headed for the door.

He met Bullock in the foyer and the pair moved outside. Without speaking, Bullock moved to the other end of the hotel's car entrance, a position that would give the two of them maximum visual coverage. They needed to spot Purchas's contact while keeping a feel for anyone looking for them or trailing the source. The adrenalin was now coursing through him. 'Game on,' he whispered to himself.

He spotted the man a few minutes later. He was exactly as Purchas had described: small, neat, tailored suit, unremarkable face and a steely expression. The source fell in behind Bullock, and he behind the source, as Bullock walked back into the hotel-casino complex and its sea of people. For a moment he felt a twinge of uncertainty; there were too many people, too much movement. It reminded him of trudging towards Wembley Stadium for the FA Cup Final as a boy, fearful of losing his father amid the hordes.

He was struggling to keep Bullock and the source in sight among the mass of Asian gamblers heading for the tables, when a group of Japanese businessmen suddenly pushed in front of him.

He swore under his breath and pushed his way through. He'd lost sight of Bullock and the source. Five seconds. Ten seconds. He pushed on, walking faster. Thirty seconds. He spotted a wide pair of shoulders moving through the crowd. Gotcha.

Five minutes later, they walked into a high-class gaming lounge with private rooms. James studied his surrounds as Bullock and the source walked into a booth and slid the curtain behind them.

They'd agreed earlier that Bullock, who had met Purchas's source before, would handle the meeting. Bullock had extensive experience with Asian informers and was one of the only people who Purchas trusted to deal with his own sources. If James barged in, it may have unnerved the source.

Instead, James was assigned to keep watch, looking to see who was looking at them, and if anyone had taken undue interest. The room reminded him of the intergalactic bar scene from *Star Wars*, a place teeming with every creature the galaxy could spew up. There were five gaming tables surrounding a bar in the middle of the room. To the side of the room was a lounge and dining area. Young prostitutes sat on the knees of men three times their age, while heavy-set men, dripping in gold, handled gambling chips as if they were worthless. The room bubbled with Mandarin, Cantonese, English and Russian.

Nobody except the prostitutes paid him any attention. A woman, who looked about nineteen with impossibly firm breasts that appeared to be holding up her cocktail dress, raised her eyes at him. He shook his head. He ordered a drink and pretended to play with his phone while keeping an eye on the booth.

The meeting Bullock was having was probably premature. The source behind the curtain could help them set up a covert laundry in a gaming room, and from there they could move money through

Macau's banking system to accounts in Hong Kong and elsewhere. But to do so, they needed to convince some sceptical Hong Kong police officers of the possible existence of a global triad business with a major presence in Hong Kong, and the merits of using a covert laundry to identify and target its operations. At an earlier meeting, the Hong Kong police dismissed the idea, claiming that organised crime and money laundering was no longer a significant issue on the island. Ever since the British had handed over Hong Kong to the Chinese, officials had promulgated the myth that the triad problem was over. It was laughable.

'If Hong Kong triads were behind your drug imports and money laundering, we would already know about it and know who they are,' one official had told them. He'd been worried that the comment might provoke an outburst from Bullock, but the Melbourne investigator had held his tongue. 'Don't worry, Jamesy. We'll be back,' he'd said quietly as they left the meeting.

He hoped Bullock was right. Without the Hong Kong authorities on board, they would never get an operating certificate to extend the covert laundry to Asia. Even tonight's activities in Macau could technically be considered a black operation.

He watched the curtain being pulled back and the source walk past without acknowledging him. Bullock emerged thirty seconds later. Bullock said nothing about the meeting until they were back in the hotel, and even then spoke quietly, briefly and only in the foyer.

'We'll be able to set up in a private gaming room on the island. The commissions are higher than we thought, and every dollar we move through the casino will be taxed by the Chinese. But no one will ask any questions about the source of the funds we move, or pay any attention to suspicious structuring. We just need the approval from Canberra and Hong Kong. Let's rendezvous as planned.'

James watched Bullock disappear and then headed to his own room. Still impeccably dressed, James lay on his bed and closed his eyes. He began drifting almost immediately. The hotel phone next to his head suddenly buzzed.

'Hello?'

'It's Mike. Bruce has already filled me on your evening. We have some good news of our own back home.' Purchas sounded unusually excited.

'The surveillance team has been covering the Chinese–Canadians behind some of the High Risk Fund moves. Turns out they are in the business of importing foot spas to use in their nail and beauty salons. We have gone back and checked the customs records and found regular consignments coming in over the last twelve months. We then had a closer look and found some of their business dealings were done through the newsagency linked to the Lam family.'

He tried to shrug off his weariness and force himself to absorb what Purchas was telling him. The Lams were a well-known Vietnamese clan who owned a thriving restaurant in Cabramatta and who were suspected to have spent years facilitating Asian organised crime activity in Australia. The Lams had moved money for some of the Gordian syndicates, and there was a longstanding drug-trafficking warrant out for one of the Lam brothers, Jack.

'We did some more snooping at a factory connected to this Chinese–Canadian group's runners, and our team found they had dumped some of their imported spa baths. The thing is, they had had their bottoms cut out.' Purchas fell silent.

'Go on, Mike. What is it?'

'Ever been in a spa without a bottom?'

He detected the sarcasm in Purchas's tone as he twigged to the significance of the bottomless spas. 'How long have they been importing them?'

'Once a month over the last six months, at least. The geniuses at customs somehow missed 'em all, but we've gone back through the X-rays and each one looks like it's packed with drugs. There are more due, so we are going to see if the feds want to start taking them out while we hover in the background.'

He now knew why Purchas sounded so excited. They needed drug seizures to keep the laundry running and the bosses at bay. And each result would buy them more time.

Hakan 'Hux' Ayik

Daux Ngakuru
(Monique Westermann,
Fairfax Syndication)

Mick Hawi, president of the Comancheros
(Lisa Wiltse, Fairfax Syndication)

Sydney Morning Herald
reporter Dylan Welch
(Fairfax Syndication)

Mike Purchas and Bruce Bullock at the Venetian Macau hotel, 2011

Mike Purchas
(Lisa Wiltse, Fairfax Syndication)

Patrick Vikingsson heading to a meeting with the World Bank in Washington DC, USA, October 2010

Senator Steve Hutchins
(Brendan Esposito, Fairfax Syndication)

Purchas continued. 'There is one other thing that has come out of left field. There appears to be an Australian guy with some sort of a financial link to some of the offshore money transfers that have popped up on our radar. We haven't got much on him yet, but we are doing some sniffin'. Looks like the NSW cops have got some holdings on him. He's probably a nobody, but you never know.'

'Good work, Mike,' he said, but by then the phone was dead.

Ayik

Breathing in, Ayik braced and focused only on the cold metal bar in his hands. As he exhaled, he pushed, feeling his chest ripple, back clench and biceps seize and twitch.

His mate stood over him, ready to catch the bar if he needed. 'C'mon, big fella … C'mon, bro. You gotta fuckin' dominate. Five more to go.'

He fought the urge to rest the bar to his chest, exhaled and pushed. By the fourth rep the twitch had morphed into a spasm.

'C'mon, you big fuckin' pussy. One more to go. Push it out.'

This time he groaned as he breathed out, straining until he'd locked his elbows, the weight at full stretch above him.

'That's it, brother. Good stuff. Lookin' good. You fuckin' pumped or what?'

'Thanks, bro.' He lay on his back, panting. 'You right with money?'

'Yeah, all good mate. Our heads are above water.'

Ten minutes later, he slid into the leather car seat and, easing the Audi into first, felt the engine rumble. He picked up the mobile he used for personal calls and dialled the chemist. 'Hey doc, it's me. Mind if I swing by?'

The chemist was a Comancheros hook-up, a guy who supplied muscle juice to guys in the club. Will had recently begun using him to help out the girls at the brothel with any health problems. He knew some guys at the gym looked down on juice, but almost everyone he knew who pumped weights seriously dabbled. If you wanted to stack on the muscle, you needed a regular taste. There was no more to it. He left the car idling as he strode inside the pharmacy.

'Same as usual, doc.' He smiled. The chemist and he were similar creatures. They saw a market and met its demands. Except, of course, his market was growing exponentially. Where the pharmacist thought micro, he thought macro. He was an entrepreneur. Anyone who disagreed didn't understand market economics.

He gunned the Audi towards the city, his sound system pumping his favourite 50 Cent track, the bass filling the car.

He pressed the accelerator, feeling the car surge forward as he zipped two lanes to the right, 50 Cent rapping about jewels and money. He wound down the window and turned up the volume again.

He revised the plan as he mimed the words to the song. It was unfolding nicely. They had proven they could move the smaller contracts with ease and, even after servicing overheads, pocket a healthy return.

The key was to keep the boys focused on business, not war. He'd shown how the patches could work together. There was enough to go around to keep all engines gunning. Ice and coke were wholesaling locally for $200,000 plus per kilo; eccies could be moved at $25,000 per thousand. He could source hundreds of kilos of ice in China for $80,000 per kilo, coke in South America or Asia for just a few thousand bucks a kilo and ecstasy for a fifth of the domestic wholesale price.

Now they were playing in a bigger league, it would require better scheming to move gear through. A few of the guys had promised some new friends on the waterfront. They already had reach in the jacks to hear if there was any bad news afoot. After giving everyone their slice and wetting Will's beak, he would be left with plenty to invest.

Large capital was best poured into property, especially given the state of the market. The rest could be spread through overseas accounts, the brothel, the gym and a few sideline ventures. If he could secure the energy drink contract in Hong Kong, he could set up there semi-permanently and loosen Will's leash to run things domestically.

Will would like that. He'd call him his 2IC, and the boy would think he'd won the Beijing lottery.

He turned up the volume another notch as the track moved to the last chorus and started singing outloud.

At the end of the track, he flicked the stereo off and, keeping one eye on the road, checked his third mobile for any messages. Still nothing. Mizza left Bankstown just after midnight and should have texted long ago. He checked his watch. It was just after 4.30 p.m., meaning the light plane should have landed at Jandakot, near Perth, an hour before.

Maybe there were strong winds, or storms. What were the chances of it going down? 'Drug plane discovered in desert.' Fuck. The media would be creaming themselves. It was probably just bad weather. Still, he should have picked up a signal airborne and texted. Mizza knew the importance of keeping to a strict routine. The gear had been packed wearing gloves; the phones were all throwaways and the sim cards subscribed to phantoms. It was clinical. Perfectly clean.

He double-parked near the university and, five minutes later, walked past the pillars and concrete lions into Chinatown. He felt a faint drizzle touch his face and wondered if the weather in Perth was the same as in Sydney. As he passed the site Will had picked out for his karaoke club, he gave it a quick glance but didn't stop walking. He held his hand on the phone in his pocket, willing a vibration, while ignoring the Asian girls spruiking early dinner.

When he walked into Macchiato's, Will was waiting for him, smiling weakly. He guessed Will still hadn't found the missing cash. Dickhead. If only he had worked as hard as he whored.

'Hey man. You found that girl of yours?'

'Still looking, Hux. I think I know where she got to. Don't worry. I will make sure we get that money.'

He could tell Will was lying and knew it would be up to him to fix. Will was now flushing red, sitting sheepishly, his shoulders slumped.

'Don't worry, bro. We got bigger things happening in Asia.'

He considered telling Will more, but then decided against it. Need to know only. That is how the coppers locked down their own business, even though half the time it was locked down to guys on his side. He could do better.

Unlocking his phone, he checked his messages again. Still nothing. They should have been on the ground at least an hour ago.

'Listen, Will. I have some cash that needs to be shifted. This time, change it up a little.' As he spoke, he noticed a large, grim-faced Tongan moving through the cafe. The Tongan's eyes locked on his own. It was one of Daux's boys.

'Fuck,' he spat out in a whisper, rising to greet the bikie. It looked like bad news.

'The plane has been busted. Daux said to tell you.' The Tongan turned and walked away.

He felt his heart rate rise and turned to Will. 'We better clean up. I've gotta do a few things. Make sure to keep your head down.'

The rain was coming down a little heavier as he walked through the city streets and up an alley. He turned around and waited, watching for any movement. He took out phone three, removed the battery and tossed it into a dumpster. He ducked up another alley, increasing his pace as though he were outrunning a shadow. He slid out the sim card, snapped it into two and tossed it.

Phone or no phone, he knew he couldn't be firmly linked to anything. He had kept clean, keeping out of the club, away from the bashings and the violence and all the other ritualistic bullshit. But he felt anxious. Maybe it was time to head back overseas, to follow through on his Chinese business visa.

Before he reached his car, Ayik threw the rest of the phone into a drain. He turned around, scanning the dark. The street was mostly quiet, streaked with lights shimmering in the rain and the patter of strangers. He took out his other two phones, slid out the batteries and sim cards and tossed them as well. It was time to start afresh.

December 2007 – August 2009

Welch

Who the hell is Big Hux? Welch sat, repeating the question in his head while watching a slab of processed, compressed meat circle slowly over the heat, its oil dripping into a tray below.

Who the hell is Big Hux?

He pushed the thought aside and concentrated on watching the slab rotate, wondering how anyone could ever, even after thirty beers, equate it to lamb. He tried to count the cycles by following an especially pink bit complete a rotation. He counted three times, settling on six seconds.

So this is what he had come to. He was a cop reporter who struggled to get north of page seven and whose supposed Deep Throat was standing him up. He'd been waiting in Kings Cross for forty-five minutes for the ex-bouncer and was becoming increasingly certain that he wasn't going to show.

The agreed meeting place was a Kings Cross kebab shop. Classy. Along with some of the dirtier strip clubs, the kebab shops were among the only places that had stayed the same as the Cross had gentrified.

One, two, three, four, five, six. Yep. Six seconds per rotation.

While waiting, he had been propositioned by a prostitute, who had asked him if he wanted to buy a blow job and then, after he politely declined, whether he had two dollars or a cigarette to spare. He had handed over a few gold coins and smiled. Who said chivalry was dead?

He knew of cops who placed bets on which street hookers would die of an overdose first. Scarecrows, they called them, or just crows. Across the street, strippers came and went to work, invariably wearing tracksuit pants with bunny ears printed on the back and hooded jumpers that hugged their cosmetically enlarged breasts. Colloquially known as 'Kings Cross bolt-ons', a stripper could pay off a pair with a couple of weeks of full-time pole dancing.

In the last twenty minutes, he'd also watched a group of fully patched Hells Angels roll slowly up and down the street before pulling up outside a strip club. Before he'd spotted them, he'd heard the low-pitched throbbing and rumbling of the Harleys. There was something about that sound, the colours and the patches that he loved. It reminded him of the outlaw gangs of old Westerns. Whether they rode in on horses or bikes, the whole town turned and looked.

Behind him, a group of British men in their early twenties fell drunkenly about each other, ordering kebabs before taking their bad breath into the next nightclub. It was their money, Welch thought, along with that of the yuppies and students who came to drink and get high that had turned the Cross into a pit of disposable income and bad habits.

'Do you know where Dreamgirls is?' asked one of the kebab-ordering men between mouthfuls of unchewed meat, garlic sauce dripping down his chin onto an English soccer jersey.

'You're staring at it mate. But you might want to change your shirt if you want to get in.' Cop reporter turns Kings Cross tourist adviser. That's what he had become.

The nightclubs and strip clubs were one of the reasons he was here. That, and a list of names of leading players in the bikie scene, some who he knew a bit about and others who he'd heard mentioned only once or twice. Big Hux was one of the former. And, as with several key figures in the bikie scene, word was he wasn't even patched. If that were so, it reflected the evolution of Australia's outlaw clubs. Some of the players in the game, of which the Ibrahim family was the most public example, seemed to run with bikies because it suited their business aspirations, not because they loved Harleys.

The man he was about to meet was a bouncer who worked several of the doors in the Cross. That made him an infantryman on the front line of one of the biggest struggles in the bikie world—the fight to control the Cross. At the very least, the bouncer should be able to confirm which bikie clubs controlled which clubs.

That is, if he ever showed up. All this fucking around for a yarn that would struggle to find a home in the pages of the *Sydney Morning Herald*. When he'd floated a feature on the evolution of outlaw bikie

December 2007 – August 2009

gangs in Australia the week before, one of the news editors had responded with the conventional newspaper wisdom on the issue. 'This is scum-on-scum stuff, mate. The public doesn't give a toss. Give me a royal commission or corruption angle, or some gangland murders in public places and you'll have yourself a feature. Remember mate: if it bleeds, it leads.' The news editor paused before delivering his next piece of wisdom. 'But if it is big, fat, tattooed and hairy and bleeds, no one gives a shit. Everyone knows the bikies are in the Cross. A story about them *leaving* the Cross ... Now that's a yarn.'

Well, the bikies were unlikely to leave any time soon. That he knew. That much was confirmed. Not as long as there were wealthy clubbers, Friday night knock-off partiers and footy teams who wanted to watch naked flesh wrapped around a pole, drink twelve beers and have a line of cocaine or speed followed by a kebab, a spew in the gutter and whatever tricks your last eighty bucks (coins included) could get you from a whore.

One, two, three, four, five, six. He was spot on. Six seconds. The meat still looked too pink. He'd give the ex-bouncer five more minutes. He knew plenty about the Ibrahims and the Cross anyhow, although the man who was standing him up might have provided some of the finer details, some of what one of the senior *Sydney Morning Herald* reporters called 'the human touch'.

Welch revised the tale in his head. In the 1990s, the Ibrahim brothers, led by John and Sam, controlled much of the Cross and ran several of the nightclubs and strip clubs, using the Sydney chapter of the Nomads, run by Scott Orrock and his associates, as security.

Around 1997, the Ibrahims decided they could save on security costs if Sam became a member of the Nomads. He patched up and within five years was a chapter president. It was rumoured he had actually paid for his meteoric rise up through the club. Whatever the truth of the matter, Ibrahim soon presided over a sudden influx of young, ambitious Lebanese men into the Nomads' ranks.

Ibrahim's acquisition of the Parramatta branch of the Nomads changed the face of Australian outlaw motorcycle clubs forever. From largely blue-collar, Anglo-Saxon brotherhoods with a racist edge and a genuine passion for Harley-Davidsons, drinking, rooting, tattoos and a little crime on the side, an increasing number of bikie outfits began morphing into multi-race or multi-ethnic clubs with a lust for big money and power.

In this new rat race, Mick Hawi was rumoured to have bought into the Comancheros, beefing up the club with Tongans, Lebanese and Turkish heavies, and pushing out most of the old-timers, including founder Jock Ross. Somewhere in this new mix was Big Hux.

Whoever the hell he was.

Clubs were moving out of their stomping grounds into other bikies' territories, crossing over suburban, and then state, lines. Comancheros who had once simply preached brotherhood started to expand on the club's motto—Always Comanchero, Comanchero Always—and began preaching power: Comanchero Taking Over Your City.

They followed the quickest and easiest path to riches. That is why the Cross was so important. What better place to sell sex and drugs? Dirty earnings could be washed through nightclub tills.

He knew the story of the Cross was worth telling because it was a microcosm not only of what was going on around Australia but also of what had already happened in countries like Canada, where the Hells Angels had battled other bikie groups to take control of the lucrative drug trade. The Angels had then wrestled to control the ports, had hooked up with other criminal organisations, and had begun moving gear out of Canada. It was now an export hub for drugs, not just a consumer market. That is what loomed for Australia, he thought. Whether it was on page one or page seven or nowhere at all.

He checked his watch and figured he was done waiting. Deep Throat was a no-show. As he moved to go, several of the bikies began starting up their machines. He stood on the street and watched them revving up and felt the air around him shuddering with the Harley's roar. He suddenly felt ravenous.

He eyed the meat on the spit again. All signs of pink had been replaced by a plastic-looking brown. It looked like a giant, simmering turd. As he walked into a blast of garlic fumes, he counted the money left in his pocket. He was two dollars short. The prostitute. Damn it. She had taken his last few gold coins. His stomach and notebook empty, he left the store and trudged down the street, eyes cast downwards and people laughing, eating and drinking all around him.

Purchas

Purchas nursed his coffee, feeling the warmth spread through the palms of his hands. He'd slept for only four hours the night before, a pattern he'd repeated regularly over the past few weeks. The laundry was now thriving, so they had decided to get selective, knocking back customers and focussing their resources on a syndicate with strong ties to China, Canada and Australia.

After uncovering the bottomless foot spa business, he and Bullock had reviewed customs records and found regular importations of foot spas dating back six months, and then called in the feds. The busts followed, one after the other: 54 kilograms of ice and coke in Sydney in the first week of May; 28 kilos of ice and coke a week later; a fortnight after that, 166 kilos of ice, coke and ecstasy powder seized in Melbourne and New York. All up, the drugs seized were worth tens of millions of dollars.

Purchas glanced over at Bullock and James, who were both fiddling with the phone system. He'd never been a fan of teleconferences between Australia's mistrustful law enforcement agencies; they often turned into a game of 'show me yours first'. He had his own way of playing them. If he knew a teleconference about a disputed operation was likely to become heated, he would fill the room with his analysts, who would quietly pass him information as required, ensuring he was never short of an answer or question. It was called 'stacking the room'. No wonder the feds disliked him, Purchas thought.

He watched Bullock cursing the equipment. It was classic modern policing: the commission could have two dozen phone taps running simultaneously yet not find the funds to pay for a working teleconference phone.

His thoughts turned to whether he should brief the feds on the latest findings of Operation Dayu's High Risk Funds Program—especially the fact that Western Union agents appeared to be sending huge amounts of money offshore with scant regard for Australian laws that required them to check the identification of the person sending it.

'Can you hear me? Hello?' Purchas immediately recognised the voice crackling through the speaker phone. It belonged to a fast-talking, brash yet dedicated federal police agent who had worked for him fifteen years earlier at the National Crime Authority. Now the agent outranked him and, like many feds, regarded him warily.

He clashed with the feds regularly, ever since he'd helped the National Crime Authority muscle in on the national law enforcement scene. In the 1990s, the feds nicknamed him 'Drip-feed' because of his refusal to share NCA information with other agencies for fear of it leaking. He still wore the tag proudly. If he hadn't been pushed by his bosses, he would have stayed completely mute: 'No-feed' was his preferred moniker. Given this mutual hostility, he'd agreed to leave most of the talking to James and Bullock. There was too much at stake.

Along with their plans to operate from Macau, he and Bullock wanted to send one of their sources to Canada to infiltrate what appeared to be an Ontario-based arm of the overseas organisation that was reaping the rewards of many of the drug imports pouring into Australia. If the Canadian Mounties and the Hong Kong police were to commit to such a truly international police taskforce, the ACC needed the feds to do the same.

But it was one hoop at a time. They had agreed to keep their discussion of the bigger picture to a minimum and concentrate on getting the AFP's assistance on an incoming import—an estimated three hundred kilograms—from the local Chinese–Canadian group.

The federal agent immediately made it clear the AFP wasn't going to buy into any grand, long-term ACC operation aimed at identifying a nebulous, offshore entity. 'I would rather bust two bunnies in a container than no one at all, any day,' he said, speaking in quick spurts.

The more Purchas listened, the more his mood soured. The message coming down the line was clear, and he wondered whether old enmity was at play. Whatever the case, the feds seemed intent on simply picking off the busts that were passed to them and move on.

Purchas cleared his throat to speak but was beaten to the punch.

'Well, you are a fucking idiot then, aren't you?' Bullock spat, his face hot with anger.

Purchas nodded in agreement while James played the diplomat and glared at Bullock. But Bullock was right. What was the point of taking out a few bunnies if they and their product were replaced overnight?

It was time to get back to work.

He arrived back at his desk fifteen minutes later to find a file on his keyboard. Purchas recognised Vikingsson's handwriting on the cover, which said 'The Australian'.

He flicked open the first page. According to the file, the Sydney man linked to some of the High Risk Funds transfers was Hakan Ayik. He was aged thirty but looked older. He was one of a number of targets in a NSW police operation, codenamed Hoffman, targeting drug trafficking by outlaw motorcycle gangs in Sydney's south-west.

Bikies. They'd been growing in numbers steadily, ever since they'd come to the NCA's attention over a decade before. Many were in it for the lifestyle: the drink, drugs and women. But the cleverest bikies used their brethren to do their dirty work. Given the propensity of some bikies for violence—he'd once investigated some bikies from the Finks who had ripped off an informer's head by tying it to a car's bullbar, his legs to a tree, and driving off—they could be handy soldiers. Was it possible that some bikies had hooked up with Asian syndicates?

The thought was interrupted by a buzzing in his pocket. It was one of the mobile phones he used for his informants. The letter code for his old source, H, appeared on the screen. He hadn't heard much from him since they'd begun the laundry. In any event, it was rare for him to call. Something was up.

The source didn't bother to greet him when he answered. 'I hear your new laundry has been busy, Mike. But I have something else for you. One of the syndicates that has moved much money to Asia is looking for help to move a big load. They need a local facilitator.'

'How much?' said Purchas.

'Five hundred kilograms of ice is sitting in China.'

He felt a rush of surprise as he heard the words. He had thought the source was referring to shifting money, not importing drugs.

'Why are you telling me this?'

For a few seconds, he heard only breathing. 'You want to take out the shipment or not, Mike?'

'I'll make some enquiries and be in touch shortly. Before you go, I need your help with something. This new laundry we've been watching is sending its money back to a few companies in Asia. They are the same companies that many of the old Vietnamese remitters are also directing cash to. Do you know who we're dealing with?'

He had tried to ask the question as if it didn't matter, but he knew from the several seconds of dead air on the phone that it hadn't worked. 'Why don't you go and ask your old friend Dai Lo Cheung about it,' the source eventually said, and abruptly hung up.

Purchas was immediately consumed by memories. Dai Lo Cheung was who the Chinese referred to as Duncan Lam Sak Cheung, a Hong Kong migrant turned Sydney organised crime boss who he'd helped to lock up for trafficking 20 kilos of heroin in 2001, in an operation codenamed Tabasco.

But he'd got away with much more. Sak Cheung was suspected of organising some of Australia's biggest heroin shipments in the 1990s, including 78 kilograms of heroin worth at least $80 million, which were seized by police in 1998. The total wealth generated by Sak

Cheung's drug importations was closer to half a billion dollars. They'd never uncovered Sak Cheung's offshore bosses, or worked out who was truly behind Ly Vi Hung, the crime boss who replaced him. Ly Vi Hung was jailed a few years after Sak Cheung for the importation of 105 kilograms of heroin into Sydney in 2005.

What was abundantly clear was that the jailing of both men had not affected the supply of drugs from Asia to the nation's distribution networks. Presumably, Ly Vi Hung, like Sak Cheung before him, had been replaced as soon as he was taken out.

Purchas forced his attention back to the file in front of him. There was something disconcerting about Ayik's photo, but he couldn't quite figure out what it was. He looked too comfortable for a person posing for a mugshot, as if he were in on a sly joke that nobody else had any hope of getting. His known aliases were 'Hux' or 'Big Hux', presumably in reference to his muscular build. He was 175–180 centimetres, olive complexion with black hair and brown eyes.

The profile described him as an Australian of Turkish descent, with dual passports. Ayik was a known associate of Joseph Micalizzi, who was arrested by Western Australia police in March at Jandakot airport during an alleged drug run for the Comancheros. He had also been linked by local law enforcement officials to the importation of 850 kilos of pseudoephedrine from Thailand to Sydney, a shipment tracked by the NSW Crime Commission, customs and the federal police. His associates included not only known bikies but also Chinese nationals. Big Hux travelled frequently: Hong Kong, Macau, Dubai, Thailand and Turkey, spending almost as much time offshore as he did in Australia.

Purchas scanned further down the page. He didn't fit the mould of a person who would run with Asians. He was thirty years old, had no university education and was linked to a bikie outfit. The Turkish-Australian was the last person he'd expect to be flagged by Operation Dayu for sending large and suspicious money transfers offshore. Australian bikies and Asian organised crime? It seemed highly unlikely. The fact that Ayik was the target of a relatively low-level state police operation suggested he was a bottom feeder rather than a serious player with international connections.

And yet there was something about him. Purchas stared at the photo again before he closed the file and headed for the door. A thorough look at Ayik's financials and associates was needed before he could discount him as a potential Dayu target.

It wasn't until Purchas reached the lift that he realised what was odd about the police mugshot. It was his eyes. Hakan Ayik's eyes were smiling.

James

James rolled off his bed, feeling the cold of the morning air bite his skin as he reached for his laptop. When the light from the screen hit his wife's face, she groaned.

'What time is it?'

'It's 4 a.m. Go back to sleep.'

She groaned again, this time with extra emphasis, and rolled over while stuffing her face into the pillow.

James felt nervous as *The Age* website loaded. When he had left the ACC Sydney office the night before, the place had been electric with whispers that the Fairfax broadsheets had somehow obtained details from a damaging Crime Commission document. The headline was the first thing he saw: 'Debus Furious over Secret Spy File.'

'Incredible,' he whispered to himself. The article revealed that one of the other ACC general managers had penned some sort of quasi-official document outlining the conduct of the federal Home Affairs minister, Bob Debus, during a dinner he had with policing officials. The file included references to the minister's drinking habits, political views and friends, and to his wife's ethnicity, and it had been stored on the commission's database. He shook his head as he read on. The commission was playing the file down as a manager's 'unofficial personal notes', but it didn't look good. Keeping files on politicians, let alone the very minister who held the Crime Commission's purse strings, had gone out of fashion with the Stasi.

'We're done for.'

'What is it, Gregory?'

He realised he had spoken aloud.

His wife rolled over again and looked at him quizzically.

'It's nothing. Just another idiot masquerading as a leading public servant. Try to go back to sleep.'

He dragged himself to the shower, brainstorming as the hot water rushed down his head and back. It was the worst possible time for the commission to be on the nose in Canberra, with the Rudd government having recently ordered all federal agencies to cut staff and save money amid the madness of the global financial crisis. There were rumours that the ACC would lose up to a quarter of its staff, including several of the seconded state police detectives working under Bullock and Purchas.

The bad news had bowled up just as Operation Dayu was gaining traction. Vikingsson's last estimate, care of the High Risk Funds Program, had put the annual drug money flow out of Australia at anywhere between $4 billion and $12 billion, at least ten times the estimates published by the Australian Institute of Criminology. The shadowy overseas entity that Dayu was tracking was responsible for an estimated one tenth of this multi billion-dollar drug flow.

And they were making significant inroads. Despite the recent terse words with the AFP, federal agents had successfully busted a 312-kilogram import of ice and cocaine. Purchas was working on a 500-kilogram shipment about to be sent from China, and Hong Kong authorities had hinted they were finally willing to back Operation Dayu. The operation was also drilling into the shady practices of several Western Union money remitters. He lingered for another few seconds under the hot water, before turning it off.

Fifteen minutes later, driving to work, Purchas's gravelly London voice blasted from his speakerphone: 'I've confirmed it. It's blue on blue. Fucking unbelievable.'

'Hang on, Mike. Slow down,' James said, wondering if Purchas had slept the night before. He sounded huskier than usual. Blue on blue was police slang for one agency trampling on the work of another. Purchas was referring to his recent suspicions that a rival agency's informer had attempted to infiltrate one of the syndicates targeted by Dayu.

'What exactly have you found?' he asked.

Purchas was livid. 'It's the feds. They've sent their own informer to target one of the Dayu syndicates, without bothering to tell us. Turns out he is a con man who took 'em for a ride.'

'You sure?'

'I'll bet my bleedin' superannuation on it,' Purchas muttered darkly. 'They flew him in from the other side of the world, paid for his airfares and let him loose. They've risked blowing our ops out of the water.'

'I'll write it up this morning, Mike. I will be at the office in half an hour, so you can give me a full briefing then. And Mike, I need you to try to get along with the feds. They are our partners, not our competitors.' A fresh round of internecine warfare was the last thing they needed.

'Get fucked,' said Purchas, hanging up.

Purchas had a point, he thought as he pulled into the agency car park. The deal they had struck with the federal police was to hand over the intelligence on Canadian imports and allow them to take out the shipments and runners while the commission stayed in the background, monitoring the bigger players and the connected money movements. If the feds had put in their own source, it seemed contrary to their agreement.

He shook his head. Police forces in Europe and the UK regularly snubbed and undermined each other, but Australia's policing agencies left them for dead. The AFP labelled the Victorian and NSW cops corrupt; the Victorians labelled the NSW police even more corrupt; and nearly all the state forces labelled the feds 'the plastics', implying that they were not real police.

Purchas was partly to blame. He wouldn't give the feds an inch, entering each meeting with the air of a zookeeper about to hand out bananas. Yet he knew that, deep down, Purchas held several feds in high regard and would reel off their names when telling his war stories: Peter Lamb, John Beverage, Bill Laing, Peter Baker, Tony Negus. Many of the AFP officers he'd worked with over the past three years were terrific operators.

The problem was institutional. As with many policing agencies around the world, the feds had put too many of their eggs in the terrorism basket. The agency had only recently begun to address the absence of experience and operational expertise in its organised crime department. Purchas's zookeeper routine wasn't helping.

As he walked past the Crime Commission reception, the security guard was reading a newspaper with the headline in full view. The guard cheekily raised a single eyebrow at James before quickly looking down again in a lame attempt to conceal a grin.

He pressed on towards his office and the tall, skinny figure lingering outside it. 'Did you manage to go home last night, Mike?'

'I sure did. But I came in early to prepare you a briefing on our friends. I have also gone to the trouble of making you a cup of tea.'

He glanced down and noticed the two steaming mugs on the table. The closest had an emblem of the ACC on its side, the other an AFP logo. Purchas's craggy face was smiling, ear to ear, like an ageing Cheshire cat.

'Very good, Mike. Very good. Now what's going on?' he said, leading Purchas into his office.

'The briefing paper I have prepared for you deals with our tussle with the feds over the Canadian imports. What we need to do now is turn our attention to a fresh matter … 500 kilograms of ice sitting on a dock in China waiting to come our way.'

'And?'

'The syndicate moving it is looking for help to clear the docks. Bruce and I have come up with a plan to provide a path of least resistance for the syndicate to tread. We will set up a company that will be a front for an import facilitator with contacts on the wharf. The laundry will then introduce this firm as skilled in expediting imports from China through the docks. This will allow us to control the importation, ensuring the feds are able to intercept it once Dayu has gathered as much intelligence as possible. The syndicate will blame the seizure on bad luck.'

Purchas was beaming, his face alive with energy. It was as if he had forgotten about their argument on the phone not half an hour before.

'Mike, now may not be the best time for the agency to be taking on more risk.'

Purchas snapped, 'We are simply manipulating the environment to identify the bigger players. It's the modus operandi of Operation Dayu. Think of it as medical research. It's about producing interim results while we stay on the main game.'

Another bloody one-liner. Purchas's weakness was not that he didn't understand the political game; it was that he didn't care to play it. The man's modus operandi was bust through or bust.

'What about this?'

He tossed down the newspaper in front of Purchas. 'We now have one less friend in Canberra, which is not ideal given we weren't that popular to begin with. The agency will not want to risk any more bad headlines. We now have very few mates where they count, be it at the AFP or in Parliament House.'

James wondered if Purchas knew how truly bad it was. If the rumours about Debus refusing to take the commission's calls last night were accurate, it meant the agency was temporarily persona non grata. He'd also heard word that the head of the ACC parliamentary committee, Steve Hutchins, had demanded a meeting with Milroy in order to dress him down. It increased the chance that whoever replaced Milroy as ACC boss would be trusted in Canberra as someone able to keep very tight control over the agency. Such a development would hardly bode well for controversial policing operations and outspoken investigators.

'You can forget about more resources for the time being, Mike. Another big seizure will be great, but unless we can sell the commission executives something they can sell their own masters, we may not have much more life in us.'

'What about ...?' Purchas started.

'Your global Asian mafia is pie in the sky right now. It is nameless, faceless men who are so far out of our jurisdictional reach it isn't funny. We are not paid to chase international ghosts. For all Canberra cares, the money trail is simply figures on a page that say we are getting flogged by organised crime. And that is a story they don't want to hear.'

For an instant, he thought he saw Purchas's face drop and his shoulders droop. But it was just for a moment.

'Leave it with me. I'll be back to you shortly,' Purchas told him.

As soon as Purchas had disappeared, he tried to call some of the senior commission managers, but their phones were all off. They were likely in lock-down, dealing with the media and political enquiries flowing from the story.

The prospect of the government abandoning the agency was real. He shuddered. If among all the bad headlines, word of the covert laundry somehow leaked and the operation was then misconstrued or misreported, it would fuel a fresh fire. In the past, other agencies had been crucified for allowing drugs to run in order to gain more evidence.

An hour later, Purchas reappeared. In his right hand he held a file.

'You mind if I close the door?'

'Sure, Mike.'

'It is up to you whether you run this up the line, but I am in the process of arranging a sit-down with Senator Steve Hutchins. Bruce is going to come with me.'

James was momentarily speechless. A senior investigator meeting the head of the ACC parliamentary committee went against every bureaucratic rule in the book. The dance between policing officials and politicians in Canberra was almost always meticulously choreographed, climaxing with a series of benign questions and answers in a parliamentary committee room. The very idea of Purchas waltzing into that dance … Sooner or later, word of the meeting would filter back to the ACC bosses.

'You sure that's a good idea, Mike?'

'Well, I am sure as hell not going to let the agency cop a flogging without pushing our own line. We are getting flogged on all sides: the feds, the politicians. They have to know we are doing something real and positive.' Purchas slapped a manila folder down on the table. 'In the meantime, here is an overview of what Dayu has so far pulled together from the laundry, our human sources and the High Risk Funds Program. It is a rough outline but it paints a powerful picture.' Heading out the door, Purchas threw a final strategic punch. 'As for the nameless and faceless men offshore, we may yet have a chance to put some names and faces to our phantoms. I'll tell you more later.'

He sat there for a few minutes, tossing up whether he should raise the alarm about Purchas's plan to meet Hutchins. As much as he wished Purchas could temper his mouth, he trusted him. If Bullock was there as well, he'd act as a steadying force. Bullock was one of the only commission staff with the ability to know when and how to interrupt Purchas.

If he chose to make a big deal of the pair's proposed meeting with Hutchins, it would almost certainly be frowned upon by the agency bosses in Canberra. Bugger it. It was worth the risk. The whole damn thing was worth the risk.

He looked at the file in front of him. Purchas's overview listed several key suspects in Australia, and contained photos, bank accounts and operational activities, including the massive liquid ecstasy seizure in January and the four seizures—totalling around 520 kilograms of drugs—connected to the Chinese–Canadian syndicate.

The briefing notes also highlighted how many of the local drug syndicates were remitting funds to the same few, and apparently linked, overseas corporate accounts, and suggested that an interconnected multinational organisation was behind the bulk of importations that had come to Dayu's attention. Dayu had also begun examining the historical links between this overseas organisation and the activities of two Asian organised crime bosses jailed several years ago: Duncan Lam Sak Cheung and Ly Vi Hung. James searched his mind. The names were vaguely familiar, but that was all.

Near the end of the document, there was a section entitled 'Australian bikie connection'. It included several photos pulled from the Facebook account of a man he'd not seen previously. He spoke his name aloud, 'Hakan Ayik', as he read a brief profile compiled by Purchas and Vikingsson.

The more he read, the more excited he became. Ayik was the target of an ongoing NSW police investigation into mid-tier drug trafficking, but he also had unexplained multi million-dollar assets. A frequent international traveller closely tied to the Comancheros, he'd made transfers to a Hong Kong-based bank account that had been flagged by Operation Dayu.

Law enforcement intelligence linked him to two previous intercepted drug shipments: a light plane stashed with drugs intercepted in Western Australia in March, and a large shipment of pseudoephedrine from Thailand in July.

As he studied the photos of Ayik next to a sports car and sandwiched between two Asian women in lingerie, he chuckled. He was everything the ACC executive would expect in a wealthy, international gangster. He oozed greed. It may have been a crude way of looking at it, but superficially, at least, this man appeared to be an ideal domestic target—the missing domestic link in the organised crime chain Operation Dayu was piecing together.

The policing of bikies was emerging as a political issue, especially in South Australia and New South Wales, where the media were reporting a surge of bikie shootings and fire-bombings. Dayu needed to use the increasing interest in bikies to its favour. It had been over a year since they had been given the authority to operationalise the concept underlying Operation Dayu. He needed something to fuel the aspirations of the agency's bosses and feed their insatiable hunger for fresh briefings. Dayu needed new promise.

Hakan Ayik could provide that.

He walked out into the office towards Purchas's desk, but it was empty.

Vikingsson sat nearby, watching him. 'You looking for Mike?' he said.

'Yep.'

'He's gone.'

'You'll have to do. You're doing great work on the money flows, Patrick, but we need to zero in on the bikie links.'

Vikingsson was smiling at him.

'What's so funny?'

'Before he left, Mike told me that you'd say that.'

He said nothing as he walked back to his office. It wasn't until his door was closed that he smiled. They weren't dead yet.

Hutchins

Hutchins had expected bikies to show up, but not like this. Earlier that morning, they'd rumbled towards Queensland's Parliament House, a rolling, thundering army of leather, muscles and middle-aged paunch.

A dozen or so now sat before him in the inquiry hearing room, variously slouching, scowling and whispering among themselves. As one turned, Hutchins noticed that the back of his head bore a tattoo of a hand extending the middle finger. The committee secretary sitting next to him gently nudged his side.

'We're almost ready, Steve.'

He would give it a bit more time. The bikies had been slowed down at the security check-in, their buckles and jewellery causing mayhem with the metal detectors. A few more minutes would give him time to steel himself.

He'd argued to allow the bikies to have their say before the committee as it examined proposals for new laws enabling authorities to have certain bikie groups proscribed, making it illegal for their members to associate. South Australia had already passed similar laws, and they were being pushed by politicians keen to display their 'tough on crime' credentials. Still, he wouldn't let the bikies hijack the hearing; the only grandstanding permitted would be that of the politicians.

The thought prompted his eyes to scan the committee table and land on Liberal MP Jason Wood, one of the politicians spruiking the new laws. There was something about the policeman turned conservative politician that irked him. It wasn't just that Wood never missed an opportunity to refer to his stint in the Victoria police's organised crime squad, or even the fact that he was a Tory. As Hutchins watched Wood out of the corner of his eye, he thought back to the Perth hearing, when a surprisingly articulate Coffin Cheater bikie, who at one point starting sprouting Nietzsche, had run rings around the Liberal MP. Hutchins had interjected, not so much to save Wood as to send the message that the bikies were on committee time and would respect its rules. He'd dealt with enough knockabouts that it hadn't rattled him.

Still, he and Wood had become allies, having been lumped into what some committee members had labelled the 'police faction'—a reference to their advocacy of increasing police powers to tackle organised crime. Despite their significant agreement, they differed on what changes were needed.

Part of the problem was that they needed ACC chief executive Alastair Milroy to brief them, but he seemed cautious and unwilling to engage. The moment he walked into the committee room, he appeared to start looking for the exit. Hutchins guessed Milroy was one of those officials who believed that the less policing oversight committees knew, the better.

Recent events didn't help. The stench from the Debus spy file affair had left the ACC out in the Canberra cold. And Canberra could get very cold. As a political bridge-burner, it couldn't get much worse.

He felt a second nudge. 'You ready, Steve?'

He nodded. Leaning towards the microphone, his eyes settled on one of the three leather-clad men occupying the witness seats. The man was sitting calmly, almost grandly, wearing a Hells Angels jacket. He guessed it was the club's Queensland president, Errol Gildea.

He held his gaze on Gildea as he spoke into the microphone. 'Ladies and gentleman, I declare open this public hearing of the parliamentary joint committee on the Australian Crime Commission. This is the seventh hearing for the committee's inquiry into the legislative arrangements to outlaw serious and organised crime groups.'

As the Hells Angels president attacked the proposed laws as an anathema to a just and fair society, Hutchins found himself inwardly agreeing. The laws were ill-conceived and reeked of political opportunism. The view had been endorsed by many of the senior police who had privately briefed the committee. They warned that the laws could drive bikie clubs further underground, or into states with weaker laws, and be subject to endless legal challenges.

Yet as Gildea rambled on, he began to wonder if the bikie's speech had an end point. 'Mr Gildea, if you could start to wind …'

Before he could finish, the bikie president had begun where he'd left off.

He would let him run a little longer. At any rate, it would give him a moment to focus on a question to cut through the spin and rhetoric—at that very moment, Gildea was comparing the proposed laws to the conduct of the Nazis during World War II.

He smiled at Gildea and cleared his throat. 'Thank you, Mr Gildea. This inquiry is into serious and organised crime. So the first question I am going to ask you is: what is the relationship between biker gangs and serious organised crime, if any?'

Gildea didn't hestitate. 'We do not call ourselves gangs. We are not. I will just show you quickly that on the back of my colours, and those of every other gentleman here, you will see the letters MC.

They stand for motorcycle club. We are not a gang. We are a motorcycle club.'

Hutchins smiled again. 'Mr Gildea, let me redraft the question then. What relationship is there between motorcycle clubs and organised crime, if any?'

'None.'

'Disorganised, if anything,' Gildea's companion chipped in.

Hutchins scanned the audience before continuing. Several bikies were craning forward, as if watching a play from the cheap seats.

'There have been plenty of reports around Australia that there is a relationship between motorcycle clubs and the distribution of drugs in this country.'

Gildea responded by demanding to see evidence to sustain his comment.

As the other committee members took over the questioning, Hutchins eyed two bikies in the gallery who were trying to contain their laughter. He glanced at the two female committee members to his side and realised the bikies were having a perv. Grins spread through the gallery as one of the female committee members started questioning Gildea.

'Do you have women in your clubs?'

The ripple of smirks intensified. 'Women?'

Gildea was now playing to the crowd.

'It's a male thing, sweetheart.'

The bikie, now emboldened, began jousting with a minor party senator.

The hearing was rapidly becoming a waste of time.

As soon as they broke for morning tea, Hutchins headed for the door, dialling his message bank and pressing the phone to his ear to avoid a couple of bikies who looked keen to chat. He'd heard enough leather-clad politicking for one day.

The first message was from his wife, the second voice mail from a colleague complaining about Rudd. The man leaving the third message spoke with a gravelly London accent. He didn't recognise the voice or the name.

'This is Michael Purchas, the Sydney operations manager from the Australian Crime Commission. I was hoping you'd be kind enough to call me back.'

Will

Walking past the international business school, Will felt a growing pang of anger. It was not without some irony that a college that purported to teach international students how to prosper in business had itself failed, taken over by administrators the year before.

The place had given him more grief than education. As soon as his fees had stopped being paid, the school's officials went scurrying off to the immigration department in an attempt to get him deported. It was the international colleges that should have been fuckin' deported.

Guys with medical degrees from India and China were forking over tens of thousands of dollars to complete the cooking and hairdressing courses that would deliver them enough immigration points to secure Australian residency. They were buying the right to stay and everyone knew it. A qualified doctor was hardly going to open a hair salon. It was nothing more than a huge scam.

And yet the fuckers had taken him not once but twice to be humiliated before the immigration tribunal, where a judge had scoffed at his school performance and told him to pack his bags.

Well, he could run a scam too. He'd tasked a good immigration lawyer to appeal, stall, re-appeal and stall some more. Now, well into 2008, he was not only still in Sydney, but living large, running a business more profitable than the school that sought to have him removed in the first place. The whole system was a cluster fuck.

If his mother could have seen him now she would have laughed at the irony. Here he was, at twenty-six, walking past the place that had failed him at business studies, with a bag containing over one hundred large in pure profit generated with zero marketing or advertising. Suck on a load of that, business school.

If only those teachers knew. It wasn't that he didn't get it. In fact, he *loved* the mechanics of demand and supply, of competitive free markets, monopolies, duopolies and cartels. It was just that he preferred to *do* rather than to listen.

His mind drifted back to one of his teachers, a man with an unpleasant Australian accent, who asked dismissively one day, 'Are you a gunna or a doer?' If that cockhead could only see him now. Given the opportunity, Will would slap him down like a bitch. That was how you rolled in his market.

It was a market riding on one of the greatest ironies of them all. Quickening his stride, he toyed with the concept in his head. He should have submitted it as his final essay. The immigration tribunal would have loved it. In banning the commodities he helped sell, the government had created an underground, tax- and duty-free market in which a supplier could do business free of any regulation or red tape. Then, if you could squash your competitors, you could build a monopoly and maximise returns. All you needed was muscle and a distribution chain.

As a business model, it was governed almost purely on the free-market laws of demand and supply. It didn't mean there were no market vagaries or industry-specific environmental factors, as his teacher called them. But, as with any good business, you had to work them into your model. Attention from the pigs could lead to loss of product and personnel. So you moved your key assets offshore and factored in the occasional loss. The current rate of shipping container interception was, at worst, around one in ten. With the profit margins they could make wholesaling imported meth, heroin or ecstasy, this hardly made for a loss at all. And you could just as easily move into something else if demand for meth were to fall off. Chuckling to himself, Will walked over the road, into the money remitting service. It would have made for one fucking dope essay.

The remittance service was made up of two small offices. The front office appeared to be a travel agency. It was depressingly drab. It contained a faded laminex desk bearing a small, plastic model of the Great Wall of China, and was decorated with a few faded posters depicting tour groups walking around Angkor Wat. He eyed the man at the travel agency desk, who in turn eyed him. He looked like a party cadre from Beijing. He wondered if he ever sold a holiday. He sure as hell looked like he needed one.

The man looked him up and down again before directing him in Mandarin to the back of the store towards a Vietnamese woman absorbed in an Asian soap opera on a small television.

'I'm here to move some money.'

She eyed him suspiciously. 'How much you have?'

'120K.' The figure sounded undeniably impressive rolling off his tongue, but the woman didn't blink. He opened his bag, displaying the twenties and fifties in neat bundles.

She looked at them, and then him, impassively. 'You want it counted?'

He wasn't anticipating the question. He'd been told nothing about a count. He reached for his mobile phone and then stopped, recalling the warnings issued after Mizza was picked up. It was probably paranoia, but he didn't want to risk pissing off Hux, not with the three hundred grand still missing.

He needed to be decisive, to take charge of the business. He could be the man for once. 'Best to do a count,' he said.

His comment triggered the first sign of emotion on the woman's face. She gave him a withering stare. Only an Asian woman could look like that, he thought. She reminded him of his mother.

'Is it dirty?' she asked.

'What?' He felt confused.

'Is it dirty?' she said, hissing more than speaking.

He narrowed his eyes and tried to look her dead in the eyes. What game was she playing? Of course the money was dirty. That is why he was here. For a second, a shot of panic ran through him, powered by a sudden fear that by some ill stroke of misfortune, he'd walked into the wrong place—into a trap.

Before he could speak, the woman rolled her eyes and grabbed a bundle of cash, whipping off the rubber band and placing it on the money machine. It whirred for a few seconds, before jamming up the machine.

'You see. Your money is dirty, too crumpled and old. It means we can't use the machine.'

'You can count it later. If it comes up different, we'll carry the loss.' He was standing awkwardly, watching the woman as she shrugged, picking up the money that had jammed the machine as if she was touching a dried turd.

'Where you sending?'

He passed over a slip of paper bearing an account number and the name of a bank in Asia.

'You got licence or passport?'

He was expecting this and handed her an expired student card which had his name misspelled and recorded an incorrect date of birth.

As she photocopied the card without bothering to check it, he noticed a sign on the wall. It read, 'Know Your Customer! Remitters must record the identity of all customers and report suspicious transactions to AUSTRAC!'

The woman noticed him reading the sign and, shrugging, scrawled down what looked to him like some sort of receipt, which she handed him along with his student card before turning back to the television.

'Fucking bitch,' he muttered as he walked out of the shop, not caring if anyone heard. What a fucking stress. Still, he'd handled it.

He avoided looking at the business school as he crossed the street, and wondered which girls would be rostered on. Would he have one or two? Either way, he'd earned himself some fun.

Purchas

Purchas looked over the members of Operation Dayu who sat before him. Apart from Vikingsson, who was fiddling on a laptop, everyone was watching him. The walls of the corridors behind them were plastered with mission statements, including one about professionalism. Whoever penned it had misspelt the word 'integrity'.

James, the most senior man in the room, sat at the back and was deep in whispered conversation with Bullock. Both men looked worried.

'I have called this briefing so I can update you on the direction of Operation Dayu,' Purchas said. 'We have ascertained the likely existence of an offshore and highly networked, multinational drug-trafficking business with significant assets in Hong Kong, Cambodia, Macau and Vietnam. We are corroborating its activities by tracking the movement of high-risk funds out of Australia and through briefings from a network of extremely well-placed sources.'

Purchas reminded himself of Bullock's instructions to avoid his usual tendency to get lost in obsessive detail and to keep it succinct, drew a deep breath and continued. 'In addition to the drug seizures so far secured, most of you are aware that we have been tracking a fresh 500-kilo importation from China. The federal police recently intercepted 80 kilos from that shipment in Adelaide … The location of the remaining 420 kilos remains a point of some dispute.'

He ignored the enquiring looks. Only James and Bullock knew about the 420 kilos that had disappeared in China when the Adelaide bust had gone down.

'There are a growing number of questions from other agencies not familiar with Operation Dayu about how we are managing to generate intelligence about these large importations. So we have taken a decision to protect the long-term integrity of Dayu. We will now begin running two new operations that we can work on relatively openly with our state and federal friends.'

He smiled at James, who still looked concerned. Pressing on, he outlined the first operation. Codenamed Agrale, it would concentrate on using Vikingsson's High Risk Funds Program to identify and target the money remitters suspected of moving the proceeds of crime. Several Western Union money remitters, who appeared to be moving large cash amounts while ignoring the know-your-customer regulations, would be among those targeted. By taking out corrupt remitters, Operation Agrale would also help draw criminals to the ACC's covert laundry. He expected Vikingsson to acknowledge the plan with a nod, but the analyst was still staring at his laptop screen.

'For Christ's sake, Patrick. Any chance of you entering our quadrant and gracing us with your attention?' Vikingsson didn't look up, so he continued. 'Our second operation will take its name from an existing state police investigation, codenamed Hoffmann. The NSW police have been kind enough to let us take over the targets of this job. In return, we will feed back intelligence that will hopefully lead them to busts and arrests, especially of outlaw bikie targets. This will give Dayu good cover. The more people who think our work is limited to a state police anti-bikie operation, the better.'

Next he unfurled a sheet of A3 paper. 'Some of you may have already seen this chart. It will be on the wall of the ops room. Get to know the faces on it. Some of you will be living, sleeping and breathing them.' The chart featured a photo of Hakan Ayik surrounded by several of his known associates. Among them were Comanchero leaders Daux Ngakuru and Mahmoud Hawi, as well as a young Chinese national, Wei Wong, who was listed alongside Ayik as co-director of a company, Multi-Capital Trading.

'At this early point in time, a central target of Operation Hoffman is Hakan Ayik. Unconfirmed intelligence suggests that he or his associates may be on the receiving end of importations sent by those overseas who are of interest to Operation Dayu. We are, of course, a very long way from proving this. What we do know is that Hakan Ayik has significant unexplained wealth and may well be a decent local target in and of himself. Our broader hope is that he will provide fresh insights for Operation Dayu.'

'Bruce Bullock will coordinate much of Operation Hoffmann. We are all going to start living with Ayik and his crew. We will run surveillance three days a week, seeing what patterns we can turn up. And we will burrow into relevant financials and phone records. In the event we put some meat on the bone, we may even end up getting a few phones tapped.'

He watched the investigators and analysts begin scrawling in their diaries. The room was filled with a silent electricity, and he was pleased. Their team was small, but its members had smarts in spades.

'If we find any major busts, we will feed them to the feds or state police and stay in the background. Remember, we are in this for the long haul, not for the headlines. The other thing to remember is the need to know.'

Raising his voice, he said firmly, 'Some of our intel reports will now be disseminated to other agencies, which increases the risk of leakage. But you too must resist the urge to gossip. Don't tell your wives, neighbours or friends. Our targets will have friends in law enforcement and they will be looking for intelligence on what we are doing.'

He briefly weighed up sharing the warning he'd received the day before from a NSW policeman about the reach of Ayik's crew into state police forces and customs, but he kept it to himself.

'That's it. Let's get crackin',' he said. Thirty seconds later he was in James's office with James and Bullock. James still looked worried.

'This is not about Hutchins is it? He has already agreed to meet and I am not about to stand him up.'

James shook as head, looking as if he was searching for words.

'Is it Macau?'

'No Mike … in fact Bruce tells me you are working on getting some of our offshore phantoms to a meeting on the island to discuss a money-laundering venture.'

Before James could continue, Purchas felt Bullock grasp him gently on the shoulder. 'The feds have raised concerns at board level about the lack of visibility on our operations. The commission is still on the outer with the new government, and Milroy wants to slow things down until he is replaced by a new boss … We have to suspend the laundry, Mike. It's too high risk.'

He felt his stomach deflate as his temper rose, but he measured his response. 'I will tell you what is high risk—letting 420 kilograms disappear off the wharf in China. That's high risk.' He had blamed the feds for the disappearing drugs after their apparent failure to engage the Chinese authorities. But the feds had hit back, questioning the commission's role in facilitating the movement of the 80 kilograms of ice to Adelaide, where it had been seized. 'That Adelaide job has turned into a train wreck. It is crucial we keep Operation Dayu on course. The Macau meeting will go ahead whether we can move a single dollar or not. Are you with me on this or not?' Falling silent, he was pleased he'd restrained himself. 'Well?'

'We're with you Mikey,' said Bullock.

James said nothing.

'Well, that's settled then. We'll push on.'

Walking back to his desk, Purchas found himself muttering fiercely under his breath. Nothing explicit had been said, but he sensed that things were changing. The end of Milroy's tenure as commission CEO was nearing, and it was rumoured his replacement would be John Lawler, a successful, clever, yet risk-averse, deputy commissioner from the AFP. It was Lawler who had cleared them on robbing the feds of a seizure when they had coordinated the liquid ecstasy bust with the NSW police.

But he and Lawler's personal history, and animosity, had started years before. His mind drifted to Washington in the late 1990s, when Lawler was serving as the AFP's liaison—after a stint as a funeral parlour director—and Purchas had flown in for a drug job. After a disagreement, Purchas had wandered whether a glowering Lawler was sizing him up for a casket. If Lawler was to become his next boss, he may as well prepare for his own funeral.

Vikingsson was waiting for him at his desk.

'They are shutting down the laundry,' he told the analyst.

'I've heard,' Vikingsson replied. The bleedin' Swede knew everything, he thought.

'I'm afraid I have some more bad news,' Vikingsson continued, handing him a memo.

As he scanned it, he felt himself bristling again. Australia's embassy in Hong Kong had just reissued a fresh passport to one of Operation Dayu's mid-tier targets, Jack Lam, despite the fact that he was the subject of an outstanding Australian arrest warrant. 'The whole world is going mad, Patrick. The whole bleedin' universe …'

Vikingsson smiled at him. 'At least we're not alone, Mike. At least we're not alone.'

Hutchins

It was spring, but a brisk southerly wind whistled down William Street, buffeting him. A stream of suits and skirts rushed by, heading home in the dimming light. Hutchins picked out the two investigators a block away. Both wore suits and grim poker faces. They appeared to have picked him as well.

The taller man extended his hand. 'I'm Mike. Good to meet you, Senator. This is Bruce, the commission's operations manager from Melbourne.'

Purchas was thinner, and older, than he had expected. Bullock looked every inch a policeman. 'Call me Steve, fellas. Good to meet you. Let's get a beer. Docklands sound okay?'

He walked next to the two men, chatting awkwardly about weather and football—avoiding raising the reason for their meeting. That could come later. The wind was colder as they neared Docklands, gaining strength as it danced across the water's surface, cutting through his suit jacket. His desire for a drink intensified as he stepped inside the restaurant.

'What can I get you blokes?' Hutchins asked.

'We'll have whatever you're having, Senator.'

Purchas sipped at his beer like a duck in a pond, and Hutchins guessed the police officer was drinking with him out of politeness.

'So what's going on fellas? You planning to write up a spy dossier on me?'

Both men flushed red. They were obviously proud police.

'It's a fiasco, Steve. The Debus dossier thing is an unmitigated stuff-up turned media beat-up … Do you mind if I speak frankly?' Purchas asked, haltingly. 'Because not everyone would appreciate us being here.'

He had earlier guessed that the pair would be taking a risk in meeting him. It was unlikely they had the nod from all of their bosses. 'Go ahead. One thing the ACC has not been good at is straight talking,' he said, hesitating. It would need to be a mutual exercise in trust. 'And from what I hear, the agency will be cold-shouldered until the author of the Debus file is carried out on a slab.'

Purchas nodded in agreement and said, 'We are here to say that the commission is doing some good things.' Purchas looked over at Bullock, who nodded, willing his colleague on. 'Senator, have you heard of Operation Gordian?' Purchas said.

Before he could answer, Purchas continued. 'What if I told you that the Asian crime syndicates importing the bulk of drugs into this country are moving out hundreds of millions of narco-dollars every few months? And what if I told you that we are working on a system to find and track that money; a system that will help us infiltrate and understand some of the major offshore crime syndicates which have transformed Australia into an extraordinary profitable market? Think of a fisherman in a lake …'

He listened and observed Purchas become increasingly animated.

'Senator, I know your committee is doing a lot around bikies. But bikies are …'

'Bikies are low hanging fruit, Senator,' interrupted Bullock with quiet assurance. 'Yet they are increasingly being used by powerful international syndicates as local distributors and stand-over merchants. If bikies can access the expanding drug pipeline into Australia, they'll progress from surburban thugs to genuine gangsters.

'But there are bigger threats. Right now, Australia faces a real risk of turning into a country that not only receives drug imports, but exports big shipments as well. The syndicates know that Australian shipping containers are considered low risk and pass through most container ports unchecked. The market here is hungry for drugs, but it is only so big. We already suspect more drugs are coming in than could possibly be consumed locally, so there is every chance Australia is already exporting gear to bigger markets.'

Purchas continued: 'What is a certainty is that the local drug market is booming. We are aware of one bikie-linked syndicate wanting to move millions of drug dollars offshore every week. In one bust alone, we found half a billion dollars worth of liquid ecstasy. We are working on ways to confront this expansion with minimal resources. But we need more support from government. Instead … instead we seem to be losing it.'

'Do you think it is possible to get a firmer figure on how much drug money is moving out of Australia annually?' Hutchins asked the investigator.

'We estimate it's anywhere between ten to twenty billion dollars annually. At best, we are intercepting 15 percent of all drug imports, but the real figure is probably much lower. Our ultimate aim is to be able to tell the government about the true size of Australia's drug problem and the real impact of organised crime on the economy. And to identify who is pocketing all the money that is leaving our shores. To do this, we need support. We need more time and more money.'

Hutchins noticed a vein sticking out of Purchas's neck as the cop finished talking.

'Time and money, eh?' Hutchins raised his eyebrows. 'They are two things that aren't thick on the ground in Canberra right now, especially with the global economy on fire.'

December 2007 – August 2009

He wondered if the two investigators appreciated the true dynamics of Canberra, the politicking, short-termism, self-interest, egoism ... He was aware that they were watching him, waiting expectantly for his response, and he felt a trickle of guilt. They weren't men with a gripe, or self-promoters looking for a hand-up. Unlike some of the public servants who turned to politicians for help, neither man had a personal grievance or a political cause. They were simply seeking help to do their jobs. To fight organised crime.

There was something at once honourable and naive about their idealism and plain talking. They had come to him because they believed their concerns weren't being heeded elsewhere. He must have appeared a stable, capable figure in a sea of mess.

And yet while he was powerful, it was in a Canberra sort of way, a New South Wales Labor Party sort of way. His influence carried to politicians and party officials, rather than to policy and funding. Especially with Rudd ascendant.

Money and time were the two things he couldn't promise.

He cleared his throat. 'You need to realise that because I am not a minister in this government, there are limits to what I can do. But I can assure you that I have listened to your concerns—and I get it. They will certainly be shared among my friends on the committee, although I can assure you that this meeting will not be disclosed.'

Rising to leave, Hutchins noticed Purchas had barely touched his beer. He shook the men's hands firmly and looked them both in the eye, trying to gauge whether they were disappointed or satisfied by the brief encounter.

'Stay in touch, fellas.'

He left the restaurant and headed back towards the bridge that would him take over the Spencer Street rail yards, to what had been the old city edge before Melbourne's CBD had begun creeping into areas once fit only for wharfies, painters and dockers. The wind was attacking him again, colder than before, yet he was still warm from the restaurant and he let it cool his body.

Perhaps there was something more he could do. Just a few weeks before, after some intense lobbying by the committee, Rudd had included a pointed reference to the spectre of organised crime and money laundering in his inaugural statement on national security. Rudd's words were not only welcomed by the growing number of police and policymakers who believed that the fight against terrorism had overshadowed organised crime, but they also created an expectation that needed fulfilling. Hutchins's bête noire had given his committee more room to move. And he'd see that the committee take the chance.

The trip. That was it. If organised crime was indeed globalising, they should see it for themselves. He'd ensure it wasn't another international junket and enlist the media. Tonight's meeting had given him a few bullets, and he knew there'd be more.

Pulling out his mobile phone, he selected the number of a newspaper journalist. 'Hi, it's Steve. Steve Hutchins. I might have something for you. You got time for a quick beer tomorrow?'

Ayik

Ayik sat in the back of the taxi scanning the day's news on his phone while attempting to block out the waves of nausea from last night's session. What a night. He was still dehydrated as fuck, the stench of cigar smoke thick on his fingers. He most definitely was no longer high. He felt like shit.

But fuck, they'd rolled big. He'd cracked two bottles of Grange. Daux had gone head to toe in his pimpin' tracksuit, and Hawi was blinged up like a pawn shop, ears, hands and neck all glistening. Hawi had travelled far since the schoolyard. They all had.

He'd bailed at about one, once Hawi and Daux had become engrossed in club business. The Hells Angels, Nomads and Notorious were all kitting up, and the boys needed to ensure the Comos had the steel to hold their own.

His crew was doing their part, and he'd put up the funds to build their defences while enlisting his nephew Erkan to sit on the arsenal. If anyone tried to rob their stashes, or get in on their game, they had to be ready. Violence was mostly unnecessary. It could be avoided with enough planning and strategising, but they could never look weak. The Comos' strength was the club's best asset and they needed it to help protect their share of the pie. The bigger it got, the more players wanted a piece. Anticipating the unknown—that's what it was all about.

That's why he had four hot cars with fake numberplates stashed away, ready for any possible turn of events. That's what most bikies failed to do. They didn't think far enough ahead. All the beef was bad for business. Fighting earned nobody money.

Flicking his finger down the screen, his eyes landed on a headline: 'Rudd Lame on Crime'. He read the article as the cab pulled into the exit lane towards Sydney airport.

> Prime Minister Kevin Rudd's position on national security has been labelled 'pretty lame' by a senior Labor MP who is worried by budget cuts to agencies fighting organised crime.
>
> Senator Hutchins, chairman of the parliamentary committee overseeing the Australian Crime Commission, yesterday warned of 'serious disquiet' in criminal intelligence agencies, which are being forced to cut jobs and scale back operations due to demands for budget savings.
>
> He questioned whether Mr Rudd was fully aware of the battle being waged by agencies against organised crime. And he warned Australia was on the verge of moving from a bulk illegal drug importer to a producer and exporter of 'some of the most dangerous, addictive drugs in the world'.
>
> 'I am not sure the Prime Minister has been told the full facts about the war against serious organised crime that is being conducted by our chief criminal intelligence agency, the ACC, along with AUSTRAC and other agencies,' Senator Hutchins said. Two months ago, ACC boss Alastair Milroy said his agency and AUSTRAC had tracked up to $12 billion in drug dollars flowing offshore annually.

Twelve billion. That was a lot of paper.

It made no sense to export from Australia, not while the Aussie dollar was strong and suckers were paying so much compared with other markets. Pills cost a few pounds in England, even less in Amsterdam, but thirty-five bucks a pop here. It was an ideal seller's market, an importer's wet dream. You just had to stay a step ahead of the pigs.

Discipline. Strategy. Foresight. Being fucking smart. That's all it came down to. He'd heard of the crime commission before, after some of the boys were called to its star chamber and forced to answer questions. They all returned, claiming they had lied to their inquisitors. But he had his doubts. There were always weak cunts out there.

An image of Will entered his mind. For a decent earn and a sideplate of flattery, Will should stay loyal. Will also had delusions of grandeur. The cunt wanted to be some sort of a nightclub gangster—part Jet Li, part Pacino. But Will didn't have the guts for it. He couldn't carry the weight, and he'd go to water after five minutes in the can.

At least his Chinese mate knew how to follow orders and didn't yap back. He'd recently stepped up Will's role, giving him responsibility for liasing with the wharf guys and running the Perth operations, reasoning that with Mizza out of the picture they couldn't let the void be filled with anyone else.

'This is fine. Pull up here. Just here.'

He'd get out at the Virgin terminal and then duck over to Qantas. If anyone was watching, they'd at least have to work to keep up. Sliding out of the taxi, Ayik glanced behind him. One of the girls he was banging had called him paranoid, but he knew what he knew. And he knew to trust his instincts. Things were starting to unsettle him.

The leaked NSW police intelligence reports showed the coppers were behind, but running hard. Thank God for those feelers, he thought; the club had friends everywhere. One of the boys ran with a police intelligence analyst who could peek into almost every job on the bikies, and the club had friends in customs and on the wharf.

Still, it was no reason to get sloppy. He'd already planned to buy his ticket at the last minute and pay for it in cash. He'd also left a motion-activated camera mobile phone watching the door. If there was any movement, it would take a picture and send it to his phone. Technology was his friend—and enemy.

'Would you like to upgrade from business to first class, Mr Ayik?'

'Sure thing, love.' He noticed the woman's face flush with suspicion as he pulled out a wad of pineapples. 'It's nice eh?' he said, motioning to the money clip. 'Real diamond as well.'

She said nothing. Cheap bitch, he thought as he handed over the cash.

At the customs desk, an officer scanned his Turkish passport and looked him up and down. He shook his head, but said nothing. After September 11, he'd started getting hassled whenever he left the country. And yet an Asian or an Aussie could fly drugs across the country without a hint of trouble. He watched the customs officer flicking through his passport.

'You do a lot of travel, sir.'

He ignored the comment.

'Is your trip for business?'

'Sure is,' he said. He'd been through this before.

'What do you do, sir?'

'Import and export, bro. You know, those energy drinks. That's my game.'

The officer gave him the once over again, handed back his passport and sighed.

'Have a nice day, bud,' Ayik said, winking at the official.

The official made no attempt to conceal his distaste as he looked away.

'Well, fuck you too, buddy.'

An hour later, he was lying on a forty-five degree angle, sipping champagne and flirting with a cute Asian flight attendant. If that pussy in a customs outfit could see him now.

He switched on his laptop and waited for the movie-editing program to load. He'd already selected the soundtrack along with some of the choicest photos from the gym and of his wheels. There'd be more to load up once he was country hopping. Between business there would be plenty of time; he had already made the key decisions. He was moving most of the key shit offshore. The next play had been staring him in the face for months, each time one of Daux's Tongan mates lumbered into sight.

'It's an island paradise, bro. No real cops, just sun and brown bitches,' one of the Tongans had told him. It sounded perfect.

He plugged in his laptop headphones and hit the iTunes icon, selecting 'Troublemaker' by Akon. He mouthed the words as he sorted through his pictures. The song was perfect for his soundtrack.

He clicked on a photo that showed him flexing his pecs and lats, veins and tendons rippling. Fuck, yeah. That looked sick.

He fiddled with the settings until he found one that allowed him to place his image on the cover of *Esquire* magazine. Nice. Sensing someone standing over his shoulder, he removed his earphones.

'Champagne, sir?'

The flight attendant, the sexy one, was looking at his screen, eyeing the photos. He gave her his special smile.

'Why not, babe? Top me up. And tell me … you ever been to Tonga?'

Bilal

The portable container that housed his desk and that of the other freight forwarders and customs brokers sat on the edge of the wharf precinct. From his desk, Bilal could see the container trucks rumbling by in a never-ending procession. It was, by any measure, a grim view, even on a summer's day, an endless industrial landscape of steel boxes, cranes and fences, permeated by the grinding sound of metal on metal, of roaring engines and squealing breaks. He knew by heart the sound of a cab engine dropping from second to first, and the make of a truck by the sound it made when reversing.

His job variously involved helping importers and exporters clear customs and quarantine, and have their goods moved to warehouses for collection. The aching dullness of his work was lessened by the kick he still got when tracking a consignment from an overseas port to the east coast of Australia, through the docks and into his custody. It made him feel like a tiny but vital cog in the wheel of international trade.

He was good at his job as well, he thought. He could now guess within two days how long a container would be delayed by weather, a port bottleneck or a union strike. He knew which ports were efficient, which were not, which were run by the labour unions and which were all machines and no humans.

'Hey, Bilal. Your cousin is here to see you.' It was the shift supervisor.

'He's what?'

'He's waiting outside, mate.'

He briefly considered staying put in his cubicle, but thought better of it and grabbed his windbreaker and headed outside. Waz was standing in the wind, shivering and nursing a cigarette in his hand.

'Hey, cuz,' Waz said, offering his hand.

He took it reluctantly, thinking how they hadn't spoken since Waz had come round to scope his new tattoo. He'd been taking care to avoid Waz, ignoring the messages left on his machine and passed through his wife. He'd also thought a lot about the money since it had run out. It was helpful, very helpful, but it hadn't been paid because of the quality of the cook. It was danger money, cash handed over by those smarter than he and Waz, guys who didn't want to do twenty years inside.

He noticed a thick gold chain around Waz's neck. One of his eyes also appeared swollen. 'What happened to you?' he asked.

His cousin forced a weak smile. 'Oh, nothing. Just got in a bit of blue. Fuck, it's blowy out here.'

'It's a port, Waz.' He stood silently, waiting for Waz to explain the reason for his visit, watching him inhale another drag of his cigarette, holding the smoke in for a few seconds before blowing it out of his nostrils in two unedifying streams.

'Smoke?'

'Nup.'

'How's your tat?'

'Same as last time I checked.'

They continued to stand in silence as Waz took another drag.

'I gotta get back to work, so if you have just come here to smoke …'

'I have another earn for you, Bilal. It's a cakewalk.'

'Forget it, Waz. My life as a cook is over.' Bilal turned to walk away, but Waz grabbed his shoulder. 'It's not another cook. I just need you to follow a few different ships and containers and let me know if customs is havin' a sniff.'

He couldn't believe what he was hearing. Had Waz not listened to anything he'd said after the cook? He'd made it abundantly clear: no more bikies, no more favours and no more fucking you, Waz!

'Forget it. No fucking way. Find some other dickhead to do your dirty work.'

'Ten grand. It's all yours.'

Waz pushed a bag into his hands. As he pushed it back he felt what must have been bundles of cash. 'No fucking w-way.' But his voice faltered and he realised he'd stuttered.

'And another ten at the end. It's a piece of piss and no risk for you at all. All you got to do is run a few checks. The boys do it all the time.'

When he turned to look his cousin dead in the face, he could see the desperation in his eyes. It hit him then that Waz had most likely already promised his services to whoever had handed him the cash. He breathed in deeply, closed his eyes tightly, and opened them as he exhaled.

'Come to my house tonight,' Bilal said, moving back towards the office door. 'And bring the whole twenty. This is the last time, Waz, I swear on my mother's grave.'

'Cool, cuz. You'll be thanking …'

Waz's last words were cut off as Bilal slammed the door behind him.

Head down, moving back to his desk, he thought of how several of the guys were making a few extra bucks by helping ease things through the port. If you knew the system and had the access, it was a piece of piss.

Yet it made him feel sick. Staring at the screen, he logged into the container monitoring system, willing himself to get lost in the numbers and lights, to blank out what had just happened, and what was yet to come.

Purchas

The main light in the ops room was off, so he worked using the glow from the computer screens. The darkness was fitting.

They had no coverage on what was about to unfold in Macau, just one pair of eyes that didn't even belong to the agency. They belonged to a high-level casino security officer, an ex-cop and friend who'd agreed to do some pro bono work; whether it was for the public good or to catch a favour down the way, he'd be watching when the meeting went down. If anyone discovered him working for the agency, losing his job would be the least of his worries. Chances were he'd end up floating in Macau harbour.

Purchas revised the plan again in his head. He'd kept it simple. While they knew their plans to run a laundry from Macau were temporarily dead, those who wanted to use their laundry thought the venture still alive. Through a number of sources and intermediaries, he'd organised a business meeting.

The man attending on the commission's behalf had no idea he was actually working for the ACC. He was just a mid-tier runner in the money game who'd agreed, after a word with the informer Bullock had met in Macau a few months before, to float the laundry's rates.

Purchas silently prayed the exercise would be worth the effort. At least the signs were right. Operation Gordian had taught them that it was usually the syndicate bosses who fronted when business decisions were made about moving multi million-dollar drug contracts.

At such meetings, nobody handled money. That was left to runners later. To that extent, the meetings were events with little risk for those in attendance. He and Bullock had also reasoned that a meeting in Macau would strengthen the likelihood of bosses attending. It was their turf.

For Operation Dayu, the meeting presented a rare opportunity: the chance to smoke out and positively identify at least a few of the syndicate's most senior players. Or, as James had put it, to put some names and faces to Dayu's offshore phantoms. Of course, even if they secured a contract, they needed a way out. Their laundry was a long way from being established in Macau, so to scotch any agreement they would have to raise the laundry's commission to an uncompetitive rate.

The Macau operation's trump card involved arranging the meeting in a secure, high-roller room, which required guests to scan their passports when entering. All they had to do was make copies. If the passports were genuine, the operation would be a success. At least that was the plan. Once it was in action, anything could happen.

Waiting for the phone call from Macau, Purchas's mind drifted to Operation Hoffman. Despite expending considerable energy, they still knew very little about Ayik. Intelligence suggested he was getting gear into the country and was able to easily absorb any losses, including a big seizure from Thailand and the arrest of Micalizzi. But there was nothing hard on him. If he was a genuine player, he played the game well: minimal phone contact, plenty of time outside the jurisdiction, an array of seemingly legitimate business interests.

And the endless stream of Asian women. The only person outrooting Ayik was Will. They treated women like commodities, things to be conquered and discarded.

He'd never chased women. One was hard enough. Especially Huong. He had seen almost nothing of her in the last six months. When he did, she bristled at the constant whispered phone calls to sources and to Bullock, and the early starts and late finishes. Work was killing his home life, and yet he struggled to imagine a life without the job. Mike Purchas, Organised Crime Investigator—that's what he was.

His phone buzzed with an incoming text. 'Op is live.'

It would all be for nothing if they didn't get the passport scans. His excitement was building. The passports could be analysed; they could unravel the men's travel movements, corporate interests and what was known about them by overseas agencies.

'Mike,' said one of the junior analysts who had just entered the ops room. 'You won't believe what we've found.'

'Try me,' he said, spinning around and radiating annoyance.

'We have accessed a certain Facebook page.'

'Go on,' he said, attempting not to betray his interest.

'One Hakan Joseph Ayik. Photos, videos and all. This guy's ego is on a rampage.'

Several investigators and analysts were hovering over a computer screen in the centre of the office. As he neared the group, he could hear the beats of a rap music track playing. He hated that music. It made him feel like a fossil.

The screen flickered with photos of Ayik in various poses: outside designer stores in Hong Kong, in a nightclub, surrounded by Asian women, on a helicopter, getting into a white sports car. There was also a photo of him meeting an imposing figure in a Comanchero T-shirt—the sergeant-at-arms Daux Ngakuru—at what looked like Hong Kong airport.

In other photos, Ayik appeared to be somewhere in the Middle East or Europe, riding a statue of a bull and enjoying a shave from a barber armed with a cutthroat razor. It looked like Turkey.

In each shot, Ayik's face stayed much the same, oozing a calm confidence. The last frame showed his bare chest, an intricate tattoo draped over his shoulder and onto one of his two bulging pectorals. Above his torso, the words 'Written and directed by Hakan Ayik' splayed across the screen.

James was right, he thought. Ayik was a musclebound monster, an archetypal modern gangster: an ideal target to sell to the bosses, even if he was only a piece of a much bigger, still unassembled puzzle.

Purchas reached for the phone in his pocket, but it wasn't there. Damn it. Half walking, half running, he headed for the ops room where he'd left it. A new message was waiting for him. It was from Macau. Opening the attachment, he silently scoured the images, feeling his heart thumping like it hadn't done in months.

Will

After squeezing his eyes shut, and then opening them as wide as he could, Will focused back on the gun sight. He hadn't slept in at least twenty-four hours. An empty 2-litre Coke bottle lay to his side. Food? Fuck food. Food was for pussies.

Behind a bombed-out building at the edge of what looked like a car yard gutted by fire, he locked in on a small figure in army greens. He carefully adjusted the crosshairs onto the man, zooming in to get a better look. It was another sniper. Motherfucker.

He let the target rest on the man's head, letting the music in his headphones fill his ears. It was a low, growling drone, a sound he had been listening to for far too long. He held his finger over the trigger button. He wanted to savour this kill.

Bang. The shot rang out as the man's head exploded into red puff, like a small firework. 'Take that bitch.'

Wiping the sweat from his brow, he paused the game. This was living. He loved days like this: he had nothing to do, no girls to check in on, no money or gear to run, just time to kill. So he killed.

December 2007 – August 2009

He knew he was addicted to his Xbox, the way it let him drift into another world, where he was king. He was already dreading reaching the end.

Clocking a game always left him sullen, anxious. Especially now things on the outside were getting heavy. A fresh run was scheduled, which meant another flight and pick-up by the new Comos interstate. He hated flying. On the last trip, a group of immigration and customs officers had eyed him strangely. He hadn't told Hux, but he'd felt … he'd felt like he had when that bitch had stolen the cash. But worse. It was one thing he and Hux had never spoken about. Getting caught.

He shuddered at the thought of it; the phone calls to his family, the shame of it all. They thought he was a businessman. And even though he was … well, his mother was unlikely to understand.

He stretched, yawned, flicked briefly onto Facebook and then onto Google News. The first headline leapt out at him: 'Fatal bikie bashing at Sydney airport'.

What the fuck? How could you bash someone to death at an airport? What about all the people, the cameras, the cops? A gun was one thing, but to bash someone to death took some effort. And at Sydney airport?

He read on in disbelief. A few hours before, a huge brawl had erupted between men who some claimed were Hells Angels and Comancheros. The crazy Comos. He knew it. He knew they were heading for trouble.

He thought back to what Hux had told him a few days before. Some of the boys were heading interstate. If it was them who were involved at the airport …

He dialled Hux on the safe phone, but it was engaged.

It had been turning to shit for the last few months, ever since more gear had begun flowing in and all Hux's boys had begun playing like gangsters. Guns were flying around and everyone was getting greedier. And the greedier they got, the more they thought they needed to tool up and expand their patches. The Comos wanted in on the Cross worse than ever. Everyone was paranoid. He knew the excuses, about protecting turf and showing other crews who was boss. But muscle brought heat, and that was bad for business. Surely they all knew that. At Sydney airport. Of all places. A fucking airport!

He shook his head, breathing in. His own crew, mostly Chinese students and gamers, kept their heads and profile low. They quietly sold gear from restaurants, karaoke joints and game parlours. Violence never played a part in what they did. Maybe bad news for the bikies wasn't such bad news. If Hux needed to fill a hole …

Flicking through different news websites, he clicked on links about the bashing. Someone said a metal bollard had been used. Another spoke of seeing a pool of blood next to the check-in counter. A female witness described the fight as a rolling ball of fury. *A rolling ball of fury.* The quote made him think of legs stomping and arms thrashing and metal flying and some guy's head—*poof*—a red explosion. But this one was real. At an airport. Not just an airport; Australia's largest airport.

Shit would now go outta control. There would be payback and cops crawling up bikie's arses. Hux would be mad if he didn't call on some of his guys, Chinese players who would float under the radar and not pump out their chests or flash their wealth the minute they got some.

He tried Hux again, but the phone was still engaged. If it was the Comancheros involved …

He had to stop thinking about it. He checked his watch and picked up the console. There was time for another game. The paused screen still showed the dead, headless soldier. The words 'perfect kill' were flashing on the screen.

He shut the laptop and headed for the door, feeling a fist of anxiety knead his innards.

Welch

'Hello?' Sleep gripped him as he fumbled with his phone.

'Dylan, it's the desk. There's been another bikie killing. A shooting we think. It's at Lakemba. We need you to get out there.'

He rubbed his eyes. 'What time is it?'

'It's 3.00 a.m.'

'I'll be there. Text me the address.'

He tried the radio in the car, but there was nothing about a shooting. The newsdesk must have picked it up from the scanner. He hoped it wasn't a dud lead. Ever since the brawl at Sydney airport a week before, the newsdesk had pounced on every shooting, bashing or incident that could conceivably be bikie-related. After months of struggling to get his yarns up, he was suddenly the go-to man. Anything bikie-related would fly, either on page one, three or, at worst, five. All it had taken was Hells Angels associate Tony Zervas to be bashed to death with a metal bollard at one of Australia's most secure sites, Sydney airport.

'If it bleeds, it leads.' Indeed. Driving through the blackness, he felt his cynicism rising, not just at the media's blood lust, but at the way the politics was playing out. Bikies were now public enemy number one. Police taskforces with a bikie focus that a few weeks back could barely muster enough men to work a surveillance crew suddenly had dozens of techs, dogs and analysts that had been ripped out of other operations.

The New South Wales government was vowing to follow South Australia's lead and introduce new laws to outlaw bikie clubs—an idea most experienced police thought was madness. Bikies were seen as thugs, cowards, animals; men who had to be stopped before an innocent ended up dead. Almost no one was asking how it had got to this and what was really driving the bikie violence.

His brain was now waking up, twitching with energy. He thought back to the hours after the airport murder, when he'd called Derek Wainahou, the president of the Hells Angels. The tension in

Wainahou's voice had startled him. 'I can't talk right now, Dylan. I have to bury a brother.'

He'd realised then it must have been Wainahou sitting on the plane with Zervas when they'd spotted the Comancheros on the same flight; Wainahou in the checkout hall with Zervas when the brawl erupted; Wainahou next to that big, rolling ball of mayhem, of flying fists, feet and metal bollards; and, at the end of it all, Wainahou's bikie brother dead, his brain caved in. Except it wasn't the end, or the start.

It was what he had been trying to tell the newsdesk for weeks, and what his police and bikie sources had been warning of for months. The surge in violence was part of a bikie evolution. Old-school, white supremacist rooting and drinking outfits and gangs were dividing along new ethnic lines and wrestling for control of the drug market and tattoo parlour and nightclub turf—big, rolling balls of money making and power. Or maybe that was too simplistic. Maybe some of it was just tribal, violent, irrational and inexplicable.

He drove towards the flashing blue and red lights, picking out a television news van, and then the small group of suited, grim-faced detectives from the Gangs Squad, talking in a huddle outside an apartment complex.

Walking towards the police tape, he noticed the car, a white Excel, on the back of a tow truck, its side panels pocked with bullet holes and forensic markings. Next to it was a puddle of dark red blood, litres of it.

'G'day, mate. I'm from the *Sydney Morning Herald*, Dylan Welch. What's happened?' he asked a uniformed officer next to the tape.

The cop greased him. 'Wait for the press conference, mate.'

Another journo wandered up to him. 'Apparently it's Zervas,' he said nonchalantly.

'Whaddya mean?' The journo must have been mistaken. Tony Zervas died at the airport.

'Not Tony. His brother, Peter.'

'You're shittin' me.'

Just two days before, he'd watched Peter Zervas send off his brother at the Euro Funeral Services building in Roselands. He had gone to the funeral to absorb the spectacle: the leather patches, the rituals, the throbbing roar of the Harleys. He remembered instead being struck by the grimness of it all, the cheap suburban solemnity, and Zervas's mother gasping for breath between sobs as her remaining son held her from falling.

Walking around the crime scene, taking notes, he looked for a friendly face among the detectives. His eyes were drawn again to the dark pool of blood. It was massive.

Suddenly the air was pierced by a woman's screams. He spun around.

'Peter! Peter! Peter!' Every face at the scene—the journalists, police and forensic officers, the tow truck driver—was turned skywards, towards a balcony in the apartment block. Again she wailed, her anguish saturating the air.

'Where is my baby, my baby?'

Welch recognised the grief-stricken face peering over the balcony from the funeral. It was Zervas's mother.

He begun scrawling in his notebook. Zervas must have been staying at his mother's house. When he'd pulled up to the driveway to the underground car park, he must have been ambushed and shot repeatedly as he sat in the Excel. All fingers would be pointed at the Comancheros.

The wailing continued, and a second woman appeared on the balcony, soothing Zervas's mother, saying, 'He's alive. He's alive. Calm down.' Peter must have survived the shooting.

The morning light was now seeping into the sky. It didn't make sense. Why the continuing violence? It would only draw more police and political heat. Was it a result of the real story—the story of the franchising and criminalisation of some bikie clubs—being ignored for too long, not just by the media but by the authorities as well?

Organised crime was at its most powerful when it was out of sight and out of mind. The pressure had been rising but no one was paying any real attention.

Well, when it came to bikies, at least for the time being, that was over. As long as they kept exploding with violence in public, they would be the stuff of page one, and remain political priorities.

He noticed two stickers on metal lockers inside what must have been the Zervas family's parking spot. They both read: 'Support Your Local Hells Angels'. He jotted the line down in his notebook, wondering if it counted as the 'human touch' he'd been taught to observe.

Hutchins

The flags hung limply, a colourful imposition on the otherwise austere background, a fusion of steel, glass and concrete melded into a huge, curved building facade. Behold the industry of international bureaucracy, Hutchins thought, following the others towards the United Nations Office of Drugs and Crime.

His legs ached from walking. In the last ten days, he and the other members of the ACC committee's overseas delegation—Labor colleague Chris Hayes, Liberals Jason Wood and Stephen Parry, and committee secretary Dr Jacqui Dewar, an erudite public servant acknowledged as the committee's driving force—had travelled to several countries and across multiple time zones before ending up in Vienna.

Waiting in the UNODC foyer, Hutchins flicked open his notebook and studied his notes. Politically, the public outcry and media attention following the bikie airport bashing were both a blessing and a curse. Organised crime was in the headlines, but the debate had been dominated by talk of banning bikie groups. It was knee-jerk, opportunistic politics at its worst.

And when the journos had started calling, he'd said so publicly, fighting rhetoric with rhetoric. The focus on boofhead bikies was a distraction from the fight against the Mr Bigs of the drug trade. It was a good line, and he'd repeated it several times.

Everywhere they had travelled, Hutchins's opposition to the bikie ban was supported.

His eyes scanned the page on which he'd scrawled his notes about the meeting with Italian officials from the Direzione Investigativa Antimafia, several of whose bosses had been blown up by car bombs.

'Criminal gangs have set up international networks—Colombia, west coast of Africa, Italy, Asia, Canada, Australia—to traffic ecstasy or ice ... The state must attack economic power. Attacking assets is key.'

His eyes moved to the top of the page, where he'd scrawled and underlined the words 'political will?' The question was still troubling him. Simply getting the committee's overseas trip approved had already exhausted considerable political capital, despite his insistence it would be no junket. There were no wives in tow, no diversions to sporting arenas, safaris or shopping malls.

They'd done almost nothing but live and breathe organised crime. Before Italy, the Royal Canadian Mounted Police in Ottawa had outlined failed efforts to ban outlaw bikie gangs expanding their business ventures with Asian organised crime groups. In Washington, senior FBI officials spoke of their 'farm-to-arm' strategy aimed at investigating not only distributors but also the original source of drug imports. One grim-faced FBI official had equated organised crime bosses with multinational businessmen, controlling networked resources and industries across international borders.

Hutchins closed his notebook as a well-groomed man quietly addressed them.

'If you could be so kind, Mr Antonio Maria Costa is ready to see you.'

Sliding his notebook under his arm, he followed the others into the office of the chief of the United Nations Office of Drugs and Crime.

Their host was straight to the point. 'You know, if organised crime was a country, it would be a member of the G20. In the last quarter-century, it has become extraordinarily organised and transnational. It has reached macro-economic dimensions; it is a global business operating in collusion with legitimate activity.'

He watched Costa as he talked. He had a graceful air, was smartly dressed and spoke elegantly, but with fierce passion.

'Organised crime has globalised much more fluently than law enforcement. It is transnational big business. In 2005, the size of the global illegal drug trade was $320 billion.' Costa paused, his eyes burning. 'Think about that figure: $320 billion. We hear now a lot about climate change, but there is another climate change. It is the disintegration of civil society caused by organised crime. In fragile states, organised crime fills the void left by unstable governments. Do you know that the economies of some countries actually rely on the capital from organised crime?'

Costa sighed. 'The financial sector is being penetrated by cash-rich organised crime groups; money laundering has never been easier, more widely practiced, and on such a grand scale. And yet international action on organised crime is disjointed or non-existent.'

Hutchins glanced at his fellow politicians. All were listening intently. If there was a turning point on the trip, it was this, he thought.

Costa's words stayed with him when they broke for lunch and he slipped out towards the banks of the Danube. The air was still cold, but the sun was now beating down. He strode on, past women in bikinis tanning themselves on patches of grass, and towards the St. Stephen's spire.

Passing through the huge, imposing entrance, he was hit by the nostalgia that always struck him in grand churches: growing up, his father, who had done a stint as an SP bookmaker, and his mother, a sometime barmaid, were regular churchgoers.

The church had always been in his life. He had become a union official on St Patrick's Day. When he fought cancer, his faith, and his wife, had helped him win. He passed his hand over the top of a pew, feeling the reassuring roughness of the wood, muttered a short prayer and walked back into the sunlight.

His mind was made up. Everyone was saying the same, from the two Crime Commission investigators he had met in Melbourne, Bullock and Purchas, to Antonio Maria Costa. It was all about money. The committee needed to focus the fight on uncovering, following and ultimately seizing the billions of drug dollars flowing around the world. The Italians were right. They had to attack the assets.

The time to strike was now, he thought. Their next report needed to be written and released urgently while the political debate was still hot. If it helped steer the debate, the committee would have achieved something.

Stepping back into the sunlight, he turned as if to farewell the church. It stood grand and tall, imposing and immovable. He felt his neck warmed by the sun. A strong report would get the support of the other politicians on the trip. Whether anyone else would pay attention once it was released was another question. Perhaps God could lend a hand. He smiled as the thought crossed his mind. Even He would struggle with Australian politics.

Purchas

Purchas rubbed his chin. 'Are you absolutely sure?'

'It's got to be. It's absolutely got to be it.'

He was still unconvinced and said, 'Let's go through it again.'

He and Bullock had been at it for hours. After several weeks of watching Ayik, the commission's surveillance teams, known as the dogs, had begun tailing his associates, including several senior Comancheros and the young Asian man, Wei 'Will' Wong, who appeared to do Ayik's running. His network appeared to stretch from Sydney to Melbourne and Perth, where the Comancheros were establishing new chapters.

They'd also been checking Ayik's phone records and, by examining the call charge records of his associates, had begun uncovering the numbers of some of his burn-and-churn mobile phones.

His dispute with Bullock involved the work of the dogs, who had been tailing Ayik's nephew, Erkan Dogan, a skinny, acne-scarred twenty-year-old who, despite his age, appeared deeply embedded in the bikie scene. The dogs had watched Erkan meeting Ayik before heading off to a block of flats in Kogarah in Sydney's south-west. As soon as he arrived, he acted strangely, ducking down lanes and employing what appeared to be amateurish counter-surveillance. He was hiding something.

Bullock had been pushing for a sneak-and-peek search warrant, but he needed to be certain. If they made a mistake they would risk spooking Dogan and, ultimately, Ayik.

Bullock drummed the table. 'It's got to be it, Mikey. There are only a dozen or so apartments linked to the garage door entrance he's been coming out of. And the dogs have already tracked him to the floor.'

A week before, a surveillance team member had bolted into the lobby as soon as Dogan had disappeared into the lift and recorded what level it had stopped at. He'd repeated the exercise twice in the last few days while the dogs watching from outside looked for any corresponding movement—a blind closing or a light being switched on. They had picked it three times. Bullock was certain they didn't just have the right apartment; they had found a bikie safe house.

'I'm telling you Mikey: it's got to be it,' Bullock said, this time injecting his words with a twinge of anger.

Purchas said nothing, but began silently working through the underlying logic again. The bikie bashing at the airport had upped the stakes significantly. Politicians were baying for blood, and several of the chief commissioners on the ACC board wanted to shake bikie trees to see what fell out. Across Australia, bikies were being charged with anything and everything, from carrying a gram of speed to running stop signs. It was largely futile and a spectacular waste of resources.

And it missed the point, thought Purchas. Several bikie clubs had morphed into slick drug distribution machines. They had more guns and money than ever before. Violence was inevitable. Locking them up for minor offences served as an irritant but did nothing to stop the cause of their enrichment.

Yet the hunger for bikie scalps also presented them with an opportunity to make Operation Hoffman's work indispensible. Their focus on Ayik's crew had left them in the box seat when it came to gathering and sharing bikie-related intelligence with state police forces.

Just two days after the airport bashing, Vikingsson's High Risk Funds Program had uncovered a significant funds transfer offshore that was linked to a relative of one of the airport murder suspects. Believing it to be either the proceeds of crime being removed out of the country before it could be seized or money sent to finance a fresh criminal venture, Vikingsson had passed it on to a grateful state police detective.

Bullock was right, he thought. The more important Operation Hoffman became to the Crime Commission's partner agencies, the more it would help to prop up the real game: Operation Dayu. Ayik was just another way into the international network.

'Alright, Bruce. Let's rally the troops. We'll hit it tonight.'

Bullock looked at him, surprised, as if he was expecting more of an argument.

'You heard me, Melonhead. Go get the team organised.'

Bullock shrugged and disappeared.

He checked his watch. It was noon, meaning the Western Union representative would more than likely already be waiting for him downstairs. Argument two for the day was about to commence.

As he headed towards the lift, he wondered whether the company had again dispatched their blond-haired, white-toothed envoy. Ever since they had begun targeting the Western Union remitters, the company had sought to ease the commission's pressure. She was the latest of its tricks. If she had lucked onto one of the younger blokes, maybe it would have worked. But he had learnt long ago to leave that part of his imagination at home. He was also no fool. Women under thirty-five were unlikely to regard him a sexual treasure chest of experience they just had to prise open. Western Union had problems, no matter how many blonde beauties they employed.

In the lift, he revised what he needed to raise. Small money remitters operating under the Western Union brand and sending their funds via a larger company agent were suspected of dealing with huge amounts of narco-dollars. What was certain was the process used by Western Union often disregarded the know-your-customer regulations. Before the lift door opened, he rearranged his moppish hair. Here comes the treasure chest, he thought.

'Hi, Mike. How are you going.'

'I'm good. I wish I could say the same thing for your subagents.'

Smiling, he extended his meat plate of a hand. She didn't flinch.

'We are working on it Mike. We have a raft of new training policies. Can I get you a coffee?'

'I'm just fine, thanks.'

They both took a seat.

'I have said this before and I want to make it clear. Many of your remitters are still dealing in the scumbag end of the market. I don't want to hear about your training and all that crap. I want to know what you have done in the last few months to address my concerns. Your subagents are still failing the know-your-customer test. Which means they may well be in breach of the law.'

It took her an hour for her to agree that Western Union would demand that its subagents do more to report all suspicious transfers to authorities and for the company to review the way it moved Australian money across the globe.

'Great to see you, Mike,' she said as she left.

'And you. It's always a pleasure.'

This time he hit the elevator down button. If the sneak-and-peek at Erkan Dogan's apartment was happening tonight, it could be a late one. Bullock could arrange and oversee the operation. He needed to recharge his system.

December 2007 – August 2009

The sinking sun transformed the sky into a pink and yellow hue and, as he pounded the road, he felt the impact of shoe on pavement shoot through his knee joints. As he ran, he wondered how long it would be before he and the new regime would butt heads. Several weeks ago, John Lawler had finally arrived at the Crime Commission as its new boss. His arrival coincided with whispers that the feds would begin taking a bigger interest in organised crime, shifting some of their best investigators from terrorism back to other areas. It would mean the Crime Commission could find itself fighting for space in Canberra.

Every day there was a new rumour of further restructuring, new managers and changes to existing operations. Dayu would not be exempt, and there was already talk that its core elements—the High Risk Funds Program, Hoffman, Agrale and the informer network—could be divided up, removed from James's administrative control and overseen by a range of different managers.

Perhaps it was why James was beginning to act oddly, coolly. It was as if he knew of bad news but didn't want to talk about it. Bullock had his own theory. There were some in the commission who didn't like the trio's influence. Breaking up Dayu would sap it.

Passing the tree that marked his halfway point, he wondered if he could step out of the life. Out of the game. If he left the commission, it would mean more time with Huong. He trusted her as he trusted few others—maybe Bullock, Adams, James, Vikingsson. Yet could he do it? Could he start a new life, outside of the job, no longer in the game? Huong was stubborn and sullen when she didn't get her own way. But so was he. She was also loyal and hardworking, a self-made person with her own thriving business. He rarely said so openly, but it was a relationship that mattered deeply to him. Away from the office, she broke up his need for order, making each day a lottery, spontaneous. She ran with her ideas, rather than long-term plans. It was different with him. But maybe it would work when he left the commission. *If* he left the commission. Or maybe they'd carry him out in a box. Lawler would get his casket after all.

It was late when he stepped back into the operations room. There were only a few investigators there, but he could tell something major had gone down. Bullock was on the phone, his face ashen, and the other investigators were all deep in discussion.

One of the techs spotted him and came over. 'Unbelievable, isn't it, Mike.'

'What is?'

The tech looked at him as though he were daft.

'No one's told you? They found a Comos safe house with enough bombs and guns to fuel one hell of a war. And that's not all. Seems like they have been getting some of their gear from guys meant to be fighting on our side.'

Welch

Welch sat at his desk, blocking out the buzz of the newsroom around him. He hated being told to wait. The more good mail you got, the more you were asked by police to hold off reporting it. Underlining this deal was an unspoken notion that a reporter's display of goodwill would, sometime in the future, be handsomely repaid. Yet the more goodwill he banked, the less he valued his deposit.

Police almost always wanted events reported on their terms. If it was bad publicity, they didn't want it reported at all. That was why it was crucial to cultivate sources in the underworld. Criminals had a vested interest, but they also viewed events through different eyes and reminded reporters that the police version of events wasn't always right.

Studying his notebook, Welch thought back to his online boss, an old British tabloid editor who had taught him about looking for the hidden story amid the crumbs a reporter gathered on their beat. The editor had given Welch the advice after he'd returned from the scene of a fire in which a charred body had been found. 'Ask the firemen how they found the body,' the editor told him. He made the call and, thirty seconds later, his story had morphed from a fire to a murder involving a body wrapped in a carpet.

The details he was holding off on this morning suggested something far bigger was afoot than the police were letting on. Police had raided a suspected Comanchero safe house and found an impressive arsenal: automatic rifles and pistols, silencers and scopes, and improvised explosive devices that a police source had told him that morning were most likely made by an ex-special forces soldier under Comancher command.

It wasn't just the size of the arsenal or the allegation that it belonged to a bikie club at war with the Hells Angels that was disturbing. The raid also uncovered gear most likely sourced by someone with access to a police store: bulletproof vests, police helmets, a ramming device, night vision goggles, uniforms and several police badges. It all pointed to a corrupt relationship with someone in law enforcement. And wealth. Not only could the Comos afford an impressive arsenal, but they were also most likely paying off someone on the inside.

Flicking through pages of his notebook, his eyes rested on the words 'Australian Crime Commission'. His police source was certain the tip-off on the safe house had come from the ACC, rather than the NSW police anti-bikie taskforce, Raptor. That meant one of the biggest hauls in the post-airport bikie crackdown hadn't come from the state police at all. The Crime Commission was a secretive agency designed to tackle high-level organised crime. Many cops were dismissive of its ability to do so, but if the weapons raid originated from the ACC's work, it was likely to be part of a much bigger operation. But what?

The last piece of notebook scrawl was the name of the man arrested in connection to the safe house: 'Erkan Dogan'. It was a Turkish name, but beyond that he was certain of nothing but the man's age—twenty years old, too young to be of any real consequence. Next to the name, he had written 'relative of Big Hux?' It was something a crook had told him that morning, although it was unconfirmed and no police source would tell him any more.

Closing the notebook, he returned to the story he was composing on his screen. The newsdesk wanted a short, punchy piece to fill a hole on page three. Keep it short and simple, he'd been told, and file no later than 7.00 p.m. He tried to focus on writing, but he was distracted. There was something he was missing. He just didn't know what.

James

Sitting in his office, James stared at the photo of his youngest son. He had done so every night since the boy had been rushed to intensive care. He was just seven years old. He hated thinking about it, but he couldn't stop his mind spinning back to him. And especially that first morning when he had crawled into their room on his hands and knees. 'I don't feel good,' he'd said. He had kissed him on the forehead and put him back to bed.

A day later, his son was paralysed from his waist down. They'd rushed him to hospital, where he'd stayed for a month. Guillain-Barré syndrome, the doctor called it. The younger they get it, the better. There is hope, he said. Well, he was young—just look at him—too young. Seven years old. The signs were better now, but no one could say if he'd walk again like other kids—like other seven-year-olds.

He knew he should be at home now, with his boy and his wife, but the peace of his office at night was soothing. It gave him time to think. Purchas and Bullock had covered for him while his boy was sick, but he'd returned to a commission that was changing. Not yet at tipping point. But heading that way. The new boss, John Lawler, had arrived, and shortly afterwards James had silently been benched—on the outer and out of favour. The whisper was that Dayu was viewed as too high risk, too resource intensive. There simply wasn't enough manpower to do what was required. Purchas was already warning Dayu staff of an impending death by a thousand cuts, and while it was still too early to tell, he may have been on the mark.

James still had some of his Financial Crimes portfolio staff, but Operation Dayu was slowing down as resources were diverted into Operation Hoffman. Hoffman had come under the control of another general manager, Jim Duffy, an experienced and respected career policeman who managed the High Risk Crime Groups portfolio, which had responsibility for the bikies.

On paper, that made sense. But it didn't account for the continuing erosion of his own standing within the agency. He'd been demoted from acting general manager, a position he had held for eighteen months, to senior manager, despite a promise from his direct boss, Michael Outram, that the general manager's job was his. His ability to protect the long-term goals of Dayu was going the way of his Crime Commission career.

The agency's senior staff were all focused on what had been termed 'a new way of doing business', a new operating model named Sentinel, aimed at reshaping the commission's handling of criminal intelligence. Despite resistance from himself, Purchas and Bullock, Sentinel was driving the increasing efforts to divide and reassign throughout the commission the various parts of Operation Dayu: Vikingsson's High Risk Funds Program, Agrale, Hoffman and the informer network.

Sentinel had its passionate defenders, but it also left many commission staff perplexed and concerned that they were witnessing nothing more than a shifting of the deck chairs. Whatever the truth, he was certain of one thing: the institutional and political tide in the commission was turning. And it appeared to be turning, if only slowly, against all that Purchas, Bullock, Vikingsson and he had fought for: long-term, high-risk operations that sought to push the limits of how law enforcement could infiltrate and analyse the criminal economy.

The covert laundry remained suspended, and the agency bosses had ordered several internal reviews of Purchas and Bullock's use of human sources, the informers crucial to setting up the laundry and infiltrating the international money-laundering sector. One had already found administrative shortcomings—shortcomings he'd argued were the product of scarce resources.

He'd also faced criticism for being too close to Purchas and Bullock when it came to overseeing the pair's operational decision-making. He suspected that it was a cover for something else: that he was considered too much of a Purchas- and Bullock-style operator, and not enough of a public service man.

His best guess was that Hoffman and Agrale would run for another twelve months while the grand plan informing Operation Dayu slowly withered. He cursed himself. He had seen it coming months before: the new regime, the lingering fear that the covert laundry would embarrass the agency, the ferocious and obstinate nature of Purchas and Bullock. The style of policing induced by a public service mentality was always going to catch up with them. The only uncertainty was exactly when it would ride them all down.

Their faults seemed to overshadow their successes. After the detection and seizure of the bikie armoury, Bullock, who'd led the operation, had been chided for breaching protocol. When they'd found the explosives, to act fast, Bullock had alerted the local branch of the state police, rather than central crime command, who later complained. Lawler had told Bullock that he'd 'stolen defeat from the jaws of victory'. It was a classic case of policing politics overshadowing results.

The successful massive liquid ecstasy seizure and the 80-kilogram Adelaide ice bust had also been diminished by complaints from the federal police, who claimed that they had been dudded or misled by the ACC.

He recalled what one of the newly promoted managers had told Purchas, Bullock and himself. 'You are poor managers and you need to remake your corporate image.' Whatever that meant. Most disappointing was the apparent and growing lack of corporate commitment to back Dayu: to invest in a concept of operations that could really make a difference to law enforcement.

James's attention was drawn to movement in the office. He thought it was a cleaner but then saw Vikingsson, his face lit up by the computer, completely absorbed. He was struck by a sudden fondness for the Swede. At work, he was brilliant, the best analyst he'd ever encountered. Outside of the office, he was less robust.

'Patrick,' he called out, walking towards him. 'What are you still doing here?'

Vikingsson looked tired, his face thin and unshaven, but his eyes still twinkled.

'I've been shaping the High Risk Funds Program. The latest modelling corroborates Dayu's intelligence that several of the major drug imports into Australia have come from the same overseas entity. A vast amount of drug money is pouring into the same companies or developments in Hong Kong, Macau and Vietnam. If you take the time to drill right down, there appear to be repeated associations between high-level government officials in Asia and the corporate entities receiving the drug money.'

He knew now why Vikingsson looked like he hadn't been sleeping: he probably hadn't been home for days.

'You know, when I sat in that briefing, I knew that they had really got it …' said Vikingsson, leaping in a fresh direction. 'I saw Lawler whisper to Bradley and then both of them, almost in unison, said, "This is going to change law enforcement. It is going to produce irresistible intelligence." And in their faces, I could see that they truly believed it.'

The excitable Vikingsson wasn't easy to follow, but James realised that he was talking about the briefing the analyst had recently given to the nation's three most powerful law enforcement figures: Lawler, Philip Bradley, who headed the NSW Crime Commission, and the newly installed AFP commissioner, Tony Negus.

'I have seen that same expression when I explain the High Risk Funds Program to other people. There is a moment when their faces light up and you know the penny has dropped.' James didn't know what to say, and there was a moment of silence between them. Vikingsson still seemed hopeful. Maybe he was giving up too easily. His eyes moved to the family photo on the desk, and Vikingsson noticed him looking at it.

'She's taken the kids back overseas. She was sick of all of this. But it is something I felt I really had to do. We've all been doing the same thing in drug enforcement for twenty years and not made any difference. Dayu can change that.'

'Go home Patrick,' he said, patting Vikingsson on the shoulder.

As he turned to leave, Vikingsson spoke again, this time with more urgency. 'I've tracked them to Japan, Gregory. They are in bed with the Yakuza.'

'Who?' said James, swinging back to face the analyst.

'The owners of those passports Mike had scanned in the Macau meeting. I did some work on their travel movements, trying to come up with some patterns, whether they travel with the same people frequently—that sort of thing. It appears they often move with some well-known senior Chinese triad figures, including figures we have identified in Gordian, or more recently during Dayu.'

'And Japan?'

The analyst passed him a newspaper article.

Ex-gangster shot by gunman in Tokyo
A man was shot and later pronounced dead on Sunday after several men opened fire on him with handguns on a street in a busy commercial district in Tokyo's Taito Ward, police said.

The gunmen fled the scene after the shooting at around 10:55 a.m. on a street near JR Okachimachi Station and the famous Ameyoko shopping market, the police said. The man, who was shot in his upper body, fell into a coma and was pronounced dead afterwards at a nearby hospital, the police said.

The police identified the man as 42-year-old Shinichi Nakanishi, a former member of a gangster group affiliated with the nation's largest gangster group, the Yamaguchi-gumi. The police are searching for the gunmen, who are also believed to be members of a gangster group, on suspicion of murder.

Before he could finish the article, Vikingsson had conjured up a map of the world on his computer. 'Some of the Operation Dayu targets appear to have travelled to Tokyo on the same day, so I checked out why. It is the day of the funeral. They must have travelled for the ceremony, maybe out of respect. Or maybe to reorganise. Who knows.'

'That's great work, Patrick. Really great work. Now go and get some sleep.' He turned to leave, but suddenly swung around to face the analyst again. 'You know things are changing here, don't you?'

Vikingsson looked at him oddly.

'It might be time to think about a different future, Patrick. If we stick at this, we might all end up wasting our time.' He immediately regretted the comment. Vikingsson was passionate about his work to the extent that others would complain about the hours he worked. They were right, of course. But now wasn't the time for grim news.

Vikingsson furrowed his brow, shrugged and wished him good night, before swivelling back to face his computer, cocooned again by the light from the screen, as if James had never been there at all.

Ayik

He'd be alright. Ayik studied the photo of the two of them, arm draped over each other's shoulders. 'My uncle and I' was the caption Erkan had put underneath the shot when he had posted it to his Myspace site.

Ayik re-read his own posting: 'Two champions at their best'.

Erkan had been inside for a few weeks now, ever since the jacks had raided the safe house stash. He knew it was heavy weight for a twenty-year-old to carry: just a kid and already facing at least a few years inside. He slid the photo back into his bag but he couldn't shake Erkan from his mind. He knew what happened inside to those without connects. But Erkan had them. He was connected to him, and the boys and everyone knew that.

He'd be fine.

Still, there was always danger, especially at the moment, the risk that a rival bikie would punch on or try to shiv him. Then there were the more mundane dangers: the prison junkies, the religious crews and the black fellas. The prison system was better than it once was, but it still teemed with cliques, gangs and violence.

At least Erkan had the inner fortitude to hold his own. Erkan had balls. He had trained with his nephew in the gym, helping him bulk up after he'd come down from Queensland. He'd morphed into a cocky little bastard, but one who still revered him.

'This is my uncle,' Erkan would tell his mates when introducing him to guys who looked like miniature versions of his own old school crew: little Dauxs and Hawis intent on hitting up girls and clubs, making a few decent earns and, with them, a name.

He'd promised his family that Erkan would be looked after on the inside and he'd already put the word out. He had friends, money and access to a phone. Most importantly, everyone knew that to fuck with him would be to fuck with the Comos. Yet he couldn't shake the vision of his nephew confined in a cell. He hated the idea that he'd come out dark and brooding, and having to tell people, 'I've been away for a while'.

The guard! He reached for his mobile. 'You know that fella who works in prison? You know, thingo's cousin. We need him to chop us out a few favours on the inside.'

'Onto it.'

After he hung up, he realised he had probably said too much. Fuck it. It was family. And there was no indication that his phones were tapped. Still, everyone was hot. One of the Comos hooked up with an analyst in police intelligence had passed back the word to the crew that they were all tropical as a result of the airport bashing. The good news was that any specific enquiries about him had apparently died a natural. Mizza hadn't burned him, and neither had the Thai gear.

Yet it was odd that they'd found the safe house. If they were watching Erkan, they would have seen him, too. He looked at his watch; he needed a clear hour to work through everything again. He pulled out his notebook, and shook off the remnants of his jet lag.

December 2007 – August 2009

The Chinese had offered him access to a stash of liquid methylamphetamine that they had stored in South Africa. The contract he and Wu had picked up involved moving the gear to Australia. They planned to secrete the gear in wine bladders, which were being exported from South Africa by the thousand every week. They'd already done a test run, sending a runner, Kelly Edmonds, to South Africa. He'd returned with two red wine bottles in his luggage, and no questions were asked.

Taking it to the next level involved sending the bladders from Capetown to Auckland and, finally, Tonga. An airfreight company contact would manipulate the computer holdings to confuse the system and make it appear as if the consignment had never existed. Once in Nuku'alofa, they would call on some of the Tongan boys, including a local customs officer, to get the gear on board an international freighter called the *Capitaine Tasman*. The crew included several friendlies, who would smuggle it to contacts on the wharf in Melbourne or Sydney once the ship arrived. All the while, their boys in the jacks would keep an eye out.

The beauty of the plan lay in its reach: from the *dai los* in Hong Kong to their runners in South Africa, Daux's friends in New Zealand and Tonga, and the club's reach into the wharves and law enforcement in Sydney and Melbourne. Five countries, three continents, several seas and oceans and $4.5 million, of which 40 percent would be repatriated back to the Hong Kong bosses. Not bad for a few weeks' work, especially given the premium they'd make on the product by selling it in Australia.

There was also talk of a large shipment of ice in China that had to be contracted out, and he'd floated to the Hong Kong bosses a venture of his own: cocaine was badly sought after in China, and he had the connects in South America, Spain and the Philippines to source it.

The loose change could prop up the brothel, which was suffering thanks to some Korean pros who'd fled their employ. He could also throw some paper Will's way and hopefully end his badgering about the karaoke bar. Will still had his sights set on becoming an Asian music promoter—he was fuckin' trippin'. He was also pushing him to invest in a second brothel venture, this one in Canberra. Could that boy not get enough sex?

He clicked up the chart of international flight times, calculating how long it would take the gear to move from South Africa to New Zealand and Tonga. The ship would take a least another week to get to Melbourne and, finally, to Sydney. That gave him some solid down time.

Pulling out the photo of his nephew again, he smiled. He would soon have the prison guard running him cash. And he'd pay for the best criminal silk. Even if he got a bad spell, he'd be looked after inside. And when he got out, he'd be ready.

He knew exactly what he'd do. Erkan loved his Audi R8. When he got out of jail he'd find a sleek, glistening machine, with its engine humming and his name etched on the key chain.

Purchas

Sliding out the magazine, Purchas checked it was fully loaded and reinserted it. For a few moments, he let the Glock sit in his hand, feeling the cold metal press against his skin as he sat in the loading room. He was glad he'd never shot anyone.

Not that the thought bothered him. If he really had to squeeze the trigger, if there was truly no other way, he wouldn't hesitate. It was just that he prided himself on never allowing a situation to descend to a level when a gun was his only option. The paperwork that came when you let a shot away could swamp a man for weeks, let alone when you actually shot a person. And he hated any paperwork that took him away from an operation.

He noticed a younger commission officer enter the loading room and watch him while he checked his own weapon. He was expecting the question when it came, yet the earnestness surprised him.

'You ever had to use it, Mike?'

He briefly pictured himself as a young detective, eager and innocent, free of the garbage that infested older cops. 'I once had a bit of an incident in the UK. The second time I was shot ... well, we don't talk about that one.'

But of course now he was thinking about it. At least the passage of three decades allowed him to see the lighter side. When he was about thirty years old in the United States, he'd holstered his weapon and it had unexpectedly discharged, sending a bullet ripping through the back of his foot. He hated lying, but made an exception when anyone asked how he came to have a limp.

'Do you think we'll crack the apartments, Mike?' the young officer asked.

'It'll be now or never.'

Heading towards the briefing room, he winced at the prospect that he and Bullock were wrong. The dollop of grief that would cover them would require a knife to spread.

He and Bullock had chosen tonight because Ayik was overseas and Will was, if he kept to his usual routine, due to head to his brothel to collect the day's earnings. And, with a bit of luck, he would engage the services of one of his unlucky female employees.

The task of inserting listening devices into Will and Ayik's apartments, situated opposite each other in a highrise block in World Square, was doubly hard. When one was out, the other was often in. Also, the Hoffman team had been warned by the NSW police about a much earlier attempt they had made on Ayik's Rockdale apartment. When they had entered, they had discovered a motion-activated mobile phone camera pointing at the door. Within minutes, a team of Comancheros, presumably dispatched by Ayik, rolled up in a glistening black Bentley.

If they were to be successful, the commission's team needed to be ready for unexpected tricks. One of the ACC techs had already devised a plan to defeat motion-activated camera phones. A phone could only handle one task at a time, so if they rang it at the precise moment of entry, it could be placed face down before the ringing stopped. Upon departure, they'd ring it again, leaving the phone in its original position.

As Purchas surveyed the five-man tech crew in front of him, he felt relaxed. They weren't much to look at. All were dressed in casual clothes, some unshaven and pot-bellied, and inflicted with the tics typical of those with a passion for covert technology. But they were also the best in the game and, when things went smoothly, could drift like ghosts, leaving a trail invisible to the naked eye: tiny hidden cameras in air-conditioners, microphones inside televisions, optic fibre cables inside pipes, tracking devices in key chains.

'We ready to go?' he asked, immediately drawing a glare from one of the senior techs.

'We're always ready, Mike.'

He should have expected that. When they rolled tonight, he would be travelling as a passenger. Nothing bothered the techs more than an investigator trying to do their job.

He sat in the back of the sedan as it pulled out of the commission car park, his knees pushing against the seat in front. No one in the car said anything, each waiting for an update to be fed into their earpieces from the dogs. The silence continued when the car pulled up at the launching spot, a Chinatown alley. As the minutes ticked past, Purchas felt the dull ache pulsing through his knees becoming increasingly intense, and he had to fight the desire to shake and stretch his legs. It was the same feeling he got on long flights.

He tried counting the number of drunks stumbling into a red neon–lit doorway, and then shifted his mind to Vikingsson's latest discovery. The passports had confirmed that those behind the offshore business identified by Operation Dayu were senior triad figures. They also knew that the tentacles of this offshore business strectched well beyond Hong Kong and China, into Vietnam, Macau, Cambodia, Asia and Canada. A new partnership between the triads and the yakuza suggested that old borders and enmities were irrelevant.

The intelligence being collected by Dayu pointed to a new path being forged by the triads. They were working with anyone, anywhere. A diversified, multinational triad enterprise comprising drug trafficking and money laundering operated in tandem with a range of legitimate multi billion-dollar business interests spanning Asia.

Yet intelligence wasn't proof. They needed corroboration. He thought back to his old source. The source knew several figures deep within Asian organised crime rackets in Hong Kong. If he could pull one last favour, it would be to get to one of those Asian players, someone who owed his source a favour and had his own reasons to talk. He wondered if he could convince him to find such a person by offering him a promise. If his source arranged the meeting, his obligation to Purchas would be fulfilled and he'd never get another call from him again.

Purchas's internal dialogue was interrupted by his earpiece.

'Target on the move.'

A surge of human electricity passed through the car. Showtime.

Without speaking, his four companions slid out of their seats. As he followed them, he felt one of his legs almost buckle. He clenched his teeth, lengthened his stride and ignored the shooting pain.

His earpiece crackled again. 'Target driving. Likely destination is brothel. Entry team is good to go.'

He watched one of the techs punch the code in the lobby door and fell to the rear of the group as it moved past the empty reception desk and into the lift.

He glanced at his watch. They had half an hour to be in and out.

Outside Will's apartment, one of the techs pulled a small toolbox from his backpack and, on his knees, attempted to defeat the lock. He swore quietly as he worked. 'Fuck ... Fuck ... Fuck ... You fucking beauty ... hit the phone jammer.'

Another operative punched some numbers into a small machine, hit enter and, when they heard ringing inside, said, 'Okay, we are good to go.'

He waited for the others to enter before he went in behind them. The apartment was small and cramped, with a bedroom and a living and kitchen area separated by a bench. A pornographic magazine featuring Asian girls lay on the floor.

'Two minutes guys,' he said, watching two of the techs search for somewhere to put a listening device. Another photographed scraps of paper removed from a bin, while a fourth ran a swab over the table and what appeared to be instruments for mixing gear.

'There's nowhere to put the audiovisual cable. It'll have to be sound only,' whispered one of techs.

'Have a look at this, Mike.'

He studied the small slip of paper the tech passed him. On one side were several mobile numbers, including one with a west coast prefix and another that looked like a Hong Kong mobile phone. Beneath it were a series of times next to the words 'Port Botany' and 'Melbourne'.

The other side of the paper was covered in Vietnamese stamps, alongside a roughly scrawled figure. Beneath that, a percentage was listed. He'd seen scraps of paper like this before: it was a receipt from an Asian money remitter. 'It's a beautiful thing,' he whispered, holding up both sides for the techs to photograph before placing it back in the bin.

After ten minutes, he and the techs closed Will's apartment and began working on Ayik's door. This time it took two of them to beat the locks. 'Check it out. The pauper and the prince,' muttered one of the techs as he disabled the camera phone and the team got to work.

Purchas studied the apartment. The place was far cleaner and bigger than Will's, with Asian-themed furniture, two laptops, a large flat-screen television and a nearly empty bottle of Grange. The bin contained some empty mobile phone boxes, which the techs photographed.

The two-apartment set-up made perfect sense, thought Purchas as he watched one of the techs slide a tiny length of wire into an expensive sound system. Ayik ran the show while Will carried the risk.

The earpiece erupted again. 'Unidentified male exiting the lift on your floor. Stand by.'

He noticed the techs immediately tense up. His own heart was pumping. Those carrying Glocks moved their hands to their sides. The air in the room was still. No one said a word.

Tap, tap, tap. They heard the sound of a door along the corridor being opened and closed, and the tension in the room dropped. I'm getting too bloody old for this, he thought.

'Right, let's go.'

He was the last one into the lift. When the door shut, he checked his watch. Twenty-two minutes had passed. The ghosts had come and gone in record time.

Will

Beep. Beep. Beep. Beep. His alarm was driving him insane. Will rolled over and checked the clock. Shit. It was 1.00 p.m. The only thing he hated more than not getting enough sleep was getting up after noon. It made him feel lazy.

He turned onto his back, staring at the roof, reliving last night. God, she was good. He wondered how many guys could go like him. The girls *always* had a good time. Then again, the chick last night technically worked for him, so it was hard to tell. One thing was certain: he'd lasted the full hour and was ready to go again minutes later.

I am the fucking bomb, he thought.

He hated chicks who tried to short-change a full booking. That was one of the good things about using his own brothel: they had to respect him, even if they hated his guts. When he was in a foul mood, he'd pick one of the haters. And he'd make sure to last the whole sweaty hour.

One of the three phones next to his head buzzed with a text: 'Hey, Big Girl. Don't forget bandages,' it read.

'Shit,' he cursed himself, rolling out of bed. He was still in last night's clothes. He rubbed his eyes and spat into the sink. He had to be on his game. The ship from Tonga was due to dock, and Kelly would be round to pick up the gear to fly it to Perth.

He headed downstairs and out into the winter chill, past his old friends the concrete dragons. Ten minutes later, bandages in hand, he was standing outside his baby. 'Cashbox Karaoke is under new management,' the sign on the door read. Finally, big things were happening. Even before they had got a sign with the name, Club de Melody, he was sounding out players in the Asian pop scene with the idea of turning the club into a hub for singers from Hong Kong, Shanghai and Taiwan.

He was getting closer to confirming the club's first big event, promoting the Australian tour of a couple of big-name Chinese pop stars. His plan was to link the tour to the club, which would promote the event with drink card giveaways, champagne happy hours, karaoke contests and—if he could pull it off—an exclusive product-signing event with both stars. The hype would be huge.

His mother and former classmates would read about him in the Chinese press. And it would blow Hux away. He dreamed up the headline as he peeked up the stairs of the club: 'New promoter makes splash.'

What's more, it would be *his* thing. Hux couldn't speak Mandarin or Cantonese, and while he could handle the Asian scene, he was still a whitey, a *laowai*, and didn't know the first thing about who was coming up in the music scene. This time, *he* would run the show. Maybe he'd even have a few Asian-friendly bikies on the door as security. Then again …

He hadn't told Hux yet, but he wanted to make a break from the imports and the money moving; as soon as the club was up and running, he would give it up. He just needed the money for the fitout, and for that he needed Hux. So he'd held off telling him all his plans.

December 2007 – August 2009

Realising he must look slightly odd, standing in Chinatown staring at a closed door, he headed back to his apartment, bandages in hand. Kelly Edmonds and another man were waiting at his door.

'Where the fuck you been, man?'

'Doing some business around my new club,' he said, doing his best to project contempt. 'Come inside.'

He retrieved the bags of powder from a backpack as both men stripped off their shirts and pants.

'You sure this shit won't go off in the scanners?'

He ignored the question and concentrated on strapping the bags to the men's bodies with the bandages.

'Watch it, little man. I've got sensitive skin.'

The sooner they were out of his apartment, the better. He avoided eye contact with them as he issued their instructions. They were in his apartment on Hux's orders, not his. It had always been that way. It was exactly why he needed his own venture.

It was a domestic flight, and aside from the airport scans, the checking was non-existent. The chances of getting patted down were one in a hundred, the chance of encountering sniffers dogs even less.

He looked the two men over as they pulled on their tracksuits and walked out of his apartment. They were hardly the best choice for couriers: too young, with short, cocky haircuts and a swagger he'd cross the street to avoid.

Neither of them said a word as they disappeared down the hallway.

'All good, Big Girl,' he punched into his phone once his door was closed. It had been Hux's idea to start calling each other 'girl' and 'darling' because he believed it would confuse anybody bugging their phones. Or maybe Hux just liked having him as his bitch.

He checked his watch and calculated that he should hear in the next hour or so if the *Capitaine Tasman* had docked and their consignment was en route. He considered downloading a new game, but settled on a feed in Chinatown. He could pop into the brothel on the way home and check the till. A surprise visit would keep the girls on their toes. Or their backs, he sniggered.

Two hours later, he was back in his apartment, having heard nothing from Edmonds or from the wharf. He was uneasy. He recognised the queasiness invading his stomach: it was that same rush of anxiety he'd felt when his girlfriend had pinched the $300,000.

He punched in another text: 'No word, Big Girl.'

A few seconds later, his phone lit up: 'Hi, darling. Let u know.'

He became increasingly rattled as he paced his apartment. Fuck it. He would use his phone and call the guy assigned with the drop-off. The idea that his phone was tapped was ridiculous. At any rate, he would be careful with what he said. 'What's going on?' The firmness in his own voice surprised him.

'No sign. We are checking with our guy.'

He hung up and started pacing again. His apartment was suddenly feeling much smaller than before, as if the walls and the roof had closed in a few inches. His stomach twisted as the phone buzzed again.

As he read the message, his heart thumped, as if it wanted out of his ribcage: 'Clean out apartments—NOW.'

Part 4
August 2009 – April 2010

James

As Purchas and Bullock sat before him, relaying the last week's events, he was hit by a wave of deja vu. While absorbing their briefing, he searched his memory for its source and landed on their first meeting, when the pair of them had first floated Operation Dayu.

Plenty had changed since then. Purchas, somewhat impossibly, appeared to have dropped a few kilos, and Bullock seemed to have gained a few, along with a fresh flush of greying hair. And he was no longer their boss. But their energy, their intensity, hadn't wavered, despite being ravaged by excessive work hours. They were addicted to the job and the feeling of grasping enough strings to make a puppet really dance.

'You can't beat bad luck,' said Purchas, repeating his latest one-liner, a sly grin on his face.

Yet they almost had. James nodded as Bullock explained how the two drug runners at Sydney airport had nearly avoided capture. Bullock and Purchas had alerted the airport police after hearing suspicious conversations in Will's apartment, but the sniffer-dog handlers had refused to conduct a targeted search because they said they didn't have due cause.

'Bruce was jumping off the bleedin' walls,' Purchas added. 'We had to call in the sniffer-dog boss and give him an earful. Of course, it was all high fives when they found the gear.'

'You can't beat bad luck, eh boss,' said Bullock.

'Indeed,' he returned dryly. 'Any update on the ship?'

James listened as Purchas explained how they'd spent hour after hour examining the movements of all vessels from the Port of Melbourne to Port Botany, trying to find a match to references Will had made about a ship and the delivery of the gear.

'There is only one vessel that fits the picture. It's called the *Capitaine Tasman* and it's steaming towards Tonga as we speak. The strange thing is, it appears they haven't offloaded any gear.'

As Bullock took over proceedings, James wondered at the chemistry between the two men. One minute Bullock and Purchas were like wolves savaging each other's throats; the next they were inseparable, the commission's own Starsky and Hutch.

'We don't exactly know why, but if our mail is right, the *Capitaine Tasman* still bears Ayik's load. Which is where you come in, Jamesy.'

Purchas re-took the reigns. 'We are after a favour. We are hoping you can call on your friends in New Zealand.'

He felt a small glow of excitement pass through him as he absorbed the request. His briefings from Purchas and Bullock were increasingly limited to whispered chats over cups of coffee. His own workload had shifted from overseeing most of the commission's major operations for over two years to signing off on badly spelled phone-tap affidavits. He was also responsible for responding to growing concerns about the unexplained wealth laws proposed by Hutchins's parliamentary committee. If they worked, the laws could be a huge aid to operations such as Dayu, allowing authorities to seize illicitly earned wealth. Yet the proposed legislation was being watered down even as it was drafted.

He'd been missing the action.

He knew why they had come to him. After working in the Pacific for a few years, he'd gathered some good contacts in the New Zealand police service. The New Zealanders had a small contingent of senior officers seconded to the notoriously corrupt Tongan police service.

'I'll put a call in.' He wasn't ready to return to his paperwork, and asked, 'Any luck with those phone numbers?' He knew the Operation Hoffman team had been working on uncovering the identities behind a list of mobile phones found in Will's apartment.

James watched Purchas hesitate—they didn't call him Drip-feed for nothing—before relenting. One of the numbers was linked to the west coast boss of the Comancheros, the other to a mid-level triad figure in China, Steve Wu.

'It appears that Wu is an associate of several of the high-level triad figures we've identified through Operation Dayu,' said Purchas.

'Does that mean ... ' He trailed off as both Purchas and Bullock silently nodded, eyes raised. Nobody spoke as he absorbed the significance of the link. Ayik's crew was not just in bed with the triads, it was also plugged into the international network uncovered by Operation Dayu.

Both men rose to leave.

'Good work. Anything else?'

'The NSW cops have picked up some minnows the bikies have been using on the wharves to run checks on customs. One of them wants to talk to someone about the Comos, so they have handballed him to us,' said Purchas.

Bullock and Purchas shook his hand and he watched them walk off. Whatever their critics said, the pair possessed a fearsome work ethic. They never stopped.

James opened his contact book and found the name he was looking for, New Zealand Detective Superintendent Bruce Goode.

The New Zealanders would jump at a good drug op in the Pacific, he thought, as he dialled the number. Of course, even if they agreed to help, there was no guarantee, especially in a country like Tonga, that they would make the bust. As the phone began to ring, he felt a ripple of excitement pass through him.

'Hello?'

Bilal

Breathe, Bilal, *breathe.* His left leg was shaking uncontrollably under the table, his chest rising in short, sharp bursts. The air was barely reaching his lungs. He had to breathe ... needed to breathe. He felt a strange taste in his mouth and stuck his finger on his tongue. His saliva was tinged red. Fuck it. He must have bitten his tongue.

Breathe, Bilal! *Breathe*, you moron, *breathe*. He laid his head on the table, pressing his cheek against the cool, smooth plastic, willing it to swallow him up.

When he'd first seen the lights streaking blue and red through the rain, he hadn't thought much of it. It had to have been another car, another driver, they were after. Even when the unmarked sedan had pulled right up on his tail, his only thought had been that he must have been speeding. He'd sworn at himself, pulled out his wallet and concentrated on appearing genuine and law-abiding.

In the side mirror, he'd been surprised to see the man who'd approached his door wearing a suit, rather than a police uniform. He'd looked like a television detective. When he'd reached the window, he had leaned against the doorframe and smiled at him, an insidious, smug smile, and said the phrase that, ever since, had replayed in an endless loop in his head.

'You must be the famous cook.'

He felt his stomach drop into a deep pit, his thoughts swinging from a desire to disappear into nothing to venomous hatred. Since then, the focus of his rage had switched from Waz to himself. How the fuck could he have been so stupid? Did he really need the money? People like him—small wimpy nothings with no gangster friends—get bashed in jail. And worse.

Breathe, Bilal, *breathe*, he repeated to himself, as he ground his cheekbone into the table.

He sat up with a start as the door opened and two suited men walked in. He thought he heard them say their names, and that they were from the Australian Crime Commission, but the words were a blur.

'Bilal?'

One of them, a tall, skinny man with a gravelly British accent, was staring at him strangely. 'Have you been listening to me, Bilal?'

He shook his head. 'C-c-c-c-c-can I have a-a-a-a-a glass of w-w-w-water?' His stutter had returned with full force and he made himself concentrate. 'And do you th-th-thi-think I can call my w-w-w-wife?'

The skinny guy smiled kindly at him, but he wondered how genuine it was.

'Of course you can, Bilal. Does your wife know you are here?'

He felt the knot in his stomach tighten as he pondered the question. She had no idea about any of it: the cook, the favours on the port for her idiotic second cousin, the reason he'd got that stupid tattoo for free. 'They, I m-m-m-mean my w-w-w-wife and my boys, they don't know nothing. I mean … I mean … one's just been born.' Every word took effort to spit out, and it was getting harder to breathe.

The skinny man smiled at him again, and as Bilal averted his eyes, he noticed the larger man looking at him with what looked like mild contempt. He would keep his eyes on the skinny man.

'What is your n-n-name again?' At least the stutter seemed to be fading, he thought.

'I'm Mike. Listen, Bilal. You are here voluntarily and are welcome to go whenever you want. The NSW police have already questioned you in connection to a drug lab, and they have released you, pending further investigation and your ongoing cooperation. But you also told them you had some information about what goes on at your work and what you know about bikies, and that is why we are here.'

'My work?'

'Yep. The ports. You remember what you told the state police?'

He knew what the skinny man was talking about. 'You help us, maybe we can see if we can help you,' he had been told by a detective from the drug squad. But it wasn't just about him. Who would look after his family when he was locked up? It was Waz's fucking fault anyhow. The idiot had roped him into this mess. So, over the course of a few hours, he had told the state police everything he knew about Waz. He turned his attention back to the skinny man, who was leaning back in his chair, waiting for him to speak.

'What do you w-w-w-want to know, and how is it going to help me get out of th-th-th …' his voice trailed off, partly defeated by the stutter and partly by the feeling that the corners of his lips were turning downwards. His eyes were watering. He squeezed them shut, tightly. *Breathe*, Bilal. He heard the sound of a glass of water being pushed across the table and opened his eyes.

'If you can help us out, we will have a talk to the NSW police. I think you'll agree you'd rather be a witness than a suspect.'

A witness. A fucking witness. He scrunched his eyes tightly again and wiped his sleeve across his face. He knew what they called witnesses in prison and in the underworld. They called them dogs.

'You should think of your family. If you want to help them, you should help us,' the skinny man continued. The other man still said nothing.

'They wanted me to access the c-c-c-consignment tracking databases and call a mate in c-c-c-customs to see if various ships and containers they had coming in were hot,' he said.

'Hot? You mean targeted for examination by customs?'

He nodded.

'When you say "they", who do you mean?' asked the larger man.

He closed his eyes again, breathed in deeply and focused on speaking slowly. He wouldn't stutter again, not if it killed him. 'Bikies. My cousin is a junior member of a bikie club. I don't know who he was dealing with, and I don't know who was calling me for the info at the ports. I just occasionally got a call from a private number asking for info about whether customs was searching a ship or container. They would call back an hour or two later and get what they wanted. If it was hot, they'd leave it alone.'

'How many times?' The bigger man seemed to have taken over.

'A few times. It only happened once or twice.'

'And what did you tell them?'

'That customs were interested. That is all I knew and all I said. Listen … they don't need me. They have enough friends on the wharves already.' He realised neither man was taking down any notes and wondered whether he was being taped.

'Who are their friends?'

They peppered him with questions for what felt like another hour, although he couldn't be sure. They asked him about corruption on the waterfront, the ease with which people could sneak out contraband and leak information, and the way wharfies sidestepped the government's maritime security identity card system. Occasionally, they looked surprised by what he knew, but mostly their faces betrayed nothing.

As the time dragged on, he began to worry that his wife would be calling around, trying to find out where he was. She might even call Waz. He couldn't have his family getting involved.

The skinny guy went to ask another question but he shook his head. 'No more. I have said enough.' He was surprised at the firmness with which the words had come out of his mouth. He could tell the two men were also surprised.

The skinny man cleared his throat. 'Fair enough, Bilal. You've been here long enough. But just one more thing. Have you seen these men before?'

He passed four photographs over the table; three were of guys who looked Arabic or Turkish, and one was of an Asian.

'Two of them are familiar, but I don't know where from.'

'Think hard, Bilal.'

As he looked at the man's face, he remembered the rock of the boat.

'I have seen these two only once. They're bikies. They were at a booze-up in the harbour with a few others. It was ages ago. My cousin took me there, but I didn't stay for long. I don't know their names, but one of them is apparently loaded. Or at least that's what Waz said.'

The skinny man stood up, followed by the larger man.

'We can get someone to drop you home, Bilal.' The skinny man paused. 'Don't worry. We'll take you from the garage in an unmarked car. No one will know that you have been here.'

'Can I ask you a question?'

The skinny man nodded.

'What happens now?'

The skinny man smiled reassuringly. 'That's up to the NSW police. But you are done with us.' He smiled again, and handed him a business card.

'Just make sure to call me if you need to. You never know when you might need a friend.'

Hutchins

Hutchins fixed his gaze on the painting on the wall of his Senate office. He once regarded it warily, but it was growing on him. It depicted the abstract shape of a figure behind a desk. The features weren't defined, but the figure's intent was becoming clearer to him the more he looked. It seemed to radiate a quiet yet unmistakable power that extended well beyond its desk.

If only it was that easy, he thought. The rumblings about Rudd's leadership were increasing as the Prime Minister blundered his way through the mounting scandals, including the millions blown on infrastructure projects. But it wasn't just the waste. It was the way Rudd was handling the issues, his arrogance and erratic micro-management. Hutchins had found himself becoming more deeply involved in the backroom whisperings, while trying to push ahead with his set tasks, but even they were being thwarted by politics.

He'd come tantalisingly close to getting support for unexplained wealth laws that police told his committee could actually work. He and fellow committee member Chris Hayes had even had a win against cautious senior bureaucrats in the Attorney-General's department by lobbying the Attorney-General himself, Robert McClelland. They had argued forcefully for the laws to be made stronger so policing agencies could more easily seize the suspected proceeds of drug trafficking and other crimes.

McClelland had backed them, but as word of the committee's intentions filtered through parliament, a trio of senior Liberal Party politicians had intervened. He'd nicknamed them 'the corporate lawyers'. They had legal backgrounds but had probably never spoken to an organised crime cop and knew nothing of the challenges they faced. One of the Liberal committee members, Stephen Parry, had quietly told him that it was this trio who'd ensured the proposed laws were fatally weakened by the time they left the Liberal Party room.

Despite all their work—committee meeting after meeting—there was now a distinct possibility that when the laws were passed in a few months, they wouldn't work. They would effectively be asset-seizure laws that still enabled crime bosses to retain their assets.

Had their trip counted for anything? The anti-mafia police in Italy had not prevaricated: the modern organised crime figure didn't care about prison. They could run their empires from inside. But strip them of their assets, and you could drain their power. Without money, they couldn't pay for muscle, defence lawyers, crooked accountants or money launderers.

And wharf workers. That was shaping as yet another battlefront. More and more senior police were beating a path to the committee's door to warn of the entrenched pockets of organised crime at the nation's major ports. Some said authorities were seizing less than 10 percent of drugs coming over the sea borders and that known organised crime figures had been given government-issued maritime identity cards. 'It's no longer a few crates of whisky, Senator. It is tonnes and tonnes of drugs,' one policeman had recently told him.

But what could the committee do? The transport minister's office didn't want to annoy the Maritime Union or the big shipping companies with more onerous security measures. Politics would surely kill off any fresh attempt to strengthen the laws.

And maybe it wasn't a fight *he* should be picking. His wife had told him she wanted to move back to Victoria and run for office, and there was talk in the party of a safe seat. It would be months away, but if she went for it, it would mean his own political career was over. He could hardly be a Senator for New South Wales living in Melbourne.

His eyes turned again to the painting on his wall. Bugger it. There was bark in the old dog yet. The committee could call an inquiry into organised crime on the waterfront and test the claims that the government was failing to deal with it. To hell with the politics. The committee's police faction would support it, as would those Libs who sniffed a chance to kick a union. An inquiry would annoy more than a few senior ministers on his own side, but it would keep the committee front and centre, tackling an issue that mattered.

Even if Rudd was slowly imploding.

Ayik

Ayik sat on the edge of his hotel bed, studying his laptop, flipping between Facebook and an online news article downloaded days before. Shit had gone awry and it needed settling.

> **Tonga police bust large seizure of drugs**
> The head of Tonga's police force says the country's biggest seizure of suspected illicit substances shows border controls must be tightened.
>
> Commander Chris Kelley says police raided two homes in Nuku'alofa earlier this week and found what they believe to be a quantity of methamphetamine of such magnitude that it must have been destined for overseas.
>
> The commander says he's determined to stop drug traffickers getting a foothold in Tonga. 'But of course these people often have very large sums of money and access to a lot for resources so it's really up to us to tighten a range of procedures.'

He'd read the article dozens of times. The home raided must have belonged to the customs officer their Tongan contacts had arranged to store the gear at upon its return. What was the point of paying these uniformed dogs if they got picked up anyway? It had to be a New Zealand police force job. Kelley was a New Zealander and the Tongan authorities wouldn't have been able to pull it off by themselves.

The Korean cutie was now humming to herself in the shower. He wished she'd shut up. Stuff it. He needed to go for a walk, get some air and clear his head. For days now, he'd been sweating on a message from Wu. A week or so ago, his friend had let him know he was in some sort of trouble, and that the bosses, the *dai los* from Hong Kong or China, were holding him over the mess in Tonga. He checked his phone again. Nothing. It wasn't a good sign.

He walked out of the lobby and fell in behind a group of Arabic businessmen, their white robes flowing grandly as they walked towards the Dubai Convention Center. Several of them carried briefcases and had mobile phones plugged into their ears. One of them turned to him and smiled. '*Assalamu alaikum.*'

'*Wa alaikum assalam,*' he answered, before dropping back 20 metres behind the men, checking his phone as he walked. Still nothing from Hong Kong. Wu hadn't been explicit, but the quaver in his voice had said enough.

On the overpass, he stopped, watching the robed businessmen disappear. Thin skyscrapers dotted the sky, towers of metal and glass shimmering in testament to unbridled commerce. He loved Dubai almost as much as he loved Hong Kong. And as much as he hated Tonga.

It was not unreasonable for the Chinese to hold suspicions about Tonga, and it was hard not to respect the way they did business. If an investment went bad, they sought to cover it. If money couldn't be found, they sought blood. Soon enough, people learnt to pay. It was never personal, only business.

The Chinese believed that the Tongans who were in on the deal may have doublecrossed them and, with the help of some corrupt Tongan police, arranged for the bust to take place.

He went over the deal again, through the things that didn't add up. A few weeks before, he had ordered Will to send a runner to Tonga to check they weren't being doublecrossed. Wu had also sent an envoy on the orders of the Chinese bosses. The reports back suggested the gear was being safely held and that a second attempt at an import was feasible. They had enough friends on the wharf and among the cops in both countries to move the gear safely and be notified if things got hot. And yet the customs officer getting paid to safeguard their gear was now banged up in a Tongan jail.

It wasn't just the Chinese who were smelling blood. Some of the boys also believed the Tongans had cheated them or, at the very least, failed to live up to their word. He'd already talked down one hit squad, reasoning that murder was bad for business. What was it with guys who thought everything could be sorted with a Glock? Look at the bikie war and the airport fiasco, he'd told the boys. Wasting a few Tongans wouldn't help anyone.

And look at Erkan. His own blood was now paying a price. Erkan had been banged up for over five months, and doing his jail time hard. The last time Ayik had visited him, Erkan looked like he had aged five years. His head was shaved and he had offered up only a weak smile when they had chatted in the glass box.

'There is nothing to do here but pump iron. Depending on how long I get, I'll be as big as you when I'm out.'

Depending on how long I get. Ayik hadn't said anything at the time, but those words had stayed in his head. The guns would get him at least two years, the gear another two. Erkan would be twenty-five by the time he was out.

A red Ferrari caught his eye as it shot under the underpass. He tried to snap it on his phone, but it moved too fast. He loved the way low-riders glided, sleek and sexy. He was due an upgrade.

Still nothing from Wu. Maybe they'd already cut him up.

Even after they had sent the envoys to Tonga, the Chinese hadn't seemed convinced. It was partly his fault. He hadn't made it clear enough to Will that they needed to weigh the drugs. The Chinese suspected that one of the Tongans had been savvy enough to dilute the gear before arranging for it to be seized, keeping the rest. They obviously hadn't met the Tongans. Unbelievably, once in Tonga, nobody could source a reliable set of scales. The industrious, paranoid Chinese didn't buy the fact that, even in a shithole like Tonga, you couldn't find a decent set of scales. Having failed to find scales themselves, they were now waiting on the police to weigh the gear. But what if the cops had a shitty set of scales? If the weight of the seizure didn't marry with the weight of their original import, suspicions would grow. He'd have to fish Wu out of Hong Kong harbour.

He thought back to what Wu had once told him. 'The difference between *dai los* and and bikie bosses is that the Australian bikies just kill those they fall out with. The *dai los* will kill someone's whole family and leave their target alive to mourn. Then they'll do him.'

Whooosh. Another sports car flew beneath him.

Re-entering the foyer of the Monarch, he ignored the suited concierge, an Indian who offered a half bow as he strode past, and resolved to extricate Wu from this mess. They would get the Tongans to use their contacts on the island to obtain the police investigation documents, which would prove the bust was genuine.

He flinched as his phone vibrated. Finally. He clenched his teeth as he read the message. It was lengthy and badly spelled. He guessed it had been written in a rush and under pressure. The Chinese wanted $1 million placed in trust until they corroborated that the loss in Tonga was genuine. When they were satisfied, they would pocket an amount to cover their loss and return the rest.

The phone vibrated again as another text landed: 'Need 400K. PLEASE.' Wu must have been 400 grand short. He frowned. He didn't have that sort of coin lying around. Wu was rapidly becoming a business liability. He could dip into the funds he had promised Will for the karaoke club, but it wouldn't be the full amount. He'd have to negotiate it down. They would understand. They were businessmen after all. And he could draw a line in the sand. He needed to get back to making money. Some of the gear coming in could still be distributed throughout Australia. They would just have to come up with a smarter way to do it. The team was strengthening interstate, and Daux was planning to recruit more soldiers. With the local economy still strong, they could sell at a premium. It would be their own gold mine.

The boys were building a base in Victoria, with a new local clubhouse, president and treasurer.

He would stay off the phones, and keep to the codes if he needed to speak. And he'd get the club to order their intelligence man to do a thorough search of what the police currently held on him. He'd keep looking ahead. Tonga was old news.

His first priority involved restoring face with the Chinese once he'd dealt with the Wu problem. He'd see about giving them access to the coke they wanted. And he'd …

Ayik suddenly spun around and eyed the concierge. India. He'd first thought of it months ago. It was badly policed, and had dirtcheap labour and a booming pharmaceutical industry. He grinned. Unlike Tonga, India was full of possibilities. And he wouldn't be relying on Wu. He'd float the plan directly with the Chinese.

He felt better as he slid his card into his hotel room door. The Korean was lying on the silk sheets—pale, naked, inviting. He shut the door behind him. It was dark outside and the lights from Dubai's skyscrapers twinkled through the large window. He was in a strange city, with a new girl, but he felt completely at home.

Purchas

Whoosh. Purchas suppressed the urge to strike the ball on the full. Moving his head sideways as it whistled past, he let it bounce off the back wall before scooping it up and flicking it into the corner to glance off both walls and drop dead. He smiled at his opponent who, dripping in sweat, smiled weakly back.

'Nice shot, Mike,' the younger man said.

He nodded, quietly buoyed that at sixty-two he could still hold his own. He'd always loved squash. It was all about angles and picking out weaknesses and opportunities. A slower, older player could still win, as long as they controlled the centre of the court and exploited their opponent's weaknesses.

Whoosh. This time he hit the ball so it hugged the left wall and dropped dead in the back corner.

'For God's sake, Mike. Give me a break!'

Grinning again at his sparring partner, he wiped the sweat off his racket handle and set up his next serve. The ball ricocheted off the side wall. He ducked his head again, this time losing the point, his attention momentarily diverted by the events of the last few days and what was still to come.

The games at the commission continued. Every day, a new angle had to be played. Under Lawler, the push to divide Operation Dayu into its various parts and send them to new managers was progressing: High Risk Funds was off to analytics; Hoffmann to the High Risk Crime Group; Agrale to Financial Crimes. On the operational front, the commission was slowly retreating as the federal police moved increasingly into the organised crime space. For years, the ACC had juggled its roles as a national intelligence creation and coordination agency *and* as a long-term operations agency.

But there were increasing rumblings among some of the managers about the need to favour intelligence above long-term operations. It was also personal. One manager had told he and Bullock outright that they had a 'disproportionate influence' in the agency. They, as well as James, were being encouraged to 'remake their corporate images'. The suggestion was worthy of his favourite one-liner: they were police, not bureaucrats.

He lunged forward, picking the ball up on the second bounce. 'Bugger,' he swore, before losing a third point, then a fourth. If the momentum turned against you in a game of squash, you either dug in or were gone. He always dug in. And for that you needed mental toughness, discipline. This time he returned the serve on the full, whipping it down at such an angle that it skidded back towards his opponent, making it impossible to play.

Ayik was disciplined. Impressively so. The commission was swimming in intelligence, but there was little hard evidence linking

Ayik to the armoury at his nephew's house or the light plane bust. It was mostly Will who'd been implicated in the sniffer-dog bust.

Ayik's assets, bank transfers, international travel and associates all pointed to the same thing, but it wasn't proof. Tonga was the first time they'd started to get close to building a circumstantial case: the coded text messages, the activity in Will's apartment, and the references on paperwork and in conversations to the times and ports that fitted the travel schedule of the *Capitaine Tasman*.

The Hoffman team had been digging around Kelly Edmonds, one of the drug mules arrested at the airport, and had discovered that he had previously travelled to South Africa and, according to customs records, returned with two bottles of red wine in his luggage. When they made the bust in Tonga, the New Zealand police discovered the drugs hidden in South African red wine casks. It was almost certainly from the same load.

They'd also confirmed that customs had searched the *Capitaine Tasman* when it had docked in Melbourne, spooking a crew member, who apparently ran over a customs officer in a car. It explained why the crew had kept the gear on board; the Tongans must have got a tip-off or encountered some other sign to spook them, something that suggested that they were being targeted.

To make a case against Ayik stick they needed more than a couple of circumstantial conspiracy charges that any experienced barrister would readily devour.

Whoosh. He played the same return that had back-footed his opponent before. Once you got the feel of a player, you could increase the chances of anticipating their next move. You then had to keep your own game disciplined and keep the centre ground, even if you were out of steam.

They needed to keep Ayik and his crew relaxed, unaware of any heat, and push on with existing and future ventures. All the while, Hoffman would tighten the net.

Because of the minimal resources, Bullock and the techs were replacing surveillance crews by plugging into the CCTV cameras around Chinatown and World Square. Phone taps were running hot, but they lacked the ears to listen, so they'd begun using investigators from other agencies in return for giving the agencies the inside running on upcoming drug busts.

Bringing in state police increased the need for him to attend to something that had been playing on his mind for months. He was almost certain that someone with access to the lower-level intelligence Operation Hoffman was sending to other agencies was leaking it to the Comancheros. He had to find the arsehole poisoning them and give him a dose of his own medicine.

He glanced at his squash opponent, who was waiting for the next missile to be launched. This time he looped a gentle serve, positioning the ball so it hugged the wall. It was designed to lure him in to take the shot on the full. It worked. The younger man jammed his racket against the wall and missed the ball.

That's what he had to do. The leaker was most likely waiting for the next Comanchero intelligence report to be lodged on a state police database. The ACC could serve up some tantalising, but false, information reports detailing the suspect conduct of Ayik and his Como associates. Something around Tonga would be perfect. The reports would be electronically tagged, so any official who accessed it would be covertly recorded.

If any chatter about what was in the report appeared over intercepted phone lines, they could immediately target any police official who had accessed the false intelligence reports. With his plan locked away in his mind, he caught his breath and served for the game.

'Shit. Nice serve, Mike. Play again?'

'I'm done,' he said panting. He hated to concede it, yet there were limits to what an older player could do. 'Besides, I have to get to a meeting. We'll hit again soon.'

He felt his suit shirt sticking against the sweat left on his skin as he drove towards the hotel where the meeting was taking place. His old source had finally come through about his request for a meeting. He had flown in from Asia and was bringing a friend with him.

'He is a retired gentleman with some scores to settle,' his source had said, matter of factly.

When he was about twenty minutes away from the hotel, he pulled over into an emergency lane and called Vikingsson. The analyst had already sent him Operation Dayu's wishlist of questions, things that needed filling in, but he wanted Vikingsson's take on the highest priority topics because the meeting could be short.

'Shit … I mean, where do I start, Mike? There is so much we don't know.'

'You've got two minutes to tell me what you most want asked. Think, Patrick. Think!'

Vikingsson talked for the next five minutes, barely catching breath as questions competed to leave his mouth. Why was the triad organisation receiving so much of Australia's drug money? Who was truly controlling the multinational businesses in Hong Kong, Macau, Vietnam and Cambodia, in which most of the narco-dollars were being invested?

'Slow down Patrick,' he said, struggling to scrawl down notes.

The analyst ignored him. What was the significance of the yakuza funeral in Japan? And who owned the Asian casinos laundering millions in dirty cash? And Ayik. Don't forget Ayik.

'Okay, Patrick. I have to get going.'

'And Mike?'

'For Christ's sake, Patrick. I have to …'

'Good luck, Mike. I just wanted to wish you good luck.'

The analyst hung up before he had a chance to respond. He turned off his phones and eased the car back onto the freeway, glancing back to see if any vehicles had stopped behind him. The road was clear. A few blocks from the hotel, he drove into a long road that turned into a cul de sac and waited. The street was quiet and stayed so. He then gunned the car straight to the hotel. He knew he was being paranoid, but he didn't want to take any risks. When it came to sources, the smallest leak could be fatal.

He walked straight to reception, checking into a suite under a false name, headed to his room and waited. And waited. As the minutes ticked by, he fought his need to turn his phone on. He began pacing the room, full of nervous energy. He hated being stood up.

The stench of his sweat from the squash game began to bother him. His attention moved to a fly moving from the wall to a window and back again. As an hour turned into two, he began to quietly curse. He didn't have two hours to spare, not with Hoffman running hot. 'This is bullshit,' he whispered. As the words left his mouth, he heard a knock on the door.

He opened it to two men. His old source's skin was blotchy and weathered, like a crumpled piece of leather, and his temples were slightly sunken. He'd aged badly in the last eighteen months. Next to him was a fit-looking Asian man who could be anywhere between fifty and seventy. He introduced himself to the stranger and shook the hand of his old source, telling him he looked well.

'Ha! We're both old men now. More wisdom than beauty.'

He smiled, withholding the urge to remark that his source's beauty, if it was ever there at all, was long ago lapped by his wisdom.

The trio drank tea and filled the air with meaningless banter until, in an effort to cut to the chase, Purchas led into the reason for the meeting. He started with some old history—Sydney crime bosses Duncan Lam Sak Cheung and Ly Vi Hung—before moving onto the flow of money to certain Asian businesses, and the unexpected appearance of bikies in the triad crime scene.

'I want to know what I am dealing with.'

His source nodded, frowning.

'You might be surprised at how much you know already,' the source said. His friend said nothing.

He studied his source's gnarled face. Something was wrong with the old man, but he couldn't tell what it was.

'Do you like to drink some more tea, Mike? We should drink some tea.'

He smiled and his source smiled back, his crooked teeth emerging like sentinels guarding a horrible cave. Purchas was used to this dance. When you had leverage, something hard and fast to hold over a person, you could make them talk. With no leverage, a source made you listen.

'Let me call up some tea. It is good to catch up.'

His source nodded encouragingly towards his friend, who responded by speaking softly, causing Purchas to lean forward.

'The people you speak about in Asia are like a …' he hesitated, speaking in Mandarin before returning to English '… like a global network … an international conglomerate.'

'There are the top bosses, the *Ong Ngoai*, and then those underneath. It has changed since I was close to some of them, but when I was, they had people everywhere—Asia, America, Europe. Everywhere. Just like after Hong Kong, when many families moved to Canada and Los Angeles, or to Sydney or Melbourne or London. The *Ong Ngoai* spread as well. There were more than twenty senior seats at last count.'

Purchas had heard the term *'Ong Ngoai'* whispered before by informers or on intercepted phones. In Vietnamese, an *ong ngoai* was a grandfather, but some old Chinese crooks had used the term as well.

'What about Australia?'

His source's friend smiled. 'Of course. The market here is small but very lucrative. They have senior men here, too, but no seats. The two you speak of, Dai Lo Cheung and Dai Lo Hung, are first contact distributors. Maybe they were seats once, but no more. Those who ride the bikes are simply wholesalers.' Without breaking eye contact, Purchas slipped a small notebook out of his pocket and began taking notes. 'You must know that it is all business nowadays. The senior people have interests in casinos, construction, governments, the military. For them, product is just another business.'

He kept scrawling, noting how the man used the word 'product' instead of drugs. 'What about Vietnam? We know that people in the government have been moving some of the profit from product out of the country or into government-supported projects.'

The man nodded. 'In Vietnam, there are some relatives of a government minister who control the money in and out.'

'What about the bikies? Why use them? Aren't they too risky?'

The man shrugged. 'The *Ong Ngoai* have people who take contracts off them to move certain product. If you have the ability to efficiently deliver on your contract, then you are offered more. These men are efficient. Same as in Canada. There are many who help out, offer their services, do business. It is everywhere and nowhere. That is how the *Ong Ngoai* operates.'

'And Japan?'

He noted the surprise register on the man's face, along with that of his now silent old source.

'Why do you say Japan?'

A knock at the door interrupted the conversation. As the old source stiffened, he instinctively reached for his side, before remembering that he was unarmed.

'Tea?'

It was room service. He watched the old man's shoulders drop, his body relax. When the room service attendant had left, his source's friend, who hadn't flinched, resumed speaking as if there had been no interruption.

'Before we talk any more, I need to see if you are interested in something. It is a job. There are some people I know who are looking to move money. My friend tells me you know of a laundry? These people need one. I would like to see them put out of business.'

Purchas nodded, but said nothing. Few sources gave information up without seeking something for themselves. The dance continues, he thought. He would need to reopen the ACC's covert laundry, a task that would not happen easily, not in the new regime. He and Bullock would need to guarantee arrests.

He tried again, 'And Japan?'

The friend looked at him curiously, and asked, 'What do you know about Japan?'

Purchas thought back to Vikingsson's work, and the yakuza boss gunned down in Tokyo. He needed to bluff, pretend he knew more than he did.

'We know about the funeral in Tokyo in 2007.'

The man appeared to plunge deeply into thought for just an instant, as if weighing his next move. 'I don't know much about that, I only know what I hear. They say some bosses went to mourn and to rearrange the seats the Yakuza control with the *Ong Ngoai*. Death means new bosses and new seats. The Japanese may have wanted another of their own rather than a dai lo.'

'And who took the seat from the dead man?'

'I don't know. There are some things that very few people know. And some things people who know will never say. It is time to go.'

He noticed the man he had been talking to, his source's companion, hadn't touched his tea. Purchas watched him step lightly, deftly to the door, followed by the older man. It would evidently be a quick goodbye. Before he left the room, his old source turned around and gently grabbed his arm and said, 'Everything's changing, Mike.' His hand was shaking and his face was still drained of colour. Purchas realised he was sick. Before he could say anything, the source passed him a piece of folded paper. 'You want to know where some of the *Ong Ngoai* money goes, Mike? You follow this down. You do it for me, eh?' Flashing a final weak smile, he walked out of the door and disappeared down the corridor, following his companion.

When the two men had turned the corner, Purchas unfolded the paper that had been thrust into his hands. It was a news article from an Asian wire service announcing that a new multi million-dollar casino cruise ship was to be launched on the Mekong River, between the Cambodia and Vietnam border. He read it again before dialling Vikingsson's number.

Welch

Sitting in the back of the Mini Minor as it sped through Sydney's outer suburbs, Welch wondered what someone peering in would think. Clutching the steering wheel was a bikie, whose vast frame and persona was markedly, ridiculously, at odds with the tiny vehicle he controlled. Next to him sat Margaret Lawson, a tall, attractive public relations consultant with auburn hair spilling onto her shoulders. She was checking her watch to ensure they didn't miss the start of the meeting.

'We're almost there,' the bikie growled, gunning the Mini into a side street and pulling up outside a small church hall in Penrith.

Stepping out, he immediately regretted wearing his Armani suit. The tattooed, thickset men milling outside the church hall were all wearing leather cuts and patches over flannelette or black T-shirts. Most had short hair or shaved heads, but a couple had long, scraggly plumages. It looked like a casting call for a *Mad Max* film.

Moving towards a group of familiar bikies, he heard someone mutter, 'Nice suit, poofta.' He picked a bikie whose face he recognised, stretching out his hand as he neared him. 'G'day mate. Dylan. Dylan from the *Sydney Morning Herald*'.

The bikie eyed him warily, two lines of cigarette smoke slowly snaking out of his nostrils as he clasped his hand. 'Better move inside,' he said. 'Meetin's about to start.'

He walked behind Lawson as she strode into the hall and wondered how a public relations consultant from Cole Lawson Communications, a firm run by a former spokesman for foreign minister Alexander Downer, had ended up advising the United Motorcycle Council. As he sat down next to her near the back of the hall, she whispered, 'You know, for all they cop in the media, some of these guys are actually okay.'

'Some of them, maybe,' he whispered back. 'But I can see two men right now who've murdered people.' Lawson's brow arched with surprise. Pulling out his notebook, Welch scanned the room: a sign near the door read, 'In case of an emergency, dial 000.' Next to it, someone had written, 'Fellowship hall, drop-in centre, play group'. He smiled and scrawled. It would make for good copy.

In the middle of the hall there was a large rectangle comprising foldable tables covered in empty pizza boxes and homebrand soft drink cans. Around it sat the members of the council, a group of bikies that had formed after the airport bashing and which represented twelve of the state's twenty-one outlaw motorcycle gangs, along with God's Squad and the Vietnam Veterans.

Across the hall from him sat Mark 'Ferret' Moroney the sergeant-at-arms of the Finks' Blacktown chapter, who was seated at the head of the rectangle. 'I declare this political meeting open,' he told the room in his throaty, ocker accent.

Welch felt the eyes of the other bikies fix on him, some with amusement, others with mild distaste, as Ferret explained that the tasty piece of jailbait wearing the suit was from the media and there to expose the government and police's unjust campaign against outlaw clubs. He smiled and waited for Ferret to seize back attention.

The bikie liked being looked at, as long as it was on his terms. He had recently complained to the *Sydney Morning Herald* that a photo the newspaper had published of his oration at the National Press Club had made him look crazy. As Welch studied him now, he wondered why Ferret had been so upset. He did look sort of crazy. The bikie's bald head glistened, his arms were wrapped in dense tattoos, and his impossibly small leather vest was straining to contain his bulging torso. The word 'unforgiven' was etched in permanent ink on his neck.

Still, he wasn't a half-bad speaker. Six months ago, as police and politicians were ramping up their zero-tolerance, anti-bikie campaign, some of the men in the room would have jumped at the slightest chance to lay a glove on each other, or worse. Now they were part of a supposed peace dialogue, a political force to confront the cops and politicians, complete with a public relations consultant. Lawson had already urged the bikies in the room to utilise social media. 'We've already got about 150 people on Twitter, so if any of you aren't, can you join?' He had scrawled down the quote, thinking how it underlined what the meeting, and the council itself, was partly about: a well-planned media assault aimed at drumming up public support.

It was a carbon copy of what had happened when bikie violence had erupted overseas. The warring groups had formed peace councils and engaged the media, pushing the line about a few bad apples and overzealous policing and politicking. Then the bikies running drugs had got back to business.

Still, at least the shootings in Sydney had temporarily ceased. If the council could halt the violence, the media and political heat would die off and the police resources would follow.

Welch glanced at the two Comancheros sitting in the group. It was their club that was responsible for much of the police crackdown, given its members' alleged role in the airport bashing and suspected hand in the subsequent shootings. They both looked bored. He guessed they were more than likely club nobodies, junior members enlisted to show up and display the club emblem.

Word was, the Comos were still expanding. He was still digging around, trying to find out how they were financing their push into Western Australia and Victoria. He'd heard about new interstate presidents and the fact that the Comos were linked to a big weapons seizure and a series of drug flights that had ended with a runner's arrest at Jandakot airport in March 2008. Yet money was still pouring in, bringing fresh recruits and clubhouses.

While Daux and Hawi strutted around as the face of the club, the real drivers were the earners. He'd thought back to the name he'd been told months before. 'Big Hux.' The name was still being bandied about, but he knew little else.

He was certain of one thing: the Comos' expansion suggested the wave of minor arrests and the thundering of politicians about banning bikie thugs 'who terrorise our streets' were failing to have any real, long-term impact.

Lawson nudged him. 'Ferret wants us out of here. They are starting a private session.'

Oh, what he would give to stay.

It was darker and colder outside than when he'd entered. A row of glittering Harleys stood like silent, menacing sentinels. Passing them, he anticipated the newsdesk's reaction to tonight's events: 'You got any good pics, mate?' Blood and colour always seemed to triumph over analysis.

The bikies story was rapidly becoming old news. Maybe it was time to think of a new challenge, a way of reinventing himself and revitalising the organised crime beat. Why not take his police round national?

'Hey, buddy?'

The bikie who drove the Mini was grinning at him. 'You want to buy me a feed?

Part 5
April 2010 – July 2011

April 2010 – July 2011

James

He knew something had happened as soon as Andrew Lee tapped on his desk. The undercover officer looked drained. Six hours before, and despite the commission's focus on Ayik sucking up almost all of its resources, Purchas and Bullock had reactivated the covert laundry for the first time in a year. They'd argued it was warranted because of new intelligence and targeting opportunities. As Vikingsson had argued, it was time to slip back into the river of slime.

If only it was that easy, he thought as Lee dragged over a chair and slumped into it. Restarting the laundry was a major feat, involving fresh legal approvals and a guarantee that any money they moved would prevent significant criminal activity. His own role had been relatively minimal, and he'd guessed the undercover was back because he wanted to talk.

'What happened?'

The undercover frowned. 'Just an uncomfortable job, that's all. Not sure I want to keep doing this.'

James said nothing. The onset of uncertainty and self-doubt could be the start of the end for an undercover.

'The thing that makes me stay at it is Mike and Bruce. They are among the best strategists I've ever seen. And Dayu is going somewhere most police have never been before.'

He nodded, not wanting to interrupt, and appreciating again the loyalty that Purchas and Bullock inspired among some of those who worked for them—a loyalty matched only by the duo's capacity to aggravate their bosses, to push an increasingly risk-averse institution to its limits.

Lee hesitated. 'You see, this time was different. I had to go to the money rather than it coming to me. And when I saw the meat cleaver …'

'Slow down, mate. What happened?'

He listened carefully as Lee outlined the operation. In the past, the crooks had come to them, but because they had been forced to shut down their covert laundry, Lee had to visit a house in Melbourne to pick up the money, leaving the surveillance and security team, along with Bullock, outside. It was ironic: their original laundry had been suspended because it was too risky, yet the replacement undercover operation approved by the commission had exposed Lee to more danger than before. After being buzzed into the house, he had walked, unaccompanied, down a long corridor.

'Something didn't feel right. I had the phone line open in my pocket and Bruce was on the other end, so I knew I was covered. But when I entered the room at the end of the passage, it was empty, save for a huge pile of money and a meat cleaver.'

Lee looked down at his shoes.

'It threw me for just a second. A Chinese guy stepped out of a side room and spoke to me in Mandarin. I pointed to the meat cleaver and asked him if he was doing some cooking. He responded by asking me if I was alone. I mean ... of course I was alone. I thought he was fucking with me, seeing if I was a cop or doing a rip-off. So I picked up the meat cleaver and put it in a cupboard under the sink, and told him that if he wanted to have me over for roast duck, he should have asked. If the money wasn't counted and ready to be moved, they could find someone else.'

He'd been right about Lee, thought James. He was a natural undercover. It would be sad to lose him.

'I mean, there was no reason to be worried. Bruce would have been in there in a flash if I'd dropped the code word ... And that long corridor. It wasn't that long at all. Just a corridor.'

'And the money?'

'Half a million. Not a dollar under. I walked it out and the guys scooped me up. They made the arrests a short time later. I mean ... looking back, I see there was nothing to worry about. I was totally covered. It was just that ...'

Lee looked at him, as if waiting for reassurance.

He searched for the right words. Lee didn't need to know about what happened afterwards, years afterwards: the paranoia, the instinct that told you never to sit facing a wall, to drive a block before parking.

And the reoccurring dreams. His involved standing on a touchline watching his son play rugby and feeling a gun pressed against his temple. As the trigger was squeezed, he saw the face of his killer in the flash, a man whose syndicate he'd infiltrated nearly twenty years ago. There was no need to tell Lee any of that.

'You've done well,' he said simply, going on to explain that, in any event, it was highly unlikely the operation would need to be repeated. Lee's reaction suggested that Purchas and Bullock were shielding him from commission politics. He wondered if Lee had heard the whisper that Purchas was likely to be replaced as Sydney operations manager by a younger NSW policeman, or about his own demise. Gregory James, Acting General Manager, Financial Crimes, was now Gregory James, team lawyer. Before Lee had appeared, he'd spent three hours editing affidavits from investigators who struggled to spell, never mind write a legal document.

'The truth is, we never had the eighteen months clear to truly operate Dayu. It has all been fits and starts. If Jock Milroy had stayed on, he would have given us time. Jock worked on the basis of confidence and trust. If I told him we could deliver a result, he'd let us get on with it. He knew we wouldn't let him down. But this regime is very different. Operation Dayu no longer has someone to fight for it. Someone to fight for us.'

As he spoke, he was struck by the thought that maybe it was he, Gregory James, who had failed the Dayu team, failed to sell the long-term plan as well as he could have. Or perhaps the police chiefs and their political masters had never really wanted to know about all the drug importations being missed at the border, the billons in tainted cash flying offshore, the offshore crime bosses protected by corrupt governments. He'd never really know.

'Operation Hoffman will keep running while it offers the promise of some big busts and a few more scalps. Agrale will keep knocking off money remitters. But the international side of things, our attempts to better understand who the major players are, how they operate on an ongoing basis … I am not sure how much further Mike and Bruce can push it.'

He saw Lee's face drop.

'Don't worry, Andrew. You've done a good job, and no one will forget it.'

As the undercover left his office, he reached for the job offer in his drawer and briefly re-examined it. He'd been offered a new start, and it was becoming more enticing as the weeks passed. He'd always spoke of the need to have an exit plan—now he had one. He put it back in the drawer and locked it. It was 5.00 p.m. and he wanted to get home. His son was back on his feet, tossing the footy and rolling in the grass.

Walking through the commission office, he noticed several members of Operation Dayu crowding around Vikingsson's computer. Nearby, the techs were standing in a group talking to Bullock. Something was going down. He guessed they'd made some inroads on the interstate drug-running, or an import, but he fought the urge to walk over. They were no longer his crew and he was never much focused on the drug busts anyway. They were a bonus in Dayu's overall scheme, a necessary way of keeping Canberra onside and thereby keeping the operation alive.

And they'd underlined the need to extend the commission's horizons—horizons that were now closing in.

Will

The steam from the soup dumped in front of him rose into his smiling face. The 300 grand had been recovered from his ex-girlfriend. The thieving bitch had been tracked down in Taiwan or South Korea, or to whatever hole she had disappeared into. He had to give it to her, he thought, gingerly sipping the broth and wincing as the heat bit his tongue—300 grand was a fair pinch. It took balls.

He glared at a couple giggling and necking next to him. The better the noodle soup, the bigger the crowd. This shop heaved like a cattle market, the chatter mixing in with the slurping of patrons squeezed onto cheap plastic stools. It reminded him of home.

He wondered if the Tongan drug bust or the arrests of Erkan and Edmonds had shaken Hux. On the surface, he exuded calmness. As long as they were earning, he seemed okay. And man were they earning; he'd been promised the cash for the fitout, and there was talk of more dough for a second brothel in Canberra.

The only time he'd seen Hux rattled was last December, when some of the bikies had got their hands on a fresh police intelligence report that referred to one of the Tongans they were running with.

Hux had lectured him about loyalty. 'You must always protect me, Will. You understand. *You must always protect me.*'

He'd reassured Hux, but the words had begun echoing in his mind. It was as if Hux knew something he didn't want to share. He knew there was action in India, China and God knows where else, but Hux was only telling him the specifics of things relating directly to his assigned tasks: fax this form here, wire this cash there. He slurped down another mouthful of soup.

You must always protect me. That was okay, but who was going to protect him? The Comos owed him nothing. If he ever got into trouble, real trouble, he would need Hux to stay true. He thought of prison and shuddered, putting down his spoon.

You must always protect me. Was there a threat hiding in Hux's pleas? What would happen if he didn't protect him? He'd never seen Hux get angry. Not violent angry. It was Hux who'd talked down those who had wanted to kill the Tongans. Hux was a businessman, a consummate professional.

He respected Hux as an entrepreneur, just as Hux respected him. Why else would he give him the capital for the club, or put him in charge of running the fresh batches of gear interstate? He'd already made a quiet vow: after the disasters of Tonga, Erkan and Edmonds, future drug runs would go smoothly.

Tipping the bowl up, he poured the last of the liquid stock down his throat.

A friend of his, a dedicated gamer who he regularly murdered online, had agreed to fly interstate to collect the cash once the gear arrived. But the brilliance of the plan lay in the mode of delivery. They purchased second-hand cars and arranged to move them across Australia on a freight train for what looked like resale. Except the panels of the cars would be packed with the gear. If anyone bothered to look, the seller and the buyer could deny all knowledge. It was an old trick pioneered by the Chinese, who stashed heroin in the panels of used rental cars and drove them down the east coast.

He pulled a clean phone out of his pocket and sent Hux a text to what he guessed was an Indian or Pakistani mobile phone: 'Hi Big Girl. Any news?' He chuckled at their code words. They were a good idea in practice, but he often confused them. Jonny meant cash; merc meant kilo; cousin was code for ice. At least that is how he remembered them. Next, he texted his man interstate: 'I have your favourite cousin.'

His next text was about the first Club de Melody promotion. He was achingly close to pulling off the deal. Once that was in the bag and the refit paid for, the club would be on its way.

He paid for his soup and headed for his apartment to get the bag he'd been told to pass to a bikie called Buds near Chinatown. He'd never liked the sound of Buds, or of the words he apparently had tattooed on his back: 'I'd rather be carried by six than judged by twelve.' He'd rather neither. Fucking bikies. Still, it was best not to keep a man like Buds waiting, tattoo or not.

Five minutes later, he was in his apartment checking his Facebook page. Ayik had posted another of his little travel videos. He clicked on it and was met with the beat of 'Troublemaker' and a headline that read 'F1 Abu Dhabi'. The opening scene showed Hux blazing away with a semiautomatic pistol at a firing range, grinning like an idiot. As he watched, he felt a sudden pang of jealousy. Hux swaggered around like a king. Whereas he, Will, was unmistakably the underling, the bitch.

The screen showed Hux posing in front of glistening sports cars; Hux on a yacht overlooking the grand prix; and Hux trackside, with Formula One cars screaming past. The online clip was fucking stupid. Real fucked up. How was it, with all the talk of keeping off the phones, that Hux was posting online films of himself acting like some jetsetting Scarface? If the cops were watching, they'd be barred up like monkeys.

His irritation grew as he walked out of his apartment. He was sick of doing the running around. He had a brothel to keep, a club to promote and several million dollars worth of gear to move across the continent.

Will shook his head. It was he who was going places, even if no other fucker knew it.

Purchas

'We nailed him, Mike.' The senior NSW police officer sounded drained. Good police hated bent cops, Purchas thought. One corrupt arsehole could sour a whole crew's work. 'We got him cold. Gregoriou was a junior state police analyst. We found his fingerprints on our documents sitting in the home of a bikie.'

'Did he take our bait?'

'Swallowed it whole. He printed off several reports. We found one at Gregoriou's house covered in the fingerprints of a bikie associate called Vassily.'

His mind whirred, trying to place the name. 'Is Vassily in property?'

'That's him, Mike.'

Vassily was a real estate agent and aspiring developer who owned a business with the one of the Tukels, brothers who ran with the

Comancheros. The connection through to the corrupt analyst suggested Ayik had almost unfettered access to the NSW police, including the operations involving Hoffman. No wonder he seemed so disciplined. He probably had a near live feed on what the NSW police were doing.

He hung up the phone as Bullock walked over to his desk. He looked like the police officer on the phone had sounded. 'What's up?'

'They've given me a promotion, Mike. But the rumours are true.' Bullock paused. 'They're planning to downgrade you. They're pulling me up the ladder while they get rid of you. They want a new manager in Sydney, although they want you to stick around for a few more months to train up your replacement.'

He watched Bullock waiting awkwardly for his reaction.

The whispers that he would be replaced had grown to a roar ever since he'd been asked to reapply for his own job. Divide and conquer. It was the perfect way to erode his and Bullock's influence. Yet it was more than that. The agency had changed. His views on policing, and the way he expressed them, were no longer welcome. He shook his head.

'I'll be right, Bruce. We knew it was coming. I'm not going to say I won't fight it,' he said, holding down a sudden welling of feeling from his stomach to the edge of his lips, 'because, God knows I'm going to dig in until we get the job done. And when I finally go down, it'll be swinging. Those pricks can't hand my job to someone else without due process. After all the years I've bled for this place. This is typical. They can't even do a fucking job on one of their own properly.'

As Bullock moved to squeeze his shoulder, Purchas brushed him off. 'We still have a job to do. If they think I'm about to be flushed like a morning turd, they're bleedin' barking. The interstate drug runs are red hot and there is the matter of a certain Cambodian cruise ship that adds another piece to the Dayu jigsaw. But first, I've got to clear out of here. Otherwise I'm likely to strangle someone … Preferably, someone from Canberra.'

April 2010 – July 2011

Within minutes, he was in sneakers and a tracksuit, dodging suited businessmen and shoppers, and grinding up the hill behind the commission, where the buildings were replaced by terrace houses and trees. Adrenalin surged through his limbs. Anger followed.

He'd worked at the commission and its predecessor since 1993, slogging away every single day. And now they were screwing him. He'd never even been in the running for his own job. It wasn't only him. Vikingsson was stewing over their failure to confirm his contract extension. James, too, was intimating his time was done. It was the price for resisting the breaking up of Dayu, of pushing back too hard.

Near the top of the hill, he turned to watch the city. Sweat was pouring off him and he could feel the full glare of the summer sun on his neck. A woman walked past with a stroller, followed by a man with a dog. It was all so suburban, so quiet, so … so bland and normal. Was this what was waiting for him?

He stretched out his legs and took off again, down the hill. Fuck it. He'd leave the commission, but he'd make sure they coughed up his due as he went out the door. In the interim, he'd dig in until the job was exhausted. If Operation Dayu was fading away, they could at least land Hoffman.

He prioritised as he ran. Bullock was due to fly interstate, where a local organised crime squad was primed to start a surveillance job on a second-hand car Will was sending from Sydney on a freight train. If it was filled with gear, as Will's coded text messages and loose talk suggested, he was a dead man walking. They just had to find the gear.

He and Bullock had had spent hours strategising how to pull off the job. The techs had hidden a tracking device in the car, and Bullock's close ties with the interstate organised crime squad were paying huge dividends—they'd even arranged for their air wing to provide cover. All that was left to do was to witness the handover to the Comancheros and make the bust. They were achingly close. The same went for some of Ayik's bikie associates. He was offshore, but the net was closing on them all the same.

Near the bottom of the hill, the Crime Commission building loomed into view. Would people start whispering about his departure? Stuff 'em. He headed straight for the showers. Water streamed down his face and back. He savoured the heat. It would be up to Bullock when he was gone, although he wondered how long his colleague would last. A single target was always easier to hit than two.

He dried himself, dressed and strode to the elevator. He moved with purpose. There was work to do, and he still had a few months left. He could at least consolidate the key Dayu findings and do some more digging around the casino cruise ship.

A few minutes later, he was back in the operations room.

'You okay?' Bullock asked

'Like a pig in shit, Bruce. What's top of the list?'

Bullock looked at him curiously, as if he doubted what he'd heard, and then handed him a file.

'Some of Ayik's crew appear to be moving gear in Sydney. We are all over them like the proverbial. And look what we've found floating in cyberspace. Our man has signed up to a Korean online dating service. He's been telling one of his Asian sweethearts that he's in India on business. He's even posted his Indian mobile phone and an email.'

He slapped Bullock on the back.

'You ever been to Mumbai, Bruce? I hope you've got a stern belly.'

Ayik

Small hands clawed at the bottom of his shirt as he walked, a jumble of tiny fingers, stroking and grabbing in quiet desperation. He ignored the children's pleas. 'You have a pen, a dollar, sweets? Where you from, mister? Where you from?' He spotted his driver darting towards him, his dhoti flowing. 'Come, come, sir. Come, come.'

He slid into the cool leather seats, savouring the air-conditioned relief. The place was a wonderful shithole, he thought as the car crawled forwards in the traffic, past peanut sellers and paper boys.

A colourful madness invaded every inch of the city. The only peace he could find was in his hotel and his car.

He noticed a small girl's dirty face at the window, brown eyes big and earnest. She was one of the kids who had followed him from his hotel. He wound down his window and passed over a tattered rupee note. He found himself smiling as she dashed away. Mumbai: the city that was going to make him rich.

The car entered an industrial district, passing a series of dilapidated warehouses and shops, some filled with a few uninterested workers, others a hive of activity. He saw the sign before his driver: Nimbus Pharmaceuticals.

Two scrawny Indian men wearing baggy T-shirts were waiting in the car park. They must be his tour guides, the runners for the Indians in on the venture.

'You Mr Akee?' one of them asked. In five days, not a single person had got his name right.

'That'll do. I'll follow you.'

The inside of the building looked impressive and his tour guides pointed out the huge metal and glass cylinders and drums lining the walls.

He found himself grinning again. The place looked more like a commercial pharmaceutical company than a meth lab. It was perfect. In the corner were several huge barrels, marked 'pseudoephedrine hydrochloride'. He did some quick calculations in his head: 2700 kilos could be converted into 1800 kilos by using the red phosphorus method.

'I have to meet my business partners to finalise the purchase. Will your people have the paperwork ready?' The two men nodded, their eyes glistening with greed. The raw ambition of India pleased him.

An hour later, in the lobby of his central Mumbai hotel, he studied his laptop. That night, he was to meet Wu and several Chinese, European and Indian businessmen. Some of them were the bosses of Wu's own bosses, *dai los* of the *dai los*. It would be an important event, signalling his progression up the ladder.

He had rehearsed his pitch. They could source tonnes of precursors in India, all legal and able to be shipped to safe countries across the world. Other syndicate members had established contacts in Thailand and the Maldives. If the Indian lab became fully operational, their conglomerate could produce hundreds of kilos of high-grade methamphetamine each fortnight. It was only when the precursors were turned into meth that the venture would move from the legal to the illicit. By then, they'd all be far from the action.

He just needed some extra cash to underpin the venture. The latest contract on offer from Hong Kong involved a big shipment. If he could find enough backers to buy into it back in Oz, and offload it quickly, he would have enough capital to underwrite his Indian adventure.

Wu would bring his own money into the business, but it wouldn't be enough. He had distanced himself from Wu ever since Tonga. Wu had had another, smaller shipment seized by the federal police a few weeks ago and some of his Chinese guys binned. Wu's crew was turning toxic; if they talked to the cops, Wu would be identified. It was another reason to keep his distance.

He studied his reflection in the computer screen as he waited for the Korean cupid to load. The tailored shirt and suit looked good. As did his face. It always looked good. He tapped in his password and clicked on the message from an admirer. The photo that appeared depicted a sexy, doll-like Asian honey. Her message was in broken English and he quickly hit reply. He knew how to play these websites in order to score.

> Hello Chaeyoung,
> I am Hakan. You are also my type, Chaeyoung.
>
> Thank you for your reply on Korean Cupid. I was very happy to receive your mail. I was in Hong Kong but I am in India now on a business trip, will be here for another week. It was great that you had help to write your email to me. It shows that you went out of your way for it. That's very nice and sweet. I think your English will get better if you talk to me. Please keep in touch and lets talk on the

phone sometime soon. Take care and I am waiting for your contact, pretty girl. Hakan Joseph Ayik.

He enjoyed the ring of his name written like that. It sounded majestic. He was about to close the screen, but decided to check the *Daily Telegraph* website. His eyes jumped to a news article and his heart quickened.

A HIGH-TECH Sydney drug lab allegedly produced large quantities of ice and other drugs which sold for millions of dollars to line the coffers of bikie gangs. Police raided two properties across Sydney yesterday and subsequently charged four men, alleged to be the 'main players' in the syndicate.

Police say they found 10kg of the drug known as ice with a street value of $5 million, plus firearms, ammunition and 4kg of pseudoephedrine commonly used in the manufacture of illegal drugs.

During the next raid at Rockdale in Sydney's south, police seized firearms, a hunting rifle, eight mobile phones, three drums of ethanol, a money counter and about $80,000 cash. The third alleged offender was arrested at the Rockdale address, while a fourth man was arrested later in Sydney city.

Fuck, fuck, fuck. Rockdale. It had to be some of the boys. Rockdale was their town. Fuck, fuck, fuck. Someone had been sloppy, or there was a dog among them.

He wondered if Daux had been picked up and was about to Facebook him, but thought better of it. He took off his jacket, feeling the lobby's air conditioning attack the sweat on his skin. Something wasn't right back home. He thought of Will. It couldn't be him; he didn't know enough about the lab or what the Comos were up to. It couldn't be.

Think. Staying seated, he flexed his upper body, holding it tense for a few seconds, until his head began to quiver and perspiration dripped from his forehead. He released, breathed out and slid a napkin in front of him.

He jotted down all the busts: Mizza and the light plane back in 2008; his cousin Erkan and the guns and police gear; Kelly Edmonds at the airport; the Tonga job; Wu's recent loss of product; and the seizure of the gear Will had stashed in the car that had been seized by the cops interstate. It was fraction of what they had moved, but it was adding up.

Will. Will had been in charge of the last interstate run, but had escaped arrest. The local Comos boss had been taken out along with one of Will's own guys, but no one had knocked on Will's door, not even to interview him. Will had insisted there was no link between him and the bust, that he'd been too careful. But Will was weak. And he was a loose end.

He slapped down his laptop, took another deep breath of chilled air, and headed for the hotel doors. Too much bad luck was falling his way. He needed to stay agile, get a few passports together and a bundle of cash. He'd pull off a few more big plays and then disappear.

The hot air immediately swamped him. He could almost taste the humidity. He turned to re-enter the lobby but felt a hand on his shoulder. He spun around to find a short but portly Indian man with slicked back hair and a flowery shirt smiling broadly at him.

'You like film, mister? You think you can play a big gangster?'

'Who the fuck are you?'

He wondered whether it was one of the men from tonight's meeting who had arrived early. Before he could speak, the man erupted into a high-pitched cackle.

'We doing a film and we need some gangsters. You know— Bollywood. You can be a big star!' The man laughed again. 'I am looking for big tough men! You know! Big gangsters! For extras.'

He eyed the man warily. He had heard about Westerners being approached to play extras in Bollywood films. The man pushed a business card into his hand and, still laughing, walked over to another hotel guest.

He smiled to himself as he walked back into the lobby. It might be a bit of fun. Who knows … he could even hit the big time. Hakan Joseph Ayik, the Scarface of Bollywood.

April 2010 – July 2011

Welch

Bugger. Welch swore under his breath as he walked down a corridor for what he was almost certain was the second time, staring at the names of senators as he passed the row of doors. He couldn't be sure. He'd been wandering the corridors for five minutes now and had lost all sense of direction. Now he was running late. Bugger.

At least it was warm inside. Canberra in June was bloody freezing. Each morning he woke up feeling cold and stiff, cursing his weatherboard house. He'd force himself out of his doona and towards the spire on the hill, a place that sometimes felt as surreal as it looked.

Bugger. Where the hell was the senator's office?

It had been the same for the last fortnight, ever since he signed onto the Australian Parliament House register as national security correspondent for the *Sydney Morning Herald* and *The Age*. During his first few days he couldn't find his new office. Forget about locating 'Aussies', the cafe where journalists, press flacks and politicians whispered and sipped coffee. He even got lost on the way to the toilet.

Finally, he spotted the sign he was looking for. Senator Steve Hutchins was one of the few parliamentarians with a genuine interest in organised crime, a man who'd labelled the push to ban bikie groups as nonsense, and had lobbied instead for better laws to seize criminals' wealth. Hutchins was one of the first politicians he'd sought a meeting with in Canberra.

As he walked into the office, Hutchins emerged from a side room, shook his hand gently and gestured to a couch next to a small coffee table in the corner of his office. A television hooked to a live feed of an empty Senate Chamber flickered in the corner. Hutchins had an open, kind and ruddy face framed by white hair.

'Welcome to Canberra, Dylan.' He was softly spoken, with none of the pomp or swagger some politicians carried. 'What brings you here?'

He took that as a prompt to begin his spiel about his role as national security correspondent, and his goal to have organised crime treated in the media as an ongoing national security issue. As he spoke, his eyes settled on a bottle of Bushnell's malt whisky on the shelf.

'It's a bit too early for a drop. Unless you're keen, of course.' The senator's eyes twinkled.

He smiled back, unsure if his host was joking, and pressed on. 'I really want to make organised crime a big part of the round. Terrorism isn't the only law enforcement game in town, and the media need to reflect that.' He hoped he didn't sound like a goose, and wasn't convinced Hutchins was even listening. 'The decision of Kevin Rudd to make organised crime a national security priority in late 2008 set the bar. But the media ... myself included, need to keep following it up.'

As he mentioned the Prime Minister's name, he thought he noticed Hutchins shift uncomfortably. He paused, then continued, explaining his desire to report on Hutchins's committee's work. He watched the senator nodding as he spoke, although he was still unsure how much Hutchins was taking in. He seemed distracted.

'How is the waterfront inquiry progressing?'

Hutchins appeared to be anticipating the question. 'It's still early days, but from what we are hearing, there are small numbers of people on the wharf in bed with organised crime figures. We are not talking about a few bottles of whisky going missing. We are talking about massive amounts of drugs being imported. I can tell you now, if we see scope to make changes, we will call for them.'

'How are the unexplained wealth laws going since they've been introduced?'

Hutchins grimaced. 'Are we off the record?'

He nodded.

'A bunch of corporate lawyers in the Opposition watered them down. From what police are telling us, the laws are too weak and difficult to use. It is a bloody shame. You know, they are saying overseas that if organised crime was a country, it would be the tenth or eleventh biggest economy in the world. Even here, some ACC investigators say there are billions of dollars in drug money leaving Australia each year. And yet, we can't pass a workable unexplained wealth law. You know …'

The Senate bells rang. Welch wondered if he was about to lose the senator to a vote.

'Don't worry. I am not needed. Now where was I?' Before he could respond, Hutchins changed the direction of his argument. 'You know, getting some of my colleagues to concentrate on organised crime is difficult in the current environment. Our leader is starting to annoy quite a few of his colleagues.'

He realised Hutchins was talking about Rudd. The senator's face was now lit up, animated.

'There are senior people meeting regularly now to discuss the state of the party under Rudd. Disenchantment is growing almost hourly. Labor is on the nose in the states and federally.'

As Hutchins pressed on, he wondered how to direct the conversation back to organised crime. He tried, but the senator wasn't interested. It was all Rudd. The Prime Minister wasn't listening to colleagues; he was arrogant, dismissive, and with fewer and fewer friends in Labor. 'There are more and more rumblings against him, you know.' He talked about Rudd for the next twenty minutes, before the bells rang again. 'I've got to run this time, Dylan. But make sure to stay in touch about the waterfront inquiry. It should be interesting.' For an instant, Hutchins eyes flashed with mischief, and Welch wondered if something deeper lay in all the talk about the Prime Minister.

Following Hutchins out, he noticed a large painting on the wall depicting a shadowy figure sitting behind a desk. There was something unsettling about the image. Was the figure pondering or plotting?

'You like it?' Hutchins asked. Before Welch could answer, he said, 'It's called *The Senator*. It's my favourite.'

Purchas

He was struck by the quietness of the office as he stood in the corner. It was in stark contrast to the frenetic activity of the last five months, with the endless stream of tapped phone calls, Facebook messages, surveillance footage, informer debriefings, operational plans and lawyers.

He wondered briefly if he'd lived more of Ayik and Will's lives than his own. Now it was about leaving it right. The surveillance net cast over their targets was as complete as it could be, given the limited resources. Every camera around their apartments in World Square fed into the Crime Commission building; every burn-and-churn mobile phone number that they could pick up from hidden bugs was tapped; every travel movement monitored; every dollar wired overseas watched. He knew the pair's favourite meals, their pet names for various girlfriends and whores, and what lies they told their mothers.

And yet, despite the near total coverage, Ayik evaded him.

It was not just that he was clever; it was more that he was simply out of reach: on Indian or Hong Kong mobile numbers, or Blackberries routed through US phone networks. Even if they could get those lines off, it would take too long. The phone would be dead by the time they were up on it. Perhaps Ayik knew he was being watched and simply didn't care, figuring that as long as he was overseas and mobile, he could evade capture.

Purchas found himself smiling. He hated to admit it, but Ayik was an impressive operator. He played his own game, knew how to control the board. If he hadn't been raised tough and schooled poorly, he probably would have made a good businessman. Maybe he already was.

Purchas hated drugs, but looking at him simply as a commodity supplier, he had to admit that Ayik knew how to meet market demands. It wasn't clear whether Ayik had pulled India together, or whether the *Ong Ngoai* syndicate or one of its tentacles was in control.

But as a business venture, it made sense: set up in a country where precursors are legal and law enforcement corruptible; buy an industrial-sized pharmaceutical manufacturer; bring others in to do the risky part of the job, turning chemicals into drugs; and then distribute them to hungry markets across the world that could be fed via an international transport chain populated with corrupt facilitators. If it turned bad, the real players would be nowhere near the mess. Ayik had read the play well.

Will, on the other hand, hadn't heeded the signs. Even after the interstate bust, when they had arrested the senior Comanchero in charge of receiving the gear, along with Will's own runner, he hadn't tried to leave Australia or source a false passport.

And even after the raid of a drug lab in Sydney in which they had arranged for the NSW police to take out some of Ayik's closest bikie associates, Will had stayed put. He may have been acting a little more cautiously, but he was still in Sydney, just a ten-minute walk from the very agency that had his apartment block wired like a Christmas tree. He was still whoring his way through Sydney's escort scene as though he had just a few days to live. Which, in a way, was true. They were bearing down. Will would soon get a tap on the shoulder. It was just a matter of when.

He'd workshopped the plan with Bullock, who had just got back from India. Taking out Will would alert Ayik that police were closer than he might yet think. He and Bullock had agreed it was better to wait and see if Ayik would return to Australia or try another import. There was intelligence coming in that, on top of the Indian venture, he was planning something big from Asia.

They both knew their views now counted for less. The job of coordinating the Indian operation had been handed by their agency bosses to the federal police. An exasperated Bullock had called him from a Mumbai hotel room to explain that the AFP appeared to be controlling, and minimising, his contact with the Indian Narcotics Bureau. The feds were playing cuckoo again, he thought; taking the credit for their work while simultaneously shitting in their nest. It was a sign of the future. The Crime Commission's new direction involved creating organised crime target packages and sending them off to other agencies to work up into operations. The feds would soon dominate the national organised crime space.

Purchas found his gaze drawn to Vikingsson's old desk. The analyst had ultimately made good on his word. The bosses in Canberra had delayed offering him a new contract for almost a year, and by the time it had finally come, Vikingsson had tired of waiting. The office had not been the same since the Swede had quietly cleared his desk two weeks before, handed in his security pass and taken the next plane to Europe.

'High-risk funds, the country profiles, the laundry … we could have changed law enforcement for ever,' a weary Vikingsson had told him before he left. He thought back to one of Vikingsson's last major breakthroughs using the High Risk Funds Program. The analyst had finally pulled off a second comprehensive case study, this time analysing all the funds being wired from Australia to the Balkans, much as he had done with Vietnam three years before. Vikingsson had eliminated all the legitimate money transfers to the Balkans, leaving only the highest risk funds. By running a further series of algorithms, he'd identified individual funds transfers to certain Balkans countries sent through companies that, upon further checking, included several linked to suspected senior organised crime figures and war criminals.

The case study had proved again that the High Risk Funds Program actually worked. The individuals sending what were likely to be narco or other crime dollars were ideal law enforcement targets, identified not through a human source or traditional investigation techniques but by analysing the flow of money out of Australia.

But Vikingsson had told him that that no one seemed willing to take the next step on the Balkans findings and target the suspect individuals and companies, which included a franchise of a well-known bank. 'It's someone else's fight now,' Vikingsson had told him as he left.

The words rang true for himself too, thought Purchas. After forty years of battling crooks, of perfecting the chess game, it was no longer his battle. He'd come to consider himself a good player, a puppetmaster of sorts, and it was hard to imagine his life with no more strings to pull. But it was time to go.

He walked back to his desk and began placing the last few items into a cardboard box. He held up a glass plaque the team had bought him and re-read the inscription: 'In appreciation. Michael Purchas, National Crime Authority, Australian Crime Commission 1993–2010.'

Next in the box was an 'I worked for Mikey and survived!' T-shirt that some of the guys had given him at his farewell lunch, a small, brief affair at a local pub. He smiled. Despite his best intentions, most had survived.

The day before, the commission chief executive, John Lawler, had extended his hand and looked him in the eye. 'I know we haven't always got along, Mike. But you worked hard up until your very last day. You were always a worker, and I respect you for it.'

The goodwill gesture hadn't stopped him telling Lawler what he thought was wrong with the place. Even in the end, I couldn't shut my bleedin' mouth, he thought to himself.

The last item he retrieved was a briefing memo, marked 'Operation Dayu and the *Ong Ngoai* Syndicate. International Overview. Highly protected.' He stood, holding it in his hands, feeling emotion wash over him. It was one of the most important documents he'd ever held. He thought back to how James had asked him during his farewell lunch whether they would ever get Ayik. He slid the brief into James's safe and stuck a Post-it note on his desk on which he had written: 'You might want to read what is in the safe. Regards, Mike Purchas.' As he walked across the office, he realised he didn't know who 'they' were anymore. Except that they were not him. A few minutes later, he drove out of the Crime Commission building for the last time. There were few cars on the road, and as he glanced out of his window, he noticed that the night sky was clear. It was a fine night for a run. Maybe Huong would be keen on a late supper.

Midway across the harbour bridge, he looked back to see the city skyline, twinkling and majestic, and realised that he wasn't feeling half as bad as he'd expected.

Will

Striding into the brothel, Will wondered how many of the girls would have seen the flyers and the posters being plastered on windows around Chinatown. The event had already made the local Chinese newspaper and was doing the rounds of Facebook and the Asian clubbing sites. It was a flying start to his business plans.

'Everything running smoothly?' he asked the receptionist, hoping to prompt a conversation. But she just gave him a blank look, nodded and said nothing. Was she deaf? Only a few days before, he'd dropped her details of the official launch and the Chinese media conference. What's more, she was a huge fan of Khalil Fong and Fiona Sit. She should have been bursting with excitement.

He tried her again. 'Hey, I'll be able to get you some VIP tickets to the Khalil and Fiona signing at the club. We had the launch on the weekend.'

'Thanks Will,' she said looking at him indifferently.

He stared at her, wondering if he should give her the promotion poster he had brought in. 'Well, tell the girls we might need to give them the night off to come to the event.'

It should be the number one rule of any club promoter, he thought: the more chicks in a joint, the better the vibe. If anyone could source women in Sydney, it was him.

She shrugged, still unimpressed. 'You'll have to pay them if they are taking the night off. And you better hope it is not a Saturday night. It is our busiest evening.'

He silently scooped up the takings and walked out without saying goodbye, poster in hand. What was he thinking anyway? Useless hoes. Most of these bitches were good for nothing. What was that line one of the restaurant guys had told him? 'You can lead a whore to culture, but you can't make her think.'

Fuck 'em. None of the pros would be getting free drink cards. He was now running the show, and no one, *no one*, would give him shit. There had already been some suggestions that they could use the club as a front for moving gear and washing money, but it wasn't going to happen. A few bad lines of publicity was all he needed to kill the club's name. It would be strictly legit. No risk, big rewards.

He checked the safe mobile and frowned. The runner should be moving the last batch by now. He had already collected the gear from the warehouse and taken it to the drop-off point. Ever since they'd lost the gear interstate, Hux had been paranoid. Tonight was no different. He was staying offshore and taking extra precautions. The the drop-off point belonged to someone with no police profile.

The rest of the gear had already gone to those who had bought into the contract, including the cashed-up dealer known as Smiley. In a week, he would have the final funds needed to cover the launch. As soon as the money was in his hands, he would tell his mother about the club. She would be impressed. They all would.

He called his runner and gave him instructions. The runner would only get a few grand for his troubles. He shook his head again. Big risk; small reward. That was him not so long ago. He had smartened up. This would be the last time he would get his hands even slightly dirty.

He pulled up under his apartment block and walked to the street exit. It wouldn't take long. The money was divided and ready, and all he needed to do was to make sure the gear was safely delivered.

The street was buzzing with the usual Saturday night energy. He felt at home here, among the Chinese and Korean students. He was hungry, but he knew it wasn't wise to eat on a nervy gut. Big imports made him queasy, especially after Tonga and the Edmonds arrest.

As he walked towards Chinatown, he noticed two of his promotion posters on an alley wall: 'Fiona and Khalil signing, Sydney 2010. Sponsored by Club de Melody.' They were plastered next to a Jay-Z album launch poster and a faded Elton John tour poster. He grinned. He would send a picture to his mother. And to Hux. He'd be pumped.

He pulled one of the mobiles out of his pocket and dialled Hux's latest number. He'd lost track of where his boss was. As he held his mobile phone up to his ear and heard Hux's familiar voice, 'Hey bro,' he caught a flurry of movement in his peripheral vision. A car was pulling up on the curb behind him.

'I'm good darling. What's going on?' he said, turning around to see two cars coming to a stop. 'Hang on a sec.'

For the first time, he noticed the lights flashing red and blue. Men were rushing towards him. He heard the words 'drug squad' and 'arrest' as his phone slid from his hand. He watched it hit the pavement, the battery splitting from the casing. He tried to reach for it, realising that he hadn't hung up, but someone stopped him from moving.

What the fuck was going on? It couldn't be ... Not now. The concert was just days away. A man in a suit was talking to him, holding a pair of handcuffs, 'You have the right to remain silent ...'

He needed his phone. Hux was still on the line. He had to hang up. He needed to fucking hang up. He tried to protest, but when he opened his mouth, nothing came out. As he was driven away, he turned to look at his poster on the wall, but it was too late.

Ayik

Ayik pulled his hat tightly over his forehead and breathed in deeply. It would take at least forty-eight hours for his name to be put on international watch lists. He had to keep moving.

Trying to look inconspicuous in the Bangkok airport queue, he went through the arrests again, his mind whirring, his heart pounding. Calm down Hux, he whispered to himself. He needed to look like everybody else. He was fifth in the line now. It would be his turn soon.

He lost count of how many times he had played the scene over in his mind. Will had had the line open when he'd gone down. He was sure he'd heard the word 'drug squad'. It was the shipment. Fucking

Will. The loose link. He should have dealt with him when he had the chance.

His older brother had been picked up and charged with trafficking heroin, and he'd also been found with several leaked police reports. His own fucking brother. He'd be joining his nephew on the inside. Calm down, Hux, he told himself.

Fourth in line.

They had also found the lab in India, seizing the gear and arresting the cooks and the runners, and taking out Wu's people too. All his hard work down the drain. Days later, the Indian newspapers were full of articles about police smashing an 'international drug cartel'. It wasn't all bad. At least he'd had time to get his papers in order and get out of the country.

His thoughts turned again to Will. What would stop him talking? Fucking Will. He shuffled as the queue moved forward, head down. Breathe in, Hux, he told himself.

Three more to go.

They had frozen Hux's assets in Australia, put a caveat on his apartment, seized his Harley. *Seized his Harley.* They must have been bugging the apartment. But how did they get up on Will's phone lines? He'd read and re-read the report in the newspaper. Memorised it: 'A man was caught with $8 million of heroin after police intercepted phone conversations in which he agreed to deliver the drugs'.

In the paper, Will had been named as a 'senior figure' in an Asian drug syndicate. Senior figure, my arse. The jacks always overstated it. But they hadn't made any mention of the gear that had got away. The shipment was massive and, according to the articles, they had only seized a few dozen. Fucking cops.

Second in line.

He lifted his chin and clenched his jaw. He had nothing to worry about, he told himself.

'Next please.'

He walked up to the counter.

'How are you today, sir?'

He forced a smile. 'Very well, thanks. Very well.' He handed over his passport.

'And where are you flying to today, sir?'

Welch

It better be worth it. Welch threw his overnight bag in the boot of the cab. 'Take me to Ultimo please'

He had got the call a few days before from one of his first bikie contacts, a man he'd spent years cultivating as a source. 'You're never going to believe what has happened,' he said. 'Meet me at the usual place on Thursday.'

As he sat in the back of the taxi, he felt grateful for the break from Canberra and the endless churn of press conferences and media releases. He was not about to complain about his first few months of his stint, though. A week after he'd met Hutchins, the senator, along with a group of influential Labor politicians, had knifed Rudd, replacing him as prime minister with Julia Gillard. He'd almost had the scoop on it, as well.

As the cab pulled up next to the cafe, he spotted his man sipping his usual drink, a bottle of Perrier. He'd barely sat down when the source leaned over to him, drawing him in, his eyes wild. 'They kidnapped Smiley and tortured him. Got all the gear. Kilos and kilos of it.'

'Slow down mate, I've got no idea what you are talking about,' Dylan said as he slid out his notebook.

'The Comos crew were behind that heroin pinch. The bloke I told you about ages ago.'

'Who's that again?'

'Big Hux. The money man for the Comos.'

He nodded, thinking briefly back to the meeting in which the name Big Hux had first been disclosed.

April 2010 – July 2011

'You heard the talk?'

The underworld had been buzzing with rumours that a recent series of drug busts announced by the police had been linked to a much bigger import. The name 'Big Hux' had come up repeatedly. Media reports had also revealed that the NSW police had issued a warrant for someone called Hakan Ayik in connection to the heroin seizures.

Hakan Ayik. Big Hux. Of course. How could he have missed it? 'Go on,' he urged his source.

'There was a shipment that came in. Worth fucking millions. Different crews had taken a piece of it. Hux's crew took their piece. And Smiley also got a share—70 kilos.'

He nodded. Smiley was the nickname of a well-known dealer in Sydney. 'How do you know this?'

'You don't need to know. Let's just say I got good sources of me own. Now to the juicy bit. Smiley stashed the gear and was about to start flogging it when Daux and Buds got word. They thought they should have themselves a chunk. And by a chunk, I mean all of it.'

The man was now beginning to relish telling his tale, and Welch had to furiously scrawl down notes in order to keep up. Daux was short for Daux Ngakuru, the Comancheros sergeant-at-arms, and Buds was a boxer turned Comos enforcer who ran with him.

'So they decide to pull a little sting. They follow Smiley out one day. As he's driving near the Owen in Rozelle, they flash a set of fake police lights. He pulls over, thinking it's the coppers. Next thing, he has a piece to his head and is being taken to a torture house. Now, according to well-placed sources,' he said, embellishing his story with jargon and movie references, 'they fitted up the safe house like a torture chamber. Sprayed pigs blood all over the joint and made Smiley an offer he couldn't refuse. They threatened to blowtorch him unless he told them where the gear was. And Smiley doesn't like fire. So he told them.'

He watched the bikie telling the story, wondering at his motives. Maybe he had a few bucks in on Smiley's stash. Or maybe he just liked telling stories. He settled on the latter as he scrawled. 'So what happened to the gear?'

'It is no doubt getting dudes high as we speak. Half of it was shipped to Melbourne, apparently to some new bikie boss that has taken up from where Hux left off. Good story, eh?'

He nodded, his mind racing to what he would need to do to confirm it. If over 150 kilos of gear had hit the streets it would be worth reporting. There would be questions asked about how it got through the wharves, and how the police had missed so much of it. And how Big Hux had got away.

Four hours later, Welch opened his laptop. Since he'd left the bikie, several more sources, including police, had confirmed the key elements of the story. It was believed to be an Ayik import, and most of it had ended up with the Comancheros' new Melbourne chapter.

The more calls he'd made, the more he had learnt. Hux, aka Hakan Ayik, had a key Chinese contact, Steve Wu, who had been arrested in Hong Kong after a big operation by the Crime Commission and an extradition request from the federal police. Ayik had somehow managed to evade capture and was now on the run.

He clicked on the cursor and began typing, describing how the Comancheros involved in the rip-off had made a 'lifetime earn'—at least $40 million worth of gear—and how rival syndicates would be nervous that underworld violence and rip-offs had reached a new high.

His fingers pounded the keyboard. He had to get his thoughts down and didn't stop writing for half an hour. He slowed down as he punched out the conclusion. It had to really say something.

> If readers take anything from this violent endpoint to the Ayik syndicate, it should be that it is far from a one-off, not an aberration in an otherwise lawful and stable world. Organised crime is growing around the world, fuelled in a large part by the affluence of bloated Western economies. Some suggest that the worldwide black economy—everything from corruption to drug trafficking—accounts for as much as fourteen trillion dollars, one-fifth of the

global economy. Despite what some politicians may tell you, organised crime is in the middle of a grand march. What are we doing to arrest it?

He read it aloud. It was good copy.

Dialling the newsdesk on his mobile, he simultaneously emailed the piece through to the day editor.

'It's Dylan. I just sent you some copy about a major underworld play. Drugs may well be flooding Melbourne and Sydney in the next few days.'

The day editor paused, and he figured he was skimming the piece. 'How long is it?' He sounded unimpressed.

'It's 70 centimetres.'

'Mate, the paper is tight as. There is no way we can fit seventy. You'll have to cut it in half. And get rid of the analysis while you're at it.'

James

It was his turn now, thought James. His turn to clean out his desk. His turn to follow Vikingsson and Purchas into the land of the civilian. He'd tried to resist having goodbye drinks, but Bullock had insisted on it. He'd even flown up that morning from Melbourne to make sure he'd show.

At least his chores were completed. He had requested a meeting with the chief executive, John Lawler, before he left, but Lawler had appeared uninterested, and he was left wondering why either of them had bothered. There had been no acknowledgement of all Operation Dayu had achieved. Or all that it hadn't but might have. In the last few weeks, Dayu, Hoffman and Agrale had begun to be rapidly wound up.

Wu had been arrested in Hong Kong over an alleged drug import into Australia, while Wei Wong and Ayik's brother had also been taken out. Yet it hadn't all gone to plan. A huge import had slipped through the law enforcement net.

And then there was Ayik. When the Indian lab was taken out, he'd disappeared, leaving the local authorities to sweep up those hired to do the syndicate's dirty work. Ayik's escape was bothering him, but not as much as what they had really lost. Operation Dayu was never about busts and arrests. But did anyone really want to hear about the true size and global nature of the narco economy, and about the public policy failures that allowed it to flourish? Maybe they were before their time. Or maybe they were just naive.

He moved to his safe and removed the contents. There were only three files left. For some reason, he'd kept them, even after he knew he was leaving. The first was Purchas's initial briefing file. He quickly scanned it. 'This agency is capable of running an operation in the mould of Gordian and aimed at better understanding the make-up of these Asian organised crime syndicates here and offshore, as well as the size of the nation's drug economy.'

James shredded the document before he finished reading it.

The second piece of paper in his safe was the one-line resignation email that he'd sent a month earlier after deciding to accept a job outside the commission. The only acknowledgement he'd received was a request from Human Resources to ensure he completed his exit proforma.

He fed the shredder again.

The last document in the safe was Purchas's final briefing. He held it above the shredder, but hesitated, moved to his seat and opened it. As he began reading it slowly, he felt gutted.

> Asian organised crime in Australia and overseas is far more integrated than perhaps at anytime in the history of the triads. This has been confirmed by a number of excellent sources the agency has recruited and the work of the covert laundry. Instead of competing and fighting amongst themselves, the old Chinese triad groups are now cooperating, franchising their operations by drawing on

April 2010 – July 2011

strongholds of Hong Kong Chinese throughout Asia and in Australia, Canada, the United States and Europe.

Most significantly, Operation Dayu identified a worldwide drug syndicate, a triad-controlled conglomerate known as *Ong Ngoai* (Grandfather Syndicate). It is likely comprised of three key bosses based in South-East Asia and at least twenty other senior figures, who occupy 'seats' or positions of influence within the syndicate.

To hold a seat, a person must prove their utility to the international operations of this syndicate, with the ability to control global drug shipments and repatriate drug money. Seats are not geographically confined, and it is not the case that one seat occupies a particular country. Seats operate wherever they have networks and ability to prosper.

This syndicate is believed to be responsible for at least $1.2 billon worth of drugs (street price) into Australia each year. The syndicate is active in at least twenty other countries, including countries in which the syndicate's activities dwarf its Australian operations.

The basic financing of the *Ong Ngoai* syndicate is as follows: for every million dollars' worth of imported drugs into Australia (wholesale price), only 40 percent is directly returned to the syndicate. Ten percent of that 40 percent is used to purchase the next shipment of drugs and to pay for transportation and the bribery of various officials. The remaining 60 percent pays for various multi-level marketing within Australia or is invested. Lower-level distribution syndicates also send their own profits offshore.

James found himself swamped by memories as he read; the meetings and arguments, the plotting and planning—a chase that actually meant something and was going somewhere.

Operation Dayu, and its offshoots Operation Hoffmann and Operation Agrale, identified drug distribution and money-laundering vehicles used by the *Ong Ngoai* syndicate and attacked these vehicles through interdiction, arrest and charging, as well as covert measures. However, these are only deterrence measures; the *Ong Ngoai* syndicate continues to traffic drugs and launder money across the world.

One of the major successes of Dayu was proving that the High Risk Funds Program works. Analysing the movement of funds out of Australia using several means allowed the agency to identify likely organised crime targets through non-traditional law enforcement techniques and to come up with a better estimate of Australia's black economy.

Purchas was right, he thought. Vikingsson's Balkans case study had proved that the High Risk Funds concept worked. It was just that those left championing it were disappearing. Bullock was the last senior official from Dayu left to fight the fight.

Returning to the file, his eyes skipped down the page, and he felt a twinge of pride at what Dayu had achieved. It had identified high-level infiltration by organised crime figures in national governments and law enforcement agencies across Asia. One of the examples cited involved a senior *Ong Ngoai* figure who was also a high-ranking Asian police official that had attended an international Interpol conference in New York.

In Vietnam, senior figures in the communist regime had helped move narco-dollars out of the country and elsewhere in Asia. The hundreds of millions of drug dollars that had remained in Vietnam were poured into major developments and businesses, including those linked to the Vietnamese government; a thriving port city was almost entirely built with narco-dollars. Drug money financed businesses, and developments had also been identified in Hong Kong and Macau.

Moving to the section covering Cambodia, James's mind was flooded with images of Phnom Penh: the scabby dogs, the prostitutes, the poverty and the pervasive sadness that hung in the humid air. There was something about the city that had stayed with him long after he and Bullock had returned from their trip to collect information for the Gordian prosecutions, something unsettling about the way the pockets of excessive wealth contrasted so blatantly with everything else.

He thought back to the afternoon their driver had taken them for a drive. It had been Bullock's idea. They'd sat in the back of a white Mercedes as it weaved and stuttered through a stream of motorbikes and four-wheel-drive Lexuses, the car favoured by wealthy and well-connected Khmers. Glimpses of the Mekong River, wide and imposing, appeared behind the markets and temples glinting gold in the afternoon sun. He and Bruce had both dressed like Western tourists in cargo pants and short-sleeve shirts dotted with sweat. That morning, both had sanitised the contents of their wallets. It was probably an unnecessary precaution, but they decided that if they somehow ended up in custody, their official commission identification could cause more trouble than it was worth. They didn't want to be accused of spying or running a black op.

When their driver neared their destination, Bullock had asked him to pull up next to a small street stall about 50 metres from a walled compound. At the entrance sat four bored-looking Khmers with AK-47s in their laps. The compound belonged to Hun To, a Crime Commission target. To was the nephew of the Cambodian Prime Minister, Hun Sen, and the business partner of Kith Meng, the founder of the Royal Group and one of Asia's richest men. Hun To had also been the target of a 2003 ACC Asian organised crime probe, Operation Illipango, which had been run by Bullock and investigated the importation of heroin into Australia.

Despite the ACC's intention to arrest Hun To, he'd escaped their net after a senior Australian official in Cambodia had learnt of the commission's plans and protested. Years on, Bullock still fumed about the incident; the official had complained that arresting the Cambodian leader's nephew would cause unwanted diplomatic fallout, and within days the Australian embassy in Cambodia had denied To a visa to return to Melbourne, meaning he was never picked up. As usual, law enforcement claimed only the scalp of a runner, Hun To's bodyguard, Phenny Thai.

As they'd sat watching the compound, Bullock had asked the driver if he knew who lived there. Everyone knows who lives there, he had replied. His eyes had stayed on the men with the automatic weapons as their Mercedes had turned slowly in the street and headed away.

James's memories were interrupted by a voice from across the office. 'Ready for the last supper, Jamesy? See you downstairs.' He recognised the voice and looked up to see a grinning Bullock. The man was still agitating the agency bosses in Canberra, although he wondered for how long.

'I'll be down in a minute,' he shot back.

He turned his attention back to the memo in front of him, focusing on a final nugget: in Cambodia, a casino cruise ship worth hundreds of millions of dollars had been identified as being among the assets of the *Ong Ngoai* empire. It had been bought by a front company, the Royal Group, which curiously shared the name of Kith Meng's firm. Among the cruise ship's investors was the Lam crime family of Sydney, who also owned a Cambodian casino in which Meng was understood to have had held an interest, and which Dayu had identified as a money-laundering hub.

He walked back to the shredder. There, he watched the last law enforcement document he'd ever hold separate into paper ribbons, and then headed to the pub. He didn't think about Cambodia until six hours later, when he found himself, arm draped over Bullock's shoulder, swaying and stumbling his way to the harbour ferry.

'There'll be no more adventures, eh?'

'Who knows, Jamesy. Who knows,' said Bullock. Then, after thrusting a small wooden plaque into his hands and squeezing his shoulder, Bullock turned and disppeared into the night.

James boarded the ferry, found a seat and closed his eyes the instant he sat down. He let his head sway with the rock of the boat. 'Stay awake,' he told himself, rubbing his eyes and looking around.

His gaze landed on a man at the back of the ferry and, for just an instant, he felt a rush of panic. It looked like … He rubbed his eyes again. Of course it wasn't. Still, the man appeared to be staring at him strangely. He was built like a body builder, and wore a singlet and a gold chain. He looked away when the man approached him. 'Hey, mate. Sorry to ask, but you don't know where I could score a little coke by any chance?' The man eyed him hopefully, and James realised he must appear the sort of Friday night drunk who was partial to the rich man's drug, cocaine.

For a moment he considered telling him he worked in policing, but instead he shook his head, saying nothing. You no longer work in law enforcement, he told himself. You're just a pissed suit heading home far too late on a Friday night.

He waited until the man had disappeared down to the bottom deck and closed his eyes again. This time he let the boat rock him half asleep. There was no need to stay alert, he told himself. He was out of the game.

Ayik

Don't look back. Keep on walking. You gotta keep walking. He felt his legs shaking. He needed a taxi before anyone had a change of mind and took him back into custody. Or put a bullet in him. At least his emergency fund had worked. Half an hour before, he'd been stopped trying to cross to the Greek side of Cyprus. His name must have been put into the Interpol database, and he'd been swarmed, surrounded by unshaven border guards poking him like a rare lab specimen.

Still no cab. He walked on, looking only at the ground.

The border guards had looked like they'd hit the jackpot after he'd slipped them his bum bag and they'd unzipped it, finding it full of tightly wrapped green bundles of US dollars.

Fuckin' dogs, he thought. He'd probably bought his freedom ten times over. A few nods and whispers later and he was out the door, past the guard box, past the barricade. He was minus a bum bag, a few phones and his laptop, as well as a safety deposit box key and the paperwork tied to his latest business ventures. But he was free, and the plans were well in train. By the time anyone figured out what it all meant, he'd be a few mill richer. He whistled.

A taxi stopped and he slid into the back seat. His legs were no longer shaking. 'Get me out of here,' he said in Turkish.

'Where to?'

'Just drive. And don't stop until I say.'

Bilal

It had been weeks, and Waz still hadn't been in touch. Maybe it was a good thing. He pressed the meat down with the back of a fork, listening to it sizzle. Leaning over the hotplate, he squinted to avoid the glare of the sun. Beads of sweat moved slowly down his face, like creeping flies.

He turned to look at his wife. She was lying on her back, their youngest on her stomach. His big brother—the six-year-old—was trying to kick a soccer ball, missing it, trying again and kicking it half a metre, and then missing it again. They had told him he would have to give evidence. That was the deal. Waz was waiting for his committal, and sometime soon, he would get the entire brief. Waz would know then how far he had gone and that he'd given a statement to the cops. The only way he would get out of giving evidence was if Waz pleaded guilty. And from what the cops had said, that was highly unlikely.

He flipped over the meat, smelling the marinade as it burnt. His eldest liked his meat well done; his wife liked it bloody. He liked it when one of them didn't complain, which was never. *Sssssssss.* He savoured the feeling of the oil biting his hand. It felt like the tiny needles burying into him in the tattoo shop. He hated the tat now. It didn't remind him of family or church or his mother or his new leaf;

it reminded him of Waz getting ... well, whatever they do to the weak in prison.

Word was that someone was funding Waz's lawyers. Probably guys scared by what Waz could say about them. It didn't bode well for him: if he was one of those whose testimony could put Waz away, then would someone try to get to him?

His wife knew about the witness statement and the court case, but he hadn't told her about his fears, even though they were killing his sleep. It had been hard enough just getting her to stay. Once she had agreed, he'd figured it was better never to speak about it unless he had to. So it lived in the background, a black stain, a never-dying reminder that he was untrustworthy, and having betrayed once could betray again. And she was right. He'd taken Waz's money and then turned into a dog. And she and his cousins and second cousins ... everyone knew it. 'Bilal the dog' is what they'd call him.

Bloody Waz. He'd never cared what Waz thought, but now Waz was ... he was morally superior. Waz had stayed staunch when it counted.

That fuckin' tattoo.

A trail of smoke began to pour from one of the steaks, but he found himself transfixed by it, not caring if the meat burnt. The cops had told him they could put him in witness protection, but even if he got into the program, it would mean putting the wife and the boys in as well, and cutting off contact with everyone. New name, new place, new life, and still looking over his shoulder, not knowing if one day, some day ...

So why not just front up in court?

The old copper had told him what to do. And when he'd finally eyeballed Waz, he'd followed the script. 'You're the one who dragged me into this shit. You're the one who made me take the risks. And you're the one who got us both fuckin' caught!'

The old copper had told him that he had to 'manipulate the environment', and that if he stuck it on Waz, he would eventually understand that he had no choice but to testify. It would be Waz's fault, not his.

Except he did have a choice. He'd *always* had a choice.

'Bilal, it's burning,' his wife yelled.

Smoke was rising thicker from the plate. He flipped the steaks, finding them charcoaled on one side, cracked and dry. At least he'd be popular with his six-year-old.

'Food's ready,' he yelled, dishing the meat onto a plate and wiping the sweat from his forehead.

Walking towards the blanket, the grass tickled his bare feet. He was momentarily distracted by a police car cruising in the distance, but then he looked away.

'It doesn't matter what anyone thinks,' he wife had kept telling him.

But it did matter. All his choices had mattered. He'd just found out far too late.

Hutchins

It was unusually quiet. Gone was the rancour and the partisan bitterness that usually hung in the air. It was all red seats and respect. It happened every three to four years, this rare show of graciousness and goodwill. It was a pity it only came on the way out: never on the way. Everyone around him knew their day would come, on their own terms rather than some other way, they hoped.

Hutchins eyed the speech in front of him, and then scanned the balcony; some of his old staffers were there, as was his family. And his wife Natalie—the only Hutchins left in politics now.

Turning his eyes back to his speech, he re-read his description of organised crime, the 'dark spectre' that lurks in our society. It sounded right. He'd focused on the committee's achievements: the unexplained wealth laws and the report, released just a few days earlier, calling for major reforms to deal with organised crime on the waterfront, including an overhaul of the federal government's maritime security identity card system.

'We gave the agencies the power to break up the baddies,' he'd written. Yet he knew he hadn't gone far enough. The waterfront report had already disappeared from the media. And the remaining committee members had recently launched a fresh inquiry into why the unexplained wealth laws weren't working.

Mike Purchas, the investigator he'd met over two years before, had sent him a text message wishing him well on his last day. He wondered what Purchas would say if they met now. Not a dollar had been seized using the laws in the year since their passage through parliament. The waterfront was still accommodating men willing to move tonnes of drugs for a six-pack and a root.

With the airport bashing a distant memory, organised crime was again slipping off the political radar. He was going the same way, he thought, revising the last line of his speech in his head: a quote from Saint Paul. When his time came, he would rise and tell his fellow senators that the apostle's words summed up not only his own feelings but those of everyone leaving: 'I have fought the good fight, I have finished the course, I have kept the faith.'

It would work well, he thought as he sat quietly, waiting for the Senate president to call his name for the last time.

Purchas

Purchas followed Bullock past the marble columns and gold leaf walls, and up into the gaming area. Located on the floor above were the private gaming rooms, including the one they had earmarked for the covert laundry.

'Shall we take a peek, Mikey?'

He nodded, and they walked to the elevator. They had taken the ferry from Hong Kong that afternoon, after he had spent the morning trying to find the building that had been his workplace two decades ago, the Independent Commission Against Corruption. They were meant to be holidaying, and Huong wasn't enamoured by the idea, but he wanted see if any of the old faces were there. Instead, he got lost. The ICAC had either moved or he'd gone to the wrong place.

He decided then that he no longer cared for Hong Kong, that any sentiment he had held for the place was gone. It seemed much bigger than before, a jumble of concrete towers crammed into a tiny area. And it still stunk.

As the elevator lifted them silently upwards, Bullock pulled out his phone and clicked on a YouTube clip. It showed Hakan Ayik being led by two scowling Cypriot police officers into court. The comments under the clip said he'd been arrested just before Christmas Day, and charged with entering a restricted military zone after evading arrest on the border two months before.

'He looks in the best shape of his life,' Bullock said quietly.

His old colleague was right. Ayik was toned and tanned, staring confidently at the camera. It reminded him of the first time he had seen Ayik's mugshot. It was as if he'd always known he'd get away. And he had. A few days after appearing in a Cypriot court, he'd been released on bail and had disappeared again. A message on his Facebook page said: 'Catch me if you can.'

'Any idea where he is?' he asked Bullock.

'Not since I left, Mikey. His Facebook page recently showed him and Daux somewhere overseas chomping on Cuban cigars … But I guess it's not our business anymore. It's someone else's job now.'

He watched his colleague as he walked out of the lift. Bullock had survived only a year longer than he, Vikingsson and James. His friend said little about his last few months at the commission, although Purchas had heard from others that Bullock had remained relentless and restless, and had kept pushing for the agency to support long-term operations. Just a few days before he announced his decision to leave law enforcement, Bullock had been told his proposal to launch a new organised crime taskforce would not go ahead.

Operation Dayu was officially dead and buried.

He walked close behind Bullock as they neared one of the high-roller rooms.

'It's coming up on the left,' Bullock said.

Two huge bouncers stood at the entrance, which was shielded by a red and gold curtain. He could hear laughter and chatter coming from inside. He slowed down and, as he walked past, the curtain parted just for an instant, exposing a smoky room packed with small gaming tables, a blur of suits and cocktail dresses.

'Anything interesting?' said Bullock once they were out of earshot from the bouncers.

Purchas shook his head. He'd seen nothing out of the ordinary. It was business as usual.

Epilogue

Operation Dayu, which also comprised Operation Hoffman and Operation Agrale, the High Risk Funds Program, the covert laundry and many other state, federal and international operations, had ceased operational work by 2011. While very few individuals are named in this book, Operations Dayu, Hoffman and Agrale could not have achieved their successes without the input of numerous other highly dedicated individuals from the ACC, AFP, WA police, NSW police, VIC police, NSW Crime Commission and overseas law enforcement agencies.

In late 2011, at the time of writing, Michael Purchas and Bruce Bullock were back working together in a risk and crisis management consultancy, with a focus on providing anti-money laundering advice to governments and big business.

Patrick Vikingsson is living in Europe and works as a private intelligence consultant. He is extending his research into organised crime and terrorism, and continues to improve his High Risks Funds methodology.

Gregory James is living a quiet life somewhere in the Pacific, where he is the coach of his son's rugby team.

Since leaving the Crime Commission, Purchas, James, Bullock and Vikingsson have remained close friends.

Dylan Welch is national security correspondent for the *Sydney Morning Herald* and *The Age* newspapers and has written a book about the Ibrahim crime family of Sydney.

The *Ong Ngoai* syndicate is believed to remain highly active across the world.

Hakan Ayik is on the run and is understood to remain an active drug trafficker. In October 2011, the NSW police added Ayik to their

EPILOGUE

most wanted list in connection to the alleged importation of 224 kilograms of heroin.

The men based on characters Wei 'Will' Wong and Steve Wu, along with more than a dozen other people investigated during Dayu, are awaiting trial for drug trafficking, money laundering or other criminal offences.

In July 2011, Erkan Dogan was sentenced to a minimum of four years' jail.

The Comancheros have a new national president and have established new chapters across Australia.

Steven Hutchins retired as a senator for NSW in the Australian Parliament on 30 June 2011 and is now living in Melbourne with his wife, Natalie Hutchins, a Victorian politician. At the time of publishing, the unexplained-wealth legislation he helped introduce had not been used and was the subject of a fresh parliamentary inquiry aimed at improving its effectiveness.

In 2010 and 2011, the High Court of Australia overturned key aspects of anti-bikie laws. New laws were being drafted in some states as a result.

In 2010, under the Australian government's new organised crime strategic framework, the AFP launched a Criminal Assets Confiscation Taskforce and the ACC launched its 'fusion' centre, which has adopted some of the work of the High Risk Funds Program. At the time of writing, the AFP was expanding its organised crime operations and investigating corruption on the waterfront.

In mid-2011, the ACC completed an inquiry that concluded that the covert laundry had been run in a proper and lawful manner. Over the three-year period in which the laundry operated, it moved $10.6 million in suspected drug funds out of Australia. Operations Dayu and Hoffman led to the seizure of $780 million worth of drugs (wholesale value), worth over $1 billion in street prices. The Hong Kong Police-controlled operation certificate to permit the laundry's operation in Hong Kong was issued but never used by Operation Dayu.

EPILOGUE

Seizures and other outcomes attributed directly or indirectly to the work of Operation Dayu include:
- a 340-litre liquid ecstasy seizure (enough to make $51 million worth of ecstasy) near Geelong in December 2006
- a 1900-litre liquid ecstasy seizure (enough to make $540 million worth of ecstasy) in January 2007
- four Canadian seizures in 2008, totalling more than 500 kilograms of drugs
- an 80-kilogram crystal methylamphetamine seizure (worth $32 million) in Adelaide in late 2008. The other 420 kilograms have never been recovered
- a large weapons seizure, including multiple pistols, shotguns, automatic weapons and explosive devices, and the seizure of 1 kilogram of base methamphetamine in May 2009 (Erkan Dogan seizure)
- an airport seizure of 4 kilograms of ice on 21 August 2009
- the Tongan seizure of 35 kilograms of liquid ice on 22 September 2009, and the arrest of a Tongan customs officer who was later convicted
- several cash and asset seizures totalling tens of millions of dollars
- a 2.7 kilogram methylamphetamine seizure in Perth on 5 December 2009
- 3.25 kilograms of methylamphetamine and 1 kilogram of cocaine seized on 15 December 2009
- the arrest of NSW police analyst Terry Gregoriou, who was sentenced to seven months' jail in 2010 for leaking police files to the Comancheros
- 50 kilograms ($20 million) of ice seized in Sydney in January 2010

EPILOGUE

- a 5 kilogram-methamphetamine seizure in Perth in mid-February 2010, and the arrest of an alleged local Comancheros boss
- the discovery of a drug laboratory and arrest of four bikies, and the seizure of 10 kilograms of ice, 4 kilograms pseudoephedrine and firearms on 1 April 2010
- a multi-million dollar heroin seizure in Sydney on 31 July 2010 and the arrest of three men. The bulk of the 220-kilogram plus heroin importation from which this seizure originated has never been recovered by police
- the discovery of 'super' drug laboratories in Mumbai, India, in August 2010 and the arrest of up to a dozen men
- the prosecution of several money remitters and reforms to Western Union's money remittance network in Australia.

Operation Gordian, which preceded Operation Dayu, remains the biggest investigation into money laundering in the southern hemisphere, leading to seventy-three successful prosecutions over the transfer of $93 million of drug money out of Australia and drug seizures worth $1 billion.

Acknowledgements

While many people contributed to this book, I want to recognise the tremendous efforts of my publisher, Sally Heath, whose advice, patience and encouragement have been invaluable; to the incredibly decent and generous Steve and Dylan, and those I can't mention (you know who you are!); to MUP's CEO and Publisher-in-Chief, Louise Adler, whose energetic lobbying got the project off the ground; to my good friend Jack O'May, whose last-minute advice was incredibly helpful; to David Poulton for his legal expertise wonderful support; to editorial manager Diane Leyman, especially for her attention to detail; to Rafael, my father, and Cam, who read rough manuscripts; to all the sources, who often took great risks to tell me the truth; and, lastly, to Puffin, whose support, advice and friendship kept the book—and me—alive.

This book is dedicated to the police who dedicate their careers to fighting organised crime, and whose contribution to this endless battle is rarely recognised.

Index

ACC, *see* Australian Crime Commission
Adams, Andrew 58–9
AFP, *see* Australian Federal Police
Age, The 114
Asian Crime Squad NSW 31
asset-seizure laws 191
AUSTRAC 46, 74–5
Australia, black economy 16, 43, 115
Australian Crime Commission
 'fusion' centre 253; limitations on 20–1; operations room 79–80; oversight committee 80, 84–6, 137–8; political pressure on 133–4; Purchas's work for 3–8; staff cuts 115; under Lawler 161, 164–5; under Rudd 229–30
Australian Federal Police
 approval needed for covert laundering 45; Criminal Assets Confiscation Taskforce 253; demarcation disputes with 89, 116–17; interference with ACC 229; move into ACC operations 197; teleconference with ACC 109–11
Australian Institute of Criminology 43
Ayik, Erkan 239–40
Ayik, Hakan 8–11
 ACC briefing on 131–2; ACC interest in 94, 111, 113–14; arrest in Cyprus 250; brother arrested 239–40; current status 252–3; difficulty finding evidence against 197–8; disappearance from India 239–40; distribution network run by 40–1; drug shipping methods 101–4; evades arrest 228–9, 234–6, 240; Facebook profile 147–8, 216–17; in Cyprus 245–6; in Dubai 192–6; in Hong Kong 63–8; in India 220–4; leaves Australia 138–42; media interest in 105–6; police dossier on 121–2; relations with Dogan 169–70; relations with Will Wong 17, 19–20, 215, 233–4; surveillance of 173–7; triad links confirmed 185

Baker, Peter 117
Balkans investigation 230, 242
banks, cooperation with ACC 46–7, 75
Bazely, James 86
beauty salons, as fronts for drug trade 89, 91–2
Beazley, Kim 11
Beverage, John 117
Big Hux, *see* Ayik, Hakan

bikies, *see* motorcycle clubs
Bilal (wharf worker)
 agrees to report Customs interest 142–5; arrest and interrogation 185–90; as informant 246–8; ecstasy prepared by 23–8
Blackburn, Harry 35–6
Bradley, Philip 167
Brighton-le-Sands, NSW 10
Buds (bikie) 216, 237
Bullock, Bruce
 Cambodian trip 242–4; confirms Ayik's involvement in drug trade 157–9; coordinates Operation Hoffman 132–4; criticised for breaching protocol 166; forms team for Operation Dayu 57–9; in Hong Kong 95–100; in Macau 249–51; interrogates Bilal 185–90; locates methylamphetamine plant 28–31; meeting with Hutchins 119–20; meetings with James 41–5, 183–5; plans covert laundry 68–71; plans for Ayik 229; promoted 218–20; Purchas's work with 3–5, 8; reopens covert laundry 212; teleconference with AFP 109–11; update on Operation Dayu 130

Cambodia
 casino cruise ship 204, 218–19, 244; James's trip to 242–4; laundered money sent to 92–3
Canada
 ACC collaboration with 110, 155; Chinese–Canadian drug syndicate 120; Hells Angels in 108; involvement in drug trade 91–2
Capitaine Tasman 171, 179, 183–4, 198
Castle Hill, ecstasy plant in 33–4
Cheung, Dai Lo, *see* Lam Sak Cheung, Duncan
Chinese–Canadian drug syndicate 110–11, 120
Club de Melody 19, 178, 216, 232–3
cocaine 102, 254
Coffin Cheaters motorcycle club 123
Cohen, Nick 57, 59, 83
Cole Lawson Communications 205
Comanchero motorcycle club 101–2
 at council meeting 207; attacks on other clubs 78; gear worn by 9–10; growth of 253; gyms run by 8–10; heroin theft by 236–8; organised crime involvement 41, 64, 108, 157; police information leaked to 199; recruits wharf workers 48–51; safe house raided by police

159–64; Sydney airport killing 149–50; tattoo parlours run by 95; weapons provided to 138–9; Will's contacts with 184
corrupt police
in Asia 38, 242; leaks from 217–18; links with Comancheros 163, 170, 199
Costa, Antonio Maria 155–6
covert laundry 78–84, 203
Criminal Assets Confiscation Taskforce 253
crystal meth, *see* methylamphetamines

Dai Lo Cheung, *see* Lam Sak Cheung, Duncan
dai los 67, 193, 195, 221–2
Daily Telegraph website 223
'Daux,' *see* Ngakuru, Daux
Da-Yu (Emperor of China) 59
Debus, Bob 114–15, 118, 135
Dewar, Jacqui 154
Direzione Investigativa Antimafia 155
Dogan, Erkan 64, 138, 169–70
arrest and jail sentence 194, 224, 253; media interest in 163–4; police surveillance of 158, 160
Dubai 192–6

ecstasy (drug)
manufacture of 23–8; plant located by ACC 28–31; seizures of 6, 33–4, 254; sources of 102
Edmonds, Kelly 171, 178–80, 198, 224

Faulkner, John 11–12
FBI, ACC collaboration with 155
Financial Crimes department 41–2
Finks motorcycle club 206

Gangs Squad, NSW 152
gei mianzi 18
Gildea, Errol 124–6
Gregoriou, Terry, arrest and sentencing 254
Guillain–Barré Syndrome 164

'H' (Chinese informant) 70–1, 112, 199–204
Hawi, Mohammed 'Mick' 10, 108, 131, 138
Hayes, Chris 154, 190
Hells Angels motorcycle club
at parliamentary inquiry 124–6; in Canada 108; in Kings Cross 105–6; Lakemba bikie shooting 151–2; Sydney airport killing 149–50
heroin, seizures of 255
High Court, overturns anti-bikie laws 253
High Risk Funds program 13–16, *see also* Vikingsson, Patrick geospatial database 91; moved to Analytics section 197; Operation Dayu proves success of 242; results of 43, 115, 230; traces links to Asian government officials 166–9; transfers detected by 39, 81, 159

Hong Kong
ACC collaboration with 90, 95–100, 115; Ayik in 63–8; laundered money sent to 93; Purchas' work in 37–8
Hun Sen 243
Hun To 243–4
Huong (Purchas's girlfriend) 7, 55, 147, 161
Hutchins, Natalie 248, 253
Hutchins, Steve
at parliamentary inquiry 122–5; chairs ACC committee 84–6; interview with Welch 225–7; meeting with Milroy 118; meetings with Purchas and Bullock 119–20, 134–7; on ACC overseas delegation 154–7; on organised crime 139; on Rudd victory 11–13; plans committee inquiry 190–2; retires from Senate 248–9, 253
Hux, *see* Ayik, Hakan

Ibrahim family 76, 106–7
ice (drug) 102, 117–18, 166, 254–5
Independent Commission against Corruption (Hong Kong) 4–5, 37–8, 250
Independent Commission against Corruption (NSW) 4–5, 36
India, drug manufacturing in 196, 220–4, 228–9, 235, 255
Indian Narcotics Bureau 229
informants
ACC internal reviews of 165–6; Bilal 187–9; embedding in police operations 47; for AFP 116; 'H' 70–1, 112, 199–204; names of concealed ix; 'Smiley' xi–xii, 236–9
interstate police cooperation 6, 116–17

James, Gregory
coordinates Tonga operation 183–5; gains approval to extend Operation Gordian 56–7; in Hong Kong 95–100; interviews Andrew Lee 71–3; involved in Debus scandal 114–22; meets Purchas and Bullock 20–3, 39–45, 132–4; plans for Ayik 231; plans to extend laundry 89–91; political pressure on 133–4, 164–9; retirement 239–45, 252; sidelining of 211–14, 219; teleconference with AFP 109–11; under Lawler 161; undercover work by 72–4; update on Operation Dayu 130
Japan, links to organised crime 203–4, *see also* Yazuka

Keelty, Mick 74
Kings Cross, NSW 105, 108
Kith Meng 243–4
Kitson, Kevin 46, 56

258

INDEX

Laing, Bill 117
Lakemba bikie shooting 151–4
Lam, Jack 100, 134
Lam family 100, 244
Lam Sak Cheung, Duncan 112–13, 121, 201–2
Lamb, Peter 117
Lan Kwai Fong, Hong Kong 66
Lawler, John
  briefing given to 167; examines AFP complaint 89; heads ACC 161, 164–5; James meets with 239; Purchas's relations with 133–4, 231
Lawson, Margaret 205–8
Lee, Andrew 71–3, 79–83, 211–14
Li (Vietnam Airlines pilot) 54–5
Lone Wolves motorcycle club 41
Long Thanh money transfer company 54
Ly Vi Hung 113, 121, 201–2

Macau 37, 90, 93, 95–100
Mandarin Oriental Hotel, Hong Kong 63–6
Maritime Security Identity Cards 50, 191
McClelland, Robert 190–1
MDP2P, *see* ecstasy
methylamphetamines, *see also* ecstasy
  ice (drug) 102, 117–18, 166, 254–5; in Tonga 192; seizures of 254–5; shipments of 171–2; sources of 64, 222
Micalizzi, Joseph 10
  arrest of 140, 224; Ayik a known associate of 113; police intercept plane 103–4; refuses to implicate Ayik 170
Milroy, Alistair 'Jock'
  at parliamentary inquiry 123; on organised crime 139; replacement of 90, 118, 213; support for Operation Dayu 45–6, 56
'Mizza,' *see* Micalizzi, Joseph
money remitters 39, 71, 128–9, 176, *see also* Western Union
Moroney, Mark 'Ferret' 206
motorcycle clubs, *see also names of clubs*
  as political issue 121–2, 158–9; at parliamentary inquiry 122–5; discriminatory laws overturned 253; involvement with organised crime 111, 136; media interest in 76–8, 106–7; violence associated with 149–54
Multi-Capital Trading 131

Nakanishi, Shinichi 168
National Crime Authority 36
Negus, Tony 117, 167
Ngakuru, Daux
  ACC briefing on 131; as Comanchero 138; drug plane intercepted 104; evades arrest 250; heroin theft by 237; recruitment plans 195–6; relations with Ayik 9–10; nicknames of ACC staff 4; 'Nike bikies' 76; Nimbus Pharmaceuticals 221
Nomads motorcycle club 78, 107–8

Ong Ngoai Syndicate 202–4, 231, 241–2, 252
Operation Agrale 131, 197, 213, 241–2
Operation Dayu
  approval for 74–5; closure of 250; concept underlying 121–2; ice imports 118; loss of support for 213–14; Macau operation 146; naming of 60; planning for 69–70; political pressure on 90–1, 164–6, 197; results of 92, 110, 240–2, 252, 254
Operation Gordian
  Asian crime syndicates identified by 38; cash tracking by 14; Hutchins briefed on 135–6; plans to extend 7–8, 41–6; results of 255; under Purchas 5–6
Operation Hoffman
  ACC takes over targets 131; Ayik a target of 111, 146; leaks in 199; moved to High Risk Crime Group 197; raids Comanchero safe house 159–63; resources diverted to 165; results of 241–2; takeover by AFP 213; traces phone numbers 184
Operation Illipango 243
Operation Tabasco 112
organised crime
  bikie links with 124–5; drug sources 102; failure of laws to prevent 249; globalisation of 156; growth in Australia 85–6; method of operations 69–70
Orrock, Scott 107
Outram, Michael 46, 56, 165

Parliament House, offices in 225
Parry, Stephen 154, 191
passport copying scheme 146
police intelligence reports, leaking of 77–8
Police Media Liaison, NSW 33
Price, Chris 57, 59
prostitution 18–19, 171–2
pseudoephedrine 25, 113, 221, 255
Purchas, Mike
  apartments raided by 173–7; confirms Ayik's involvement 157–9; covert laundry operation 56–9, 68–71, 78–84, 91–4; in Hong Kong 37–8; in Macau 145–8, 249–51; interrogates Bilal 185–90; interviews Van Dang Tran 52–6; leaves ACC 228–31; locates methylamphetamine plant 28–31; meeting with Hutchins 119–20, 126; meetings with James 21–3, 41–5, 183–5; meets with Harry Blackburn 35–6; on Chinese–Canadians 100; on demarcation disputes with AFP 116; on

INDEX

High Risk Funds program 13–16; plans Operation Gordian 38–40; sidelining of 217–20; teleconference with AFP 109–11; under Lawler 197; update on Operation Dayu 130–4; work for Crime Commission 3–8

Raptor taskforce, NSW 163
Rebels motorcycle club 41
Rockdale, drug lab in raided 223
Rogerson, Roger 36, 86
Ross, Jock 108
Royal Canadian Mounted Police 155
Rudd, Kevin
deposed as PM 236; Hutchins' role under 84–5; leadership problems 190; on organised crime 137–9, 226–7; wins ALP leadership 11–12
Rudd Labor Government 90–1, 115, 119

second-hand cars, drugs concealed in 216, 219, 224
shipping containers, drugs smuggled in 136
shui niu 18
'Smiley' xi–xii, 236–8
South Africa, drug shipments from 171–2
spa baths, drugs imported in 100, 109–11
surveillance 132, 173–7, 198, 224, 228
Sutherland, Bob 58
Sydney Airport 149–50, 183
Sydney Morning Herald 31–5, 106–7, 206, *see also* Welch, Dylan

Taskforce Wickenby 20–1
tattoo parlours, bikie involvement with 77, 94–5
Thailand, laundered money sent to 93
The Age 114
Tonga
drug seizures in 192–5, 254; drug shipments via 171; involvement with organised crime 142; police cooperation with ACC 184–5
triads
expansion of business by 174–5; in Hong Kong and Macau 37–8; involvement in organised crime 240–1; links to Australian drug running 168–9; operatives for 18
Tukel brothers 217–18

unexplained wealth laws 184, 190, 226–7, 253
United Motorcycle Council 205–6
United Nations Office of Drugs and Crime 154–7

Van Dang Tran 53–5
Vietnam 93, 202–4, 242

Vietnam Airlines, involvement with organised crime 14, 53–5
Vietnamese in Australia 89, 91–2
Vikingsson, Patrick, *see also* High Risk Funds program
develops High Risk Funds program 13–16, 81, 83; information required by 200; on Lam passport 134; on results of laundry 91–4; post-ACC career 230, 252; recruited for Operation Dayu 57; sidelining of 219

Wainahou, Derek 151–2
Wallace, Deb 31, 33–4
waterfront workers, involvement with organised crime 142–3, 191–2, 226, 249, 253
'Waz,' *see* Wissam
weapons 138–9, 254
Welch, Dylan 31–5
becomes national security correspondent 225–7; bikie contacts 75–8, 105–9, 205–8, 236–9; journalism career 252; on Comanchero safe house raid 162–4; on Zervas shooting 151–4
Western Union
disregards recognition laws 110, 115; links with organised crime 131; pressure on to enforce rules 159–60; reform of 255
'Will,' *see* Wong, Wei 'Will'
Wissam ('Waz') 23–8, 48–51, 94, 143–5, 187–9
Wong, Wei 'Will'
ACC briefing on 131; after airport bikie killing 148–50; arrest of 229, 232–4, 239–40; awaiting trial 253; Ayik's relations with 11, 65, 102–4, 177–80; business model 126–7; contacts of traced 184–5; involvement in crime confirmed 157; money remitted by 128–9; money stolen from 16–20, 214–17; role of enlarged 140; sends runner to Tonga 193; surveillance of 173–7, 224
Wood, Jason 123, 154
Wu, Steve
arrest of 239; awaiting trial 253; links to Ayik 66–8, 221–2, 238; trouble with *dai los* 193, 195–6; Will's contact with 184–5

Yakuza, linked to Australian drug trade 168–9, 174–5, 203–4

Zervas, Peter 152–3
Zervas, Tony 151